VIKING VOYAGERS

VIKING

Alan Binns

VOYAGERS

Then and Now

HEINEMANN : LONDON

William Heinemann Ltd
10 Upper Grosvenor Street, London W1X 9PA
LONDON MELBOURNE TORONTO
JOHANNESBURG AUCKLAND

First published 1980

SBN 434 07120 X

Phototypeset in V.I.P. Sabon by
Western Printing Services Ltd, Bristol.
Printed in Great Britain by
Caledonian Graphics Limited

Contents

Author's Note

This is not a book about the Viking Age in general, nor about Viking ships as museum objects. There are enough good books about both. It is deliberately confined to one aspect of the Viking Age, though the most important, neglected and misrepresented one, its voyages, in the spirit of an observation by W. L. Renwick in 1939 which decided me on my future studies: 'Technique can be learned, but three-quarters of our study must always be the attempt to re-acquire the traditional content of the imagination: this is true at all times in the study of Dryden and Wordsworth as well as Cynewulf.'

The re-creation of the imagination in this sense was one of the aims of the project, and for voyaging it can only be done at sea.

A.L.B.

Foreword

by His Excellency the Lieutenant Governor of the Isle of Man,
SIR JOHN PAUL, G.C.M.G., O.B.E., M.C.

I count myself very fortunate to have been Lieutenant Governor of the Isle of Man during the celebrations of the Millennium of Tynwald, commemorating the long and unbroken tradition of democratic government introduced by the Vikings around the year AD 979.

It was also my good fortune to be the Patron of the Manx Millennium Viking Voyage carried out in this historic year. It is fair to claim that the voyage of the *Odin's Raven* from Trondheim to the Isle of Man was the most significant single achievement in our Millennium celebrations in that it was a voyage carried out in the same way, over the same seas, calling for the same degree of skill, courage and spirit of adventure as was displayed by those Vikings who, a thousand years or more ago, brought the Court of Tynwald to the Island together with certain other aspects of Norse tradition and culture. As it is with Tynwald, many other elements of the Viking legacy are still in evidence throughout the Island today and there is no doubt that the outstanding success of the voyage has served to strengthen still further the close and long-established links which bind the Kingdoms of Norway and Man.

In an age and in a continent where there is little inducement and, indeed, little need to subject ourselves to physical hardship, danger and adventure, the Manx Millennium Viking Voyage has proved a most heartening and inspiring enterprise.

I, as Patron, and my wife as Godmother to the *Odin's Raven* are proud to have been associated with this venture. We are also delighted that this audacious re-enactment of history should be recorded in this book as a tribute to all those who made the voyage of *Odin's Raven* a possibility; even more so, of course, it is a tribute to the sixteen man crew of Manx and Norsemen and, in particular, their 'Chieftain' Robin Bigland, who together made it so splendid a reality.

PART ONE

VOYAGING IN
THE VIKING AGE

1

Introduction

The last twenty years have seen a good deal of new work on the vikings, both in their homelands of Norway, Sweden and Denmark, and in their many settlements, in Shetland, Orkney, Faeroe, Iceland, Greenland, Newfoundland, England, Ireland, Man, Normandy, and the towns of the Russian river routes Novgorod, Staraya Ladoga, and Kiev. At the same time new discoveries and the re-interpretation of old ones have thrown new light on the ships. This book is an essay on the theme which involves and unites all these three topics, homeland, settlements and ships, that is the voyages which connected the first two in the third. These voyages are the essential characterising feature of the viking age, and if we do not understand them properly, in all their wide ranging variety, we are in danger of misunderstanding the age as a whole.

The variety of voyages is the most important feature. The ship hunting whale and walrus off the North Cape of Norway, the one hauling through dense forest up the rapids of a Russian river, the one carrying sheep or goats to pasture on an off-shore island – or to Greenland –, the one carrying a king and a hundred of his men to a fleet battle, the one with a crew of two dozen pirates beating round Finisterre, the one desperately rowed off an English beach by five wounded survivors a very long way from Norway, were all engaged in very different voyages, and one can only wonder at the number of historians who seem to have thought that the Gokstad ship was

involved in all of them. Presumably the ships, rigs, rowers, problems, hoped-for returns, attitudes, navigational resources were all
very different too. If we are aware of this, we can distinguish many
voyages and voyagers and recognise that what is true of some of
them is, partly for that very reason, not necessarily true of the rest.

Because the voyages are so central to the viking age, there is some
danger of exaggerating the contrast between them and their fore-
runners. But already in the Bronze Age coastal voyages from the
Mediterranean along the Atlantic coast of Europe were being
undertaken. These carried people as far as the Hebrides and
Orkney, though not, as far as we can see at present, any further. We
do not know what sort of ships were used for these voyages. The
Ferriby boats from the north bank of the Humber, excavated by
E. V. Wright, are the oldest plank-built vessels of Europe and date
from this period, but they seem at once too heavy and too shallow,
with too little freeboard, to be at all suitable for long-distance
voyaging along the steep Atlantic coast. It seems more likely that
some skin-covered vessel like a curragh, or else an expanded dug-
out with added side-strakes, was used, particularly because the
means of propulsion must have been paddling, which requires a
low, light and narrow craft. The only ocean-going vessels of this
kind are the outrigger canoes of the Pacific which made their
trans-ocean passages under sail, and we have no evidence at all for
vessels of this kind in Europe at any period. Our earliest evidence
for sail on the Atlantic coast is the heavy leather-sailed craft of the
Venetii reported by Julius Caesar from Gaul. The Bronze Age
voyages were not of great duration and must have been done in
short stages in settled weather to be successful. Their light and
buoyant craft (for a well-finished expanded dug-out is no heavier
than a skin-covered frame boat) were the ancestors of the later
viking ships.

The Roman empire depended on the regular transport of vast
amounts of corn in merchant ships, some of which were larger than
any that were to be seen again for a thousand years, and these were
protected by a navy whose ships, though initially of Mediterranean
type, were capable of circumnavigating the British Isles. Two separate finds of Roman coins on the south-east coast of Iceland
perhaps suggest that two were capable of reaching there, though we
do not know that they were capable of returning: probably not,

from that inhospitable coast. Until the end of Roman Britain the fleet, operating from bases well fortified against much more serious attacks than could be mounted from paddled war-canoes, defended the coast and the trade in corn, lead and silver against Saxon and Anglian pirates. If we are to believe the cheerful admonition of a Roman poet writing from a comfortable distance, these pirates regarded a shipwreck as merely an opportunity for practice, and were to be looked for most when the weather was worst. It appears that some Roman crews had their faces and arms coloured as sea camouflage, and this, if it is not simply British tattooing, seems more likely to be the sort of trick picked up by regulars from pirates than vice-versa. If it was really true that descents on the coast were *more* likely in strong winds, I suppose the implication is that some of the voyages were over distances long enough to make the help of a stern wind desirable: if the possibility of wrecking the ship was really contemplated calmly, I suppose it is evidence of light and easily replaceable vessels and of their crews' conviction that they will be able to find some safe haven in some region of the coast they are attacking. Neither assumption seems particularly far-fetched at the end of Roman Britain, when there seem to have been areas in which Angles and Saxons (and other Germanic tribes, Swabians, Allemanni, Frisians, on the evidence of place-names) were well established. It has been pointed out that the names of some of the Saxon Shore forts in Latin (Anderida, Regulbium) look as if they are only Latinisations of Saxon or at least Germanic personal names (Ande-rid, Raculf) and a shipwrecked Anglo-Saxon voyager, if indeed he did not wish to settle in Britain, could presumably either join Raculf's troop or at any rate eventually return home with one of the ships bringing him reinforcements.

Some of the first Anglo-Saxon settlers may well have arrived in Roman ships, coming to serve as Roman auxiliaries, whilst those who arrived later, in the period of the Roman withdrawal, must have made the voyage in their own vessels. They did not necessarily cross direct from Jutland or the Elbe-Weser coast of North Germany and I doubt if they had many craft capable of doing so as a regular thing, though some have found that the settlement of the north-east coast of England included an element that may have done so. The extent to which the literature and culture of pre-viking England share common elements with Denmark and Sweden supports the idea that a significant part of the population was descended from a group which had formed part of a world in the western Baltic, centred on the Sound. These were presumably Angles living on the east coast of Jutland, in the modern Schleswig-Holstein. Their voyage to England probably began by coasting northwards, through the Limfjord when possible, but sometimes round Skagen. One might see some suggestion of this route in some of the finds from Lindholm Høje, overlooking the Limfjord, and in the cremation pottery and wrist-clasps common to a region of SW Norway and the Anglian parts of Eastern England but not recorded elsewhere. The most direct route into the North Sea would have been down the river Eider, emerging just north of the Elbe mouth and there joining the stream of Saxon shipping through the sand banks of the Waddenzee. Stopping places were presumably the Frisian islands and *terpen*, the latter artificial mounds which raised villages safely above the tidal marshes in Friesland. How far southwards down the coast this route went before heading out for England we have no direct evidence, but the characteristic Anglian and Saxon pottery is found in a coastal belt throughout Frisia and round the shores of the Zuider Zee so it seems that the usual departure was about in the latitude of Great Yarmouth, where the crossing is about a hundred miles. But early cruciform brooches on the north Kent coast, and other connections between the culture of Kent and the Rhine mouth at this period, suggest that some ships went down to the Hook of Holland before crossing, not to East Anglia, but to the Thames estuary. The early entries in the Anglo-Saxon Chronicle show that it was believed in the ninth century that some went much further, and entered Britain by way of the Isle of Wight and Southampton Water, presumably crossing the Dover Strait and coasting along the south coast. If we are prepared to allow any weight to the coincidence of name between the Hengest of the Hengest and Horsa story of King Vortigern, found in Gildas and Bede, and the Hengest of the fight at Finnsburg reported in *Beowulf* and the *Finnsburg Fragment*, then some of the earlier settlers in Britain had been involved in fighting and temporary and broken truces in Frisia in the course of a voyage whose start and finish might have been separated by many years.

It is noticeable in this forerunner of the viking age in the fifth and sixth centuries, that the voyages for which we have evidence involve being out of sight of land only on crossings of less than a hundred miles, sometimes much less, and are all in the southern North Sea, between 50° and 52° North, the area most heavily trafficked by Roman shipping. The early literary evidence of Nennius, Gildas, Bede and the early annals of the Chronicle present the first settlers as arriving in a Britain which the Romans were in process of abandoning, yielding their military protective role to the Anglo-Saxons. If these really were to assist the Britons against attacks from the north by Picts and Scots they would presumably use their ships to coast northwards, and there is archaeological evidence of attack (presumably seaborne) on look-out posts both on the northeast coast and above the headwaters of the Humber. Those involved in the latter had successfully passed the former Roman port of Brough, which presumably no longer held any of the warships they would have had to fear in the previous century.

To say the attack was presumably seaborne, and the look-out posts were set to watch the coast and estuary, does not require that the enemy came across the open sea. Whereas in the Roman Empire the quickest and most secure route lay along the roads, interrupted by the shortest possible water crossings, it is characteristic of the succeeding age that the quickest and most secure route led along the longest possible stretch by water. But this must often have simply substituted a coastal voyage for the earlier stage system along the Roman roads. Some crossings from the region of the Texel, where the eastern shore of the North Sea once more trends away to the south, might have been set to the northward by the ebb tide off the Norfolk coast, and thus made the Wash or the Humber direct, a day later than they had expected to be on shore, but it is difficult to see why anyone should have set out deliberately to do so straight from the homeland in Jutland or north Germany. A ship bound to Britain from the Eider, Elbe or Weser is deviating little from the direct course to Yarmouth by coasting as far as the Texel, and then making a crossing of one hundred miles, whereas to head direct for the Humber or Flamborough Head involves an open sea crossing of three hundred miles. For ships without compass, chart or weather forecast, the first route with the shorter crossing of under twenty-four hours' rowing seems infinitely preferable. In the southern North Sea the weather can usually be predicted for the next twenty-four hours from the look of the sky on the western horizon and the state of the sea. By leaving from the Texel or south of it in reasonably settled-looking weather any ship capable of five knots could certainly expect to be well under the lee of the Norfolk coast before any bad weather with its accompanying southwesterly headwind could develop. The crossing was of an area where over twenty-four hours the two tidal sets, north on the ebb and south on the flood, cancel out so that they can be ignored, as they still are to this day by many small ships. The route from Elbe mouth to Texel is signposted by the chain of Frisian islands, and in the shelter behind them it would be possible to make continued progress even in strong northerly winds which raised too much sea outside. The voyage is in these respects completely comparable to the route south down the Norwegian coast to the jumping-off point for Britain so important in the later viking age. In the Frisian islands it must always have been preferable for a fast passage, even under oars, to stay outside the islands, as the high sandbanks behind them form tidal watersheds only one of which can be crossed on each tide, even today.

I doubt whether in the face of these obvious advantages any fifth-century large oared vessel bound from the Elbe to England could possibly have preferred three days of open sea on a voyage on which the weather almost certainly would change and the tidal sets certainly would not cancel out and were at all angles to the course. For a well-found sailing vessel with a relatively small crew all accustomed to indefinite periods at sea, the situation would be different, at least in an established anti-cyclone giving light north-easterly winds, but such vessels belong to the viking age not the fifth century. Such a vessel might well prefer to get clear of the islands and stand out to sea. The difference between the English coast north and south of the Humber is easily recognised, and in practice it would be relatively easy to coast from any landfall south of Flamborough into the Humber, Wash or Thames. These seem significantly to have been the favourite Anglo-Saxon entries to Britain, and north of Flamborough Head the settlement is sparser and later. Its more purely northern character however, as long as we have no evidence for Anglo-Saxon sail in the fifth century, can scarcely be used to argue its direct settlement from Jutland. Two Roman ceramic fragments from the Rhine suggest that many Germanic raiding vessels at this time still depended on paddles, so it is fortunate that we have the archaeological evidence from Nydam and Sutton Hoo to show that large seagoing oared ships propelled by thirty oarsmen and thus disposing of ten horsepower over long periods, or fifteen in a spurt, were available to carry the Anglo-Saxons across the North Sea. Nydam dates from AD 300, Sutton Hoo from AD 600, but there is little development between them in concept or construction, so we can be reasonably certain that this type represents the vessel for these pre-viking age voyages. It seems to have survived with very little change, and that only of constructional technique rather than basic concept, up to the very eve of the viking age in such craft as the Kvalsund ship from Norway. We might well choose to connect the viking age with the replacement of this ship type by its successor round about the end of the eighth century.

Once again however it is important not to exaggerate the nature of the change. Both Nydam and Sutton Hoo, at 23 m and 27 m long, are longer than any other surviving ships before AD 1000: Oseberg and Gokstad are only 21.5 m and 23 m. The ships of the viking age were in important respects, but certainly not in speed under oars, an advance on Nydam and Sutton Hoo, but this appears in the beam and depth of the hulls. Nydam is 3.25 × 1 m, Sutton Hoo 4.25 × 1.4, Oseberg 5 × 1.5 m and Gokstad 5.25 × 2 (see illustrations on p. 92). These differences may not seem very great, but it is the area of the midship section which reflects the real size relationship to one another of hulls of roughly similar form. The midship section is not of course a rectangle of breadth times depth, and there are very important differences between the midship sections of the pair of Anglo-Saxon ships and the two viking ships. The Nydam ship in fact only occupies about one-third of the rectangular prism with the same length, breadth and depth. But if we multiply the breadth by the depth we get a rough indication of the true relationship of size, the volume or displacement: the figure for Nydam is then 3.25, for Sutton Hoo 6, almost twice the size of Nydam, for Oseberg 8.5, or just under three times the size of Nydam, and for Gokstad 10.5 or over three times the size. If anything this underestimates the differences between these hulls as presently exhibited, and it is evident that the two from the viking age are fuller bodied and able to carry heavier loads, whether of goods, men, ballast or sail pressure when heeled. Their development away from Nydam and Sutton Hoo is thus towards a hull which, whilst it has a lower maximum hull speed (which depends on waterline length) is much more suitable for longer voyages under less favourable sea conditions. This may have been the result of continuous improvement of the light raider hull, but it seems more likely to have been influenced by features of the trading or work-boat type which must always have existed alongside the warship, but was for obvious reasons less often used to bury kings. Our knowledge of the raider comes from royal graves, but we only know the workboat from wrecks or abandoned broken hulls, none earlier than AD 840 ± 75 (Äskekärr) unless we are prepared to accept the Grestedbro ship of which only three pieces survive, as a workboat, Carbon 14 dated to AD 550 ± 100. Its stem is joined to the keel by a horizontal scarf, not a vertical one as in the later ships including Äskekärr, but the planking is trenailed to the frames not lashed to it as in Nydam, Sutton Hoo and the other warships. This trenailing of the planking, involving a more rigid and therefore necessarily heavier structure, with greater carrying power but lower maximum speed for a given power is later typical of merchantmen, like Äskekärr, as against the warships and it has therefore been argued that the Grestedbro fragments belong to a trading vessel contemporary with Nydam, which might have made its North Sea voyages under sail, as presumably traders could not economically employ the large crews of sixty or more oarsmen required by the warships. This is an interesting speculation, but we have no idea of the hull of the Grestedbro ship except that it was, to judge by the surviving frame, somewhere between Nydam and Sutton Hoo in length, and had 8 strakes of planking a side, 3 more than Nydam and therefore with a greater freeboard and the possibility of much greater beam amidships: the surviving frame comes from the ends. The Gokstad ship has twice as many planks a side and it is striking that in Ole Crumlin-Petersen's reconstruction the Grestedbro hull has the same unattractively slab-sided wedge-shaped form as Nydam has now. One consequence of the flexibility of these hulls is that they are easily distorted by earth pressure when buried and the shrinkage consequent on drying out when excavated, and the present form of Nydam has some puzzling features. The sharpness of the ends is very understandable in a sea-going rowing-boat of this size, but the way in which it continues with more or less flat sides through the midship section seems improbable, as it detracts from both strength and stability without any corresponding advantage. It is notoriously difficult to allow for the effect of shrinkage which varies with how planks were cut from the original log, and Åkerlund (1961) reconstructs Nydam to a length of 23.7 (22.85), breadth of 3.75 (3.26!) and depth of 1.20 (1.09!): Johannesson's measurements of 1931, on which the 1936 replica was based, are given in brackets, and it is clear that if one accepts Åkerlund's figures there is a great gain in seaworthiness, and the performance of the replica is unlikely to be much guide to that of the original, whose breadth × depth now give 4.5 not 3.25, much closer to Sutton Hoo, and a half rather than a third of the Gokstad figure. This is just as well, as the replica of Nydam, like that of Kvalsund, had alarming and disappointing features which ought to make one wonder whether in that form they could have accomplished the voyages that we know were made. In particular the instability and need for ballast of 1 ton (most unusual for oared vessels!) of the Nydam replica, which canted dangerously if one man shifted position, is not true of the beamier Åkerlund form. The depth of hull, freeboard and therefore windage, all suggest that the traditional view of Nydam as a sea-going oared ship for North sea voyages is correct, as they are all greater than could be required for work among the Danish islands in the Sound, and rather greater than is entirely convenient for the oars found with it. These are short (3 to 3.5 metres), for the freeboard at a displacement of 6 tons, made up of the hull weight plus thirty oarsmen, is as large as that of the later Kvalsund boat in which some have seen a vessel capable of carrying sail. If it did so it can I think only have been for occasional use with the wind dead astern where heel and stability were not important, but the point is that Kvalsund, a late transitional hull is no better than Nydam from this point of view. The hull of Nydam is so deep, and the thwarts so near the gunwale, to permit the use of short, steeply angled oars (very suitable for rowing in a choppy North Sea overfall, but surely longer for smooth sheltered water?) that in spite of some specialists' denials there must have been floorboards or stretchers for the oarsmen's feet. In the space between these and the bottom of the hull two tons of stores could be carried to advantage, and in Nydam I think we have a good representative of the raiding ship at its best before the viking age. We can see from Old English texts reflecting the developments of the seventh and eighth centuries that there were improvements upon it, but we do not know that they were war-vessels and the most natural interpretation of the texts is that they were not. It seems clear from the Sutton Hoo burial and from the poem *Beowulf* that there was a continuing interest in what must once have been a very successful voyage from Sweden to East Anglia, and it is presumably not coincidental that it is in *Beowulf* that we find the first hint (though relegated to an implausibly remote past) of the long-distance sea-worthy expeditionary sailing vessel which is the staple craft of the viking age. As this Old English material is our best and in many respects only contemporary source for the viking age and the voyaging of the period immediately before it, it deserves a separate chapter.

2

Before the Vikings

It is natural from a British point of view to date the beginning of the Viking Age from 789 when three Norwegian ships from Hordaland were involved in trouble at Portland or somewhere else near to Dorchester. It was the duty of the reeve to control foreign traders, and he 'tried to compel them to go to the royal manor, for he did not know what they were, and they slew him'. The authenticity of this account has been doubted by some, I think without sufficient reason, and others have made the poor reeve into a sort of post-humous buffoon by assuming that he could not tell the difference between innocent merchants and three Gokstad ships full of men armed to the teeth. Some writers like historical periods to begin in a nice decisive way. I think the interesting thing about this incon-venient entry is that it chimes so well with what has recently emerged about the voyaging that was the essential feature of the age. The three ships had presumably crossed from Norway to Shetland and then made their way by the Hebrides down the Irish sea. The first raid on the Isle of Man was in 798, Lambay island north of Dublin was raided in 795. There are just enough early viking finds in Shetland and the Hebrides to suggest that they were being used as staging posts, and in the light of this I do not find it at all unlikely that three ships having followed this route were bound to the eastward along the south coast of England in 789. And bearing in mind the type of vessel required for such a long voyage, necessarily under sail for most of the time, and crossing very exposed and turbulent water, I do not find it surprising that a south coast reeve should assume, until it was too late, that he was dealing with merchantmen. From a much later period there are instances in the sagas of warships successfully camouflaging themselves as merchantmen, and if the ships were bound home or to the markets of France or the Low countries they presumably had goods on board, whether one calls them cargo or booty.

Those who reject the 789 annal prefer to start with the raid on Lindisfarne in 793, where I suspect they find the pillaging of a monastery a more fitting opening than a slight but fatal misunderstanding with the customs. The Laud chronicle dates the raid on January 8th but this is usually held to be a mistake for June 8th. To arrive there, by way of Shetland, Orkney and the East coast of Scotland on the eighth of January would involve leaving Norway at the latest by the middle of December, and though there is often a very stable extension southward of the polar high pressure area giving light favourable north-easterly winds which an opportunist might have used, it does seem on balance unlikely that anyone would deliberately embark on such a difficult passage, with long stretches with no shelter, at a time when daylight was so short and the risk of depressions bringing storms so great. Even a century later Ohthere did not sail at night (though Wulfstan did), and as most trade seems to have been conducted at summer markets a voyage at that season would only make sense if it was designed from the beginning as an attack on some spot which was fixed and always contained wealth, such as a monastery. To assume that such early voyages were so meticulously planned involves assumptions about intelligence, and about independence of ordinary agricultural and fishing concerns, I find unlikely.

Before this widespread outburst at the end of the eighth century we have very little evidence of North Sea voyaging after the end of the fifth-century raids and settlements of the Anglo-Saxons, and these three centuries are the real Dark Age as far as voyaging is concerned. The Sutton Hoo ship was presumably afloat some time in the first of these centuries before being buried about AD 620, and I suppose she may even have crossed more than once, perhaps carrying a king's son through the Limfjord and round the southern North Sea to England, but in the main we have to glean what we can from literary sources, some as apparently unpromising as the account of Bishop Aidan's miracle, between AD 642 and 645, which Bede gives in his *Ecclesiastical History* of 735. He had the story from his friend Cynimund, who had it from Utta, the man involved, so the authority is unimpeachable. Utta was to go down to Kent by land to bring back a princess as bride for his sovereign, but was to return by sea with her, an interesting light on the relative comfort, safety and reliability of sea and land transport, and perhaps the relative costs as well. Aidan foretold that on the return journey Utta would meet a storm and contrary wind, so evidently the vessel was a royal sailing ship, a century and a half before the vessels of similar type required for voyages from Norway to our south coast. It turned out as Aidan had predicted. 'For first the waves of the sea raged, and the sailors attempted to ride it out at anchor, though to no purpose, for the seas sweeping over the ship on all sides they perceived that death was at hand as the ship filled with water. At last Utta took the flask of oil which Bishop Aidan had given him and poured the oil onto the sea, which at once ceased its uproar as had been foretold. Thus Aidan by the spirit of prophecy had foretold the storm and though absent in the body was able to calm it when it had arisen by the same spirit.' Bede attributes the effect to Aidan's miraculous powers, but as the Admiralty Pilots advise us in beautifully measured nineteenth-century prose that itself owes much to the Authorised Version, another view is possible. 'Use of oil for modifying the effect of breaking waves: many experiences of late years have shown that the utility of oil for this purpose is undoubted, and the application simple. Attention is called to the fact that a very small quantity of oil, skilfully applied, may prevent much damage both to ships (especially the smaller classes) and to boats, by modifying the action of breaking seas.'

The generation round about the year AD 800 seems to have seen the beginning of the ship-borne expansion. As well as the Irish Sea and south coast raids related above, we have the Lamlash grave from Arran which is datable to the end of the eighth century, and a good number of similar graves from after 800. Ten years after we are told that King Gotfrid of Denmark invaded Frisia with two hundred ships, and the Swedish vikings voyaging eastwards must have been beginning to establish their settlements in Russia, for in 839 some of their ambassadors turned up in Ingolheim on the Rhine on a somewhat circuitous route back from an embassy to Constantinople. Evidently the river route down which they had made their way there had been cut in the interim, or their ships had been lost or were not easily taken back upstream. It will be observed that all this activity in this generation is from widely separated areas and is preserved in different and independent historical traditions, so that we may feel some confidence in making it the beginning of the viking age. We can have no such confidence if we seek to ascribe it to particular reasons, whether of over-population, inheritance systems which produced estates not capable of alone supporting their owners, reaction to political pressure from the south, change of natural resources by fish migrating to the westward, or technical development of a viking ship capable of making the voyages. All these have at one time or another been suggested and all probably played some part, though only the last requires serious consideration in dealing with the voyages. I think myself that the Old English literary evidence, though far from conclusive, suggests that such ships had already been developed earlier at any rate in the southern part of the North Sea area. The outburst round 800 then perhaps reflects a development by which they became generally available, and Scandinavia began to realise how vulnerable to them the coasts of neighbouring countries were.

Even such a summary account shows that all the peoples of Scandinavia were involved, Norwegians, Swedes and Danes, making voyages of different kinds in very different contexts, so we should be reluctant to seek one single explanation. The Norwegian long-range, small-scale voyages from Hordaland across open ocean, the Danish short-range, large-scale voyages down the sheltered waters of the Waddenzee, the Swedish long-range river journeys, would all require quite different vessels, types of organisation and navigational techniques. Only that involved in the Norwegian voyages was necessarily new. Gotfrid's invasion of Frisia may or may not have had more sophisticated motives, but in scope, armament and ships it need not have differed from previous incursions in the Migration age. It is only when similar-sized Danish fleets cross the North Sea, half a century later, that we are in the presence of voyages essentially different. This only means that the onset of the true viking age, if we use voyages as a criterion, came at different times in different places. I do not think that the sources, though they show it as widespread, show it as particularly abrupt, as it is often represented, probably following Alcuin's perhaps deliberately rhetorical lamentations. After the first wave in AD 800 the next does not occur for another generation when there is a peak in the 830s only surpassed by the great fleet of the 860s. Not all the early voyages were successful, and Alcuin was not the only one with reason to lament. The Laud Chronicle entry for 794 (actually 796) begins with the often-quoted, 'Northumbria was ravaged by the heathen, and Ecgfrith's monastery at Jarrow looted'; but it continues: 'There one of the leaders of the heathen was slain, and some of their ships shattered by storms: many of them were drowned there, and those that came ashore alive were soon slain at the river-mouth.'

The gradual build-up of the features we regard as characteristic of the viking age suggests that what we see about the year 800 is more likely to be the acceleration of a steady development between 600 and 800 than any dramatic novelty. Our best guide to this development is in those Old English texts which seem to refer to this period, and by using them with due caution we can produce a picture of the seafaring of these two relatively peaceful centuries between the two turbulent ages of conquest and raiding. Some is prose, some poetry and they complement one another: the texts were not written to communicate to us information of this kind, but some of the pictures they present, like that from Bede already quoted, have a value for us if we take them quite against the original author's intention. The poem *The Seafarer* as we have it is a Christian meditation about the instability of earthly life which is put in the mouth of a fictitious professional seafarer whose reflections on his situation are given wider reference by the poet. We cannot take it as the genuine autobiography of a genuine seafarer, in spite of the claim in the first line: 'I can make about my voyaging a ballad that is true'. But the description of the poem given above would also fit 'McAndrew's Hymn', in which Kipling is doing much the same, and from the wealth of accurate technical detail in that poem we can produce a complete picture of a steamship engine-room at the end of the nineteenth century. As well as that, if the original poet's sympathy with his subject was good enough, we can get something more valuable, an insight into the minds of the men who ran these engines, or at least into what their contemporaries expected them to think. Can we learn anything about the voyaging and voyagers of these two centuries, 600–800, by using this approach to Old English poems such as *Beowulf, The Seafarer, The Wife's Lament* and *The Husband's Message*? The last two give immediately recognisable expression to the human tensions involved in the inevitable separation. The first two seem to give us indispensable information about the ships and their navigation which does not always agree with recent theories. They give us much else as well of course, and to use them in this way on the narrow question of voyaging does not suggest that it exhausts their interest. But they may be more documentary than literary critics looking for allegory are inclined to suppose. The authors, like Kipling in 'McAndrew's Hymn', were concerned to do a good deal more than describe the ship of their own day, but that does not mean that their irreplaceable observations are any less true than his.

There are great difficulties of dating involved, which must affect the usefulness of the material, but we must remember that the date of the Kvalsund ship is even more uncertain than that of *Beowulf* and *The Seafarer*. *Beowulf* was probably written in the first half of the eighth century, but claims to be describing events of two centuries earlier, the beginning of our period, in southern Scandinavia. It is striking that the author assumes that his hero used for the voyage from Götaland (the west of modern Sweden) to Denmark a ship quite unlike the Sutton Hoo ship which actually comes from this period. Beowulf's ship is driven mainly by sail, not oars, and therefore has a crew of only fifteen, like *Odin's Raven* which it possibly much resembled in size, construction and rig. This is a considerable advance on Sutton Hoo which, without sail, requires thirty oarsmen who need food and water and some reliefs. Beowulf's ship is described in line 216 as 'wudu bundenne' 'the tied-together timber' and the obvious interpretation of this is that it refers to the lashing of planking to frame which distinguished the raiding-ship from the heavier, nailed, sailing merchant-ship. There is no reason to believe the poem implicitly, that this type of vessel uniting the best features of both types had been developed as early as AD 600, but it does suggest that they were no longer a novelty in AD 750 or whenever the poet was writing. If they were known to everyone to be recent introductions, I do not think the *Beowulf* poet, who shows great interest in the material aspects of his reconstruction of the past, would have made Beowulf's ship of this type. He quite clearly assumes that royal and princely vessels have had masts and sails from a very remote past, and I cannot see why a man so knowledgeable about the ring-swords and helmets appropriate to the time of his story should make a mistake about something so conspicuous. The fact that the ship in the Bede quotation above, from AD 645, looks most likely to be of this type thus predisposes me to accept *Beowulf* as evidence that these ships were well established by 700 in the southern North Sea. It is possible to argue that 'bundenne' is merely a conventional term to be understood vaguely as 'decorated' but when it is applied in *Beowulf* to swordhilts it is evidently to be understood in its usual sense, as hilts are elsewhere 'wirum bewunden' 'wound round with (gold?) wire'. The use of a reasonably large sail area to propel a long, light warship whose length was only made possible by the lightness and flexibility of its lashed construction also I think gives more precise meaning to line 1906. In this we are told that on a fast homeward passage under sail 'lyftgeswenced' 'pressed on by the wind' the sea-wood thundered 'sundwudu thunede'. I think this refers to the characteristic vibration of the bottom planking of these flexible craft at critical speeds when they become what Shetland sixareen sailors called 'water-loose', as we experienced it in *Odin's Raven* and as is discussed in detail in part two. Obviously both phrases may be merely conventional (though even conventions require some starting-point) but as they correspond exactly to characteristic features it seems unnecessary to assume so. How much the poet knew about the navigational side of the voyages is another matter. It has often been speculated that he got his knowledge of the ships from being present at a heathen burial such as Sutton Hoo: that evidently would not account for the interpretation of 'thundered' offered above. There is perhaps a hint in line 209 of a pilot or professional skipper (if it is not Beowulf himself as most assume) and line 219 shows that the voyage includes a night at sea with an estimated time of arrival on the second day at which the voyagers do indeed see the broad headlands with their steep cliffs shining ahead of them. This does not of course sound very like anywhere in Denmark, and there is reason to believe that the poet is thinking of the North-East coast of England as he evidently is when he pictures the departure from a sandy beach beneath high cliffs where strong tidal currents run.

Some of the language is certainly stylised, but there is nothing in Old English sea language to suggest, what must seem intrinsically improbable, that after the settlement the Anglo-Saxons turned their backs upon the sea.

It might be expected that a poem called *The Seafarer* would have even more to tell us, but this is scarcely so, at any rate about such technical aspects of construction and navigation. The sense of real experience makes Professor Whitelock's suggestion that it represents a voyager whose motives in leaving his native land for a life at sea were religious rather than commercial much more attractive than the idea that he is simply an allegorical invention. The freezing cold nightwatch in the ship's bow as she seems on the very point of striking on the rocks in the confused sea (reflected back off the cliffs?) which he was perhaps in the bows to observe more easily, rings true, suggests sailing vessels on sea voyages which could not stop each night, and finds some support from the practice of the Polynesian illiterate navigators described by David Lewis, who spent long periods in the bow reading the swell to locate the vessel. A similar use of the swell is said to have survived in Shetland into the eighteenth century, the 'moder-di'. The later Norse 'Seaman's Law' describes in detail the different jobs on board and their allocation among the crew, who are divided into four groups: bow, midships forward of the mast, midships aft of the mast, and stern. It is interesting that the only time we find in Old English laws a man whose oath needs the support of four other 'oath-helpers' it is the captain of a viking ship in Æthelred's code of 991. In a world very different from court or monastery it looks very much as though the testimony of all four watch-leaders is required to support the skipper. We now know how few men these hulls require, and one watch, a quarter of the crew, would be able to assure the safety of the ship if the others were asleep or ashore.

The first job named is the 'lookout for rocks', the duty of the bowmen. Those immediately aft of them had two duties, watching the yard (presumably tending the braces) and baling at sea. Those aft of the mast in harbour tended mooring ropes and gangway, at anchor the anchor-cable. The stern men looked after baling in harbour to ensure the cargo was not spoiled. Evidently the experienced seamen were forward of the mast and those less skilled who worked in harbour aft of it. It is thus thoroughly in place for an experienced seafarer to stress at the beginning of the poem that he is habitually in the bow of the ship in the freezing cold when it is near the coast at night, the most anxious and responsible time for the 'rock lookout'.

What is called in Hakluyt 'the counter-suffe of the sea' as waves reflect back from the coast has a continuous history of usage from the viking age to the North Sea mariners of our own day. Magnus Olsen recorded in 1916 that he had heard an old fisherman tell how in the old days on the coast of Möre (about 1860?) his skipper had 'listened his way in' through thick weather. He put his ear to the ship's gunwale as he sat at the helm, saying 'There goes the Goose', meaning that they had now passed the rocky skerry called the Goose, which he recognised from the characteristic sound, transmitted back through the water and amplified by the wooden hull, of the waves breaking on that particular skerry. Olsen suggests that this difference in sound may explain names like Goose, Cock, Grindstone.

The change in the ship's motion produced by intersecting wave patterns off a steep-to coast is sometimes quite marked, and I have myself been told, in the messroom of a small homeward-bound trawler, by men who had been talking there for the last three hours, 'Now we're abeam of Flamboro Head' as they noted a change in the motion of the ship which I could not sense. It is tempting to speculate that the different terms for the sea swell and waves in Old English are not all simply empty poetic variation but the clues are lost to us, and we have no similar system to which we can assimilate them, as we can for instance Ohthere's 'west ond hwon northan' 'west and a little north' when we wonder if it equals west by north (or even west half north) and thus indicates a division into points or half-points of the full circle of the horizon already in Alfred's day. The birds mentioned in *The Seafarer*, which have been the subject of a special study, may also have navigational significance: they were certainly so used in the later viking age. Probably the most significant feature of the poem is the empirical scepticism about the usual social virtues which its seafarer shows, and is sometimes recognisable in his twentieth-century successors. He knows that the careful conformity guaranteed to keep you out of trouble ashore is quite unable to protect you against the one seafaring certainty – that something unexpected will happen. His impatience with landsmen who do not believe his stories, even though they have not shared his experiences, may also strike a chord. The social imperatives, whose observance allows the landsman to feel reasonably safe, mean much less to the seafarer who must depend much more on his own shrewd intelligence and God's grace. His recognition that he is quite unable to control, or even earn the favour of, the forces with which he must work every day, gives him a freedom to recognise the artificiality of the conventions the landsman must (or can afford to?) take seriously. It will be evident that this provides a good starting-point for the philosophising of the second part of the poem, but that does not mean it is unacceptable as presenting one of the intellectual consequences of the developing voyages of the period before the viking age proper. The real difficulty is to know how far the highly educated and intelligent men whose works we read represent the day-to-day practice of their working fellows. Bede for instance carefully distinguishes as directions (in Heaven!) summer sunrise, sunrise and winter sunrise which suggests that inter-cardinal points were recognised long before the magnetic compass: the cumbrous Latin terms do not necessarily reflect colloquial English which may well already have said north-east, east and south-east. A similar difficulty arises about Alcuin's formal descriptions of the sea, whose Latin hints at vernacular terms we would love to know. He evidently sailed on Ohthere's 'all night in' system, as in his second book against Elipandus he says 'Arriving at the wished-for port we lower sail and sleep until the next dawn when we continue our voyage.' His reply to the query 'What is the sea?' includes 'The road for daring, the divider of regions, a sure refuge from danger (!) a delight in enjoyments (gratia in voluptatibus).' Some of these seem somewhat surprising even at the beginning of the viking age: there is no question of yachting here, but an understanding of the satisfaction to be had in a well-found vessel contending with the waves, an enjoyment of voyaging and a perception of its advantages, not only for daring but also for safety when a superior but landbound force appeared. Much of this is the feeling we get later in Norse verses of the viking age and it is striking to find it expressed, in Latin, already at the end of the eighth century by a churchman like Alcuin. In the ninth and tenth century the increasing number of viking voyages produces an increasing amount of material, including such detailed voyage reports as those of Ohthere and Wulfstan, but not until the verses in the sagas (with few exceptions) do we get as much indication of the feelings of the voyagers as we can glean from the earlier Old English material.

3

The Early Viking Age

The dating of the Gotland stones, and the two very different types of ship they show, one no more advanced than Nydam, the other a fully developed sailing warship, with complex arrangements for controlling the sail, is no more certain than that of the Old English poems. The arrangements for varying the flow of the sail show that a boom across the foot of the sail was not usually used, though some have claimed to find evidence for it on some stones. It may have been used occasionally when before the wind, as a simpler way of extending the foot of the sail than booming out each corner separately. This is how it was used in nineteenth-century collier brigs, which had the same problem of setting a wide sail. The advantage of the separate booms was that they could also be used to get the tack of the sail well out to windward when on the wind as well, which not only improves its efficiency but reduces its heeling moment. This is probably why the hulls not really designed for sail like Gokstad have the blocks to support such beating-poles.

How long did the evolution of such advanced vessels take? The Old English material suggests to me that the traditional late-eighth-century date for such stones as Hejnum (Plate 1) is quite acceptable, and that if people wish to revise the views of Sune Lindkvist and Haakon Shetelig on the dating it should be on some other ground than any implausibility in the ships. Ships like Hejnum make the raiding voyages typical of the first half of the

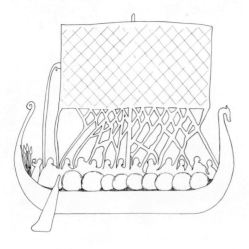

HEJNUM STONE, GOTLAND

The priare (left-hand corner) tied together; compare the Hejnum Stone. The double rope round the shroud is the rakke downhaul. The three blocks of the duva can be seen below the dragon head.

The priare. The wooden block can be moved up and down the centre rope to vary the tension in the side arms, which can also be passed through it.

Drag chain at the launch

Lady Paul launching *Odin's Rav*

Moulds and sheer batten in building stage

Heavy weather in Oslofjord during the first week of trials

Running at 10 knots under reefed main before a force 5

ninth century more easily understandable than if we suppose them to be made in narrow warships like Ladby, under oars and occasional and risky downwind sailing, or complex and relatively heavy displacement, large-crew Gokstads. If they were about 15 m only, the exaggeration of the relative size of the men on board is not intolerable, as a glance at any photo of *Odin's Raven*, also 15 m, will show.

It would not be surprising if the development in Gotland and South Sweden was relatively advanced. Coin-hoard evidence must be used with caution, for the deposit of hoards depends upon other factors apart from the wealth people possess. The likelihood of raids to frighten them into burying their wealth is an obvious one, and in areas remote from main routes this was less. But when all allowances are made it is striking that the ratio of foreign coin-finds from viking-age Scandinavia may be roughly stated as from Norway over five thousand, from Latvia-Estonia twice as many, from Denmark three times as many and from Sweden twenty times as many. This suggests clearly that the Baltic not the North Sea was the real centre, which English historians often forget, naturally impressed by the vociferous complaints of articulate western chroniclers. For the Baltic we have scarcely any written evidence. Another thing that emerges is the different aims and products of the voyages in the two seas. For many Norwegian and even more Danish vikings, the product of their voyaging was an estate in upland Britain, or, for Norwegians more often than Danes, one in Orkney, Shetland, Faeroe or Iceland. The Swedish voyages on the other hand involved hugely profitable trading (often under arms) and then a successful return home with the proceeds. Evidently not many Swedes expected to settle for the rest of their lives in the exotic eastern lands where they were a tiny minority among a vast, incomprehensible and alien population. There were many places in the west where the Danish or Norwegian settlers formed the majority of the population, and in those where they did not they were living among people whose culture, language and literature and legal systems were only in detail different from their own. The only exceptions, Ireland and Wales, have, significantly, little more than a few early and mainly coastal place-names to mark two centuries of Scandinavian presence.

Another important difference which the concentration of wealth in Sweden suggests is the very different nature of communication with the homeland. From viking settlements in the west the sea road was always open in both directions for a constant flow of men and materials. Once a ship had cleared out to sea, her chances of getting near home without being forced to pay tribute or attacked must have been good. But the Swedish vikings, whose voyages took them through forests and river rapids where the ship had to be towed by the crew or even dragged through swamps, can scarcely have had regular lines of communication in the ordinary sense, only the possibility of being able to push through a well-armed squadron once or twice a year, much as the wealth of the New World or the East was brought back to a later Europe by similar treasure fleets. The situation in northwest Europe was evidently different. This first half of the ninth century which saw such an increase in overseas raiding voyages also saw a great increase in seaborne trade, for it is the time of the rise of the great trading ports. What had previously been annual seasonal markets of only local or regional significance developed soon after AD 800 into year-round towns where goods brought great distances by sea were sold and exchanged. It has been suggested that the replacement of the earlier site of Helgön (where a mysterious little silver Buddha was found) in Lake Mälaren by the famous port of Birka was involved with the use of a new type of ship for which the very shallow beaches of Helgö were unsuitable. It is true that the first graves from Birka date from about AD 800, and that it had apparently artificial facilities for discharging cargo from ships drawing over one metre. Grobin, on the south coast of the Baltic, has evidence of viking contact, trading as well as military, from 800 to 850, and Hedeby at the foot of the Jutland peninsula near modern Schleswig seems to have started about the same time. The evidence from the Norwegian trading port of Kaupang is less clear, but not very different. We have from the second half of the century voyage reports giving routes and times from which we can see how these ports were linked in the trade of exchanging Scandinavian trade goods, and gold (often no doubt ill-gotten) for luxuries and coin from Southern Europe and further afield. The taste for luxuries thus engendered, without any regular source of income with which to buy them was no doubt, as we can see in our own day, a strong contributory factor to the search for money by hook or by crook which was the motive for many viking raids.

The fact that these two movements, the growth of trading ports in Scandinavia and the growth of viking raidings, both happen in the same half-century does not mean either that they must depend on one another, or that they are both consequences of the same thing, but obviously neither could have happened until ships and voyaging in them had reached a certain standard: one which I have shown reasons for believing was in fact reached in some parts of Scandinavia by the last quarter of the eighth century at latest. It is possible to suggest that the increase in viking raiding voyages was promoted by an increase of rich merchant ships to be preyed upon en route, and there is some late literary evidence in the sagas that such piracy could on occasion be lucrative. The trading ports themselves are fortified, with careful look-out arrangements, which we see reflected in some fortified cliff-top headland sites in the Isle of Man excavated by Peter Gelling. It is also significant that the major ports are all a little remote from the main open sea routes, up a side fjord which a raider without local knowledge would be unlikely to find by accident. But the viking raids do not seem to have been to any great extent piratical attacks on ships at sea. The evidence for this assertion is admittedly negative: such attacks are not mentioned in sources, and those which might be expected to refer to it, if it had been a great problem, do not. Travel by sea was evidently regarded as less likely to be disturbed by brigandage than that by land, and even after making allowance for the unchanging dangers of bad weather and stranding was regarded as no less safe.

Some of the reported attacks on large cities in the first half of the ninth century were probably attacks on the seaborne wealth at the point where it was most concentrated and convenient. There can scarcely have been a great enough density of merchant ships at any point at sea to make it worthwhile to cruise to raid them. Their voyages and timing were at the mercy of the wind and they could not be found on any regular routes for they had no buoys or lighthouses to aim for as a landfall, and no compass to steer for it if they had. A base installed, preferably on an island, in the approaches to a foreign trading centre might often show a better long-term profit than an attack on the city itself, and such bases, of which we have numerous examples, were presumably intended for the piracy of passing ships and would eventually become not mere summer anchorages but overwintering places as well, with sheds under which the ships could be hauled up, and enough possessions to require defending in their turn, sometimes against other vikings hired by the locals to displace the original pirates. This sort of bargain often seems to have been a good one though it paved the way to the later Danegeld system of simply paying them to go away: presumably a hungry viking was an aggressive viking, and he was after all at the end of a food-chain: by taking the booty from his predecessors he was securing the gold in its most concentrated form possible, the proceeds perhaps of many months' raids on merchants. With such great rewards on the horizon it would not be surprising if the development of long-range, seaworthy and above all fast ships of handy size was very much accelerated in the middle of the ninth century, so that many men of moderate station in Denmark or Norway, who disposed of forty men or so, would acquire a ship of this type and take her each summer on an extended voyage of three or four months.

This must have put a powerful new resource into the hands of the king, who could now, as well as calling his thanes to follow him to war with their men, tell them to bring their ships and thus advance his foreign policy by the threat of seaborne invasion. In the first half of the century there is no need to exaggerate the difference between the operations in Western Europe and those in Russia. Many of the former also evidently involved light and fairly small craft capable of penetrating far inland up rivers, and not necessarily facing long, open-sea voyages.

Examples of the first sort of voyage, to attack a city and the wealth to be found there, are probably to be found in the attacks on Dorestad in the Low Countries in 834, Southampton with 33 ships in 840, Seville in 844, Hamburg with 600 ships in 845 and Paris with 120 ships, also in 845. Some have found the fleet of 600 at Hamburg so incredible as to cast doubt on the chronicler's veracity, and so it would be if they were all Gokstad ships with a hundred men on board. But when one remembers that Hamburg is scarcely more than a day's row with favourable tide (let alone wind) from a protected assembly area behind the fortified frontier of the Dannevirke it does not seem impossible that 600 of the sort of thane who had a thirty-man boat would turn up on such an easy and attractively lucrative enterprise. It can also be seen as the national army embarked. Gotfrid of Denmark who invaded Frisia built the

Dannevirke probably about 800 though its dating is being continually revised by ever more subtle techniques: I was present on one
occasion when irreverent historians, presented with a new dating of
one stretch to 792, demanded to know what month. But both the
defensive wall and the aggressive attack on Hamburg reflect Danish
anxiety about the powerful neighbour to the south.

The second sort of voyage, which resulted in the establishing of a
piratical base in the foreign country, is represented in England by
the attack on the Isle of Sheppey in 835, commanding the rich trade
of Kent and the Thames estuary (perhaps carried in the Graveney
boat!) and in France by the occupation of Noirmoutier 'as if they
meant to stay for ever' in 843. From the latter the Westfaldingi
(Norwegians from the west side of the Oslofjord) raided as far as
Tours and Chartres. By the middle of the century all the great
trading towns of the Empire had been plundered, some more than
once. This repeated destruction has been said by some historians
to cast doubt on the reports. How, they ask, can it have been
worth while to devastate Dorestad three times in five years? I do not
find it difficult to understand: 'Dorestad' to the chronicler presumably means not particular buildings but an institution, the market of
Dorestad with the shipping and merchants attending it.

The base in Sheppey was presumably established by Danes following the usual clockwise circulation round the southern North
Sea which had earlier brought the Anglo-Saxons to the same spot.
But what route brought the Norwegians to Noirmoutier? They too
may have coasted from the Oslofjord down the North Sea's eastern
shores, rounding the difficult headlands of Normandy and Brittany,
and perhaps joining in attacks on Quentowic and Rouen on the
way. But a much more direct and navigationally attractive route is
down the Irish Sea, from the Norse kingdom already established in
Dublin. The great pirate host which came to Cornwall in 838 and
supported the Celts in unsuccessful battle against the English was
perhaps also from Ireland.

The middle of the century marks a change in the previous pattern
of widely scattered brief attacks. The Old English Chronicle annal
for 850 tells us that in this year for the first time the heathen
remained over the winter. No less than three hundred and fifty ships
attacked the mouth of the Thames and Canterbury, successfully at
first but defeated at the unknown site of Acleah (Oak Wood) in the

end. And in a successful sea battle the English fighting in ships for the first time destroyed a viking force at Sandwich, capturing nine enemy ships and driving off the rest, perhaps to travel on to try their luck elsewhere, in Normandy perhaps.

The changes of importance are in the weight of the attacks, in both numbers of ships involved and continuity, and the indications of successful Anglo-Saxon counter-action at sea, perhaps hinted at again in the Chronicle's record that many were slain and drowned on each side in the battle at Thanet. The first overwintering sites, Thanet and Sheppey, are the sort of marsh-surrounded islands, more easily reached by water than land, which later Scandinavian raiders even after the Norman Conquest were to exploit success-fully against William the Conqueror's highly professional army two centuries later. The area of the engagements, round Sandwich, is also a foretaste of the frequent appearance of the port in the naval warfare of the eleventh century. Its strategic importance was pre-sumably because a position near the North Foreland enabled a defensive fleet to cover both the Thames and East coast and also the Channel and South coast, against an invader coming south down the Dutch coast and unwilling to make a crossing of more than about twelve hours. The attraction for the invader was presumably that by making landfall there he could, depending on wind and weather, raid either the East or Channel coast. It may seem a long way round from Denmark to the former, and I think it is significant that in the later viking age direct crossings with smaller fleets of more seaworthy ships do occur, but at this early date and once again in the eleventh century, the size of the fleet and type of ship seem to make coastal passages preferable. This anticipation of the eleventh-century strategy does however suggest how little the leaders of these mid-ninth century fleets had left to learn about their correct employment. That too I think helps to support my belief that the development of this type of ship began in the early eighth century, as *Beowulf* seems to indicate.

We must not exaggerate the importance of ship-types and voyag-ing in the viking impact on Europe: there is certainly no need to do so. One noticeable aspect of developments in the second half of the century, 850–900, is the increasingly land-based activity, relegating the ships to the secondary role of transport or landing-craft. Along with this we notice a steady growth in Anglo-Saxon defensive power afloat. In 875 'King Alfred sailed out to sea with a fleet and fought against seven ships, capturing one and putting the others to flight' and in 882 'King Alfred went out to sea with ships and fought against four ships of Danes: two were captured, the men aboard were killed: two surrendered, the men were severely wounded before they yielded'. Æthelweard in his Latin Chronicle (based on a better O.E. Chronicle than any that survives) tells us that in 884, off the river Stour, 'a fleet was sent by Alfred, sixteen ships met them, but were cleared by force of arms and the leaders killed. The rest of the pirate fleet came on its way, they plied their oars, put aside the thole-pins, the waves shone with clashing arms'. We cannot be quite sure that he always understood the Latin technical terms with which he adorned his prose, perhaps in imitation of Old English verse style, but the last phrase about thole-pins suggests the ships were rowed from the rail, perhaps with the oar held to the thole by a hide loop, and not through oarports as in the Gokstad ship. This would mean a rail low enough for effective rowing, and vessels with less freeboard than Gokstad and presumably somewhat smaller, certainly less capable of open-sea sailing, for which more freeboard is required.

The three engagements just described, show that the old-style freebooting small fleets of viking ships had little to look forward to in the North Sea on unco-ordinated raids, and the point is made even more clearly by the better-known entry of 896. In that, the Chronicle tells us that Alfred's ships were twice as long as the Danish ships, and faster, steadier, and higher, some with sixty oars, some more, and as they seem to have been commanded by Frisians who were highly competent professional seafarers, they must have been deadly opponents to meet at the end of a North Sea crossing.

The great storm off Swanage in 876, in which 120 viking ships were lost overnight, must also have pointed the dangers of using ships developed in sheltered waters on coasts exposed to the seas raised by Atlantic westerly gales. The wheel seems to have come full circle when we read in 910 that the viking host from Northumbria advanced south into Mercia and King Edward mustered a fleet of a hundred ships from the South coast and sailed to meet them: 'the host, believing that the chief strength of the king lay in his ships, thought they could harry (on land) where they pleased'. It is obviously possible for a modern historian to dispute the accuracy of this assessment, but on the face of it this and other entries do suggest that by the end of the century the initial advantage of the viking ships in their sudden impact on the Irish Sea and the North Sea had been lost. The area within which their voyaging remained the decisive activity shrank back northwards to the later Scandinavian world of the Northern Isles, Faeroe, Iceland, Greenland and Vinland (Newfoundland), in a type of ship differing from the oared warship, which first returns to prominence after AD 1000. The first half of the next century, 900–950, was a period of the re-conquest of viking settlements in England, but without any opposition at sea the traditional viking ships were still able to preserve kingdoms based on Dublin, Man and York.

That the viking activity in the second half of the ninth century was largely land-based did not make it less dangerous either in Europe or in England. There is, as far as I know, no evidence on which anyone could have concluded that they were facing a different sort of threat when the Great Army (as the Chronicle calls it) arrived late in 865 in East Anglia. Those maps of viking attacks on England which show it as an arrow arriving from a generally north-easterly direction (straight from Denmark?) are probably misleading. Large fleets and armies can certainly not have been raised exclusively from the barren west coast of Jutland. In later centuries the large fleets assembled about midsummer day, an easily ascertainable date, in some sheltered central location, before moving off on their campaign. The arrival in East Anglia was so late that all that was done was to secure horses and winter quarters. As the ultimate aim was York, it seems unlikely that a direct crossing from Jutland to a coast more easily and safely reached by coasting would be undertaken, particularly late in the year. The fact that the Great Army campaigned for the next ten years without making any significant use of its ships also tells against the idea of it being an army of long-distance voyagers. When we do hear of the ships again it is in the disastrous shipwrecks off Swanage in 876: not surprising that there is no more activity at sea reported of the survivors, who after 876 settled in Northumbria. It is almost the end of the century before we hear again, in 893, of ships from Northumbria, and then they are, as the O.E. Chronicle rather patronisingly observes, 'warships built many years before'. If they were indeed survivors of the original fleet then they and their crews were thirty years older, and becoming obsolete.

The venture on which they set out in 893 seems to have been both generous in concept and successful in execution. A hundred ships attacked Exeter and forty the north coast of Devon, drawing King Alfred and his field army away to the west, and lifting the pressure on the viking army which the previous year had arrived in Kent from the Continent. It had been immediately very closely contained and continually harassed by the Anglo-Saxons and had suffered heavy casualties for little return. The forty ships which attacked in the Bristol Channel presumably came down the Irish Sea rather than passing through the Channel, along the South Coast and round Land's End. There certainly was viking shipping in the Irish Sea at this time, and much activity in the Northern Isles. I assume that Northumbrian here means 'Scandinavians (and perhaps some Angles) North of the Humber' and there is enough evidence of trans-Pennine activity to make it possible to believe in forty ships leaving from the Morecambe Bay area. Fifteen years earlier a similar attack on north Devon with twenty-three ships coming from South Wales had lost 800 men. It did not necessarily have any very permanent home in South Wales, but shows the sort of force that could be raised in the Irish Sea area. The hundred ships attacking Exeter and coming from East Anglia had, it is worth noting, rowed or sailed past their distressed kinsmen without directly intervening either to reinforce or evacuate them, another instance of the comparatively sophisticated exploitation of the possibilities of long-range action open to a fleet.

There may have been special reasons why the arrivals from the Continent in 892 had to depend on those vikings already here to raise whatever sort of fleet was possible to restore the traditional advantage. They had been defeated in the eastern part of the Empire the year before, far from the coast. King Arnulf at the head of an army of East Franks, Bavarians and Saxons had attacked them before their fleet with reinforcements could make its way to them, and they were in retreat when they arrived at Boulogne and embarked for England. The Chronicle mentions particularly that they came over in one lift, horses and all, in 250 ships. As they had, like the Great Army in England, been operating for a long time as a cavalry army away from their ships, I doubt if we can assume that they made the crossing in warships which carried a horse (or two?) for each man, nor that the warlike fleet of the 'ship host' normally included a fleet train of transports capable of lifting the whole 'mounted host' in one lift. It certainly would have presented little threat to the sort of defending fleet it might expect to meet in the southern North Sea if it did.

It is noticeable that the successful use of ships against viking fleets at this period, as far as we can read it in the Old English sources, does not involve cruising at sea or waiting off the coast, though I think there is some literary evidence that that might have happened (under Alfred's personal command) on at least one occasion. But the usual tactic seems to have been an attack on a small group of viking ships once they had entered an estuary and were committed to a landing, or were indeed halfway through it. At this stage any viking advantage of superior seamanship or sailing skill (if by this date it existed against the Frisian skippers directing the English ships) would be at a minimum, but the troops on board would be at their most vulnerable before they had time to form up on shore. The Æthelweard account almost looks like a blockade of the selected river entrance which sixteen viking ships had to put back to raise if the rest of their fleet was to make further progress.

The literary evidence which makes me speculate that Alfred had awaited at sea, probably among sandbanks, the arrival of viking ships, is one of his original additions to his translation of the soliloquies of St Augustine. Where the latter simply says that we should direct our mind's eye upon God, Alfred expands this to a most compelling and I think authentically experienced image: 'If a ship is out in the sea among the waves, beaten upon by surf, yet it can remain safe and unbroken if its anchor-cable holds, for one end of it is fast to the anchor in the seabed and the other to the ship and it is stretched out straight between them and the ship is safe, if the cable holds.' I find Alfred's injunction that we should turn our mind to God as directly as the anchor-cable stretches between ship and anchor much more intelligible if one of his Frisian skippers had explained to him how to tell if the anchor was dragging, and Alfred had himself experienced the alarming realisation that the safety of the whole crew hung by a thread, or an anchor-rope. One hopes that it was one of Ohthere's really high-class walrus-hide shipropes which he had recommended so warmly to 'his lord King Alfred'.

The conclusion of all this is that it must be doubtful whether viking fleets contained vulnerable carriers which might need towing in calms or restricted waters, and restrict the manoeuvrability of the fleet. Of the 250 ships in 892 some, perhaps the majority, were locally obtained trading craft, not necessarily of viking type. It is worth noting that the Chronicle does not say, as elsewhere, 'returned to their ships' but 'wurdon gescipode' 'were provided with ships'. The ships may well have been the hulks, keels and cogs, to use the current terms, which were regularly engaged in the carrying trade to England. We note that on arrival there the ships had to be towed (not rowed) four miles up the river from its mouth.

The settlement of the Northern Isles, Faeroe and Iceland was going on at roughly this time, and required the transport of live-stock over much greater stretches of open water and therefore greater risk of bad weather, than between Boulogne and the Lympne. Evidently vessels of viking type were capable of doing this: the question is whether they regularly formed part of fighting fleets, or whether anyone could rapidly collect a large number of them and dispatch them to a rendezvous at Boulogne. The fact that the Ladby ship has proved, in modern facsimile, capable of loading four horses in sheltered water does not really help to explain the 892 annal unless we suppose that the number of mounted warriors was absurdly small.

I therefore think that the majority of the 892 ships were probably not of viking type. But Ohthere's certainly, and Wulfstan's prob-ably, were, and the accounts of their voyages given to Alfred in the last quarter of the ninth century are our best sources for the viking seafaring of the period, infinitely preferable to deductions from imaginative works written four centuries later. They both show very well the typical mixture of interests, adventurous exploration, profitable trade, and observation of those features of the local society which might later be exploited. They also make it possible (in a way archaeological finds never can) to enter into the minds of the men who sailed the ships and see the sort of factors which they took account of. Interpreting what they have to say inevitably involves not only knowledge of their ships but also of the relation-ship between Old Norse and Old English: they were close but not identical, and the changes involved in moving from one to the other can also tell us something about the voyaging.

Ohthere does not tell us what sort of ship he used when he sailed north from his home, probably Senja in Halogaland. When he was hunting for whales up to fifty ells long (75 ft), the thickness of the walls of Babylon according to the same text!) and killed 60 in two days he was one of six. The boat may have been a sixareen, or six-oared boat, perhaps the size of Waterwitch (illustration p. 93) roughly the same as the later whalers launched from eighteenth-century ships. Probably for a voyage into the unknown 'further than the whalehunters went at their furthest' he used his larger boat: a man who owned 600 reindeer, 20 oxen and 20 sheep and twenty pigs must have had more than one boat. To collect his tribute from the Lapps in walrus-hide ropes, furs and eiderdown he probably needed a good general-purpose craft which could sail with a certain volume of goods (not very heavy or large in relation to their value) with a big enough crew to provide an armed escort. Such a vessel would be suitable for the three voyages we know he made, to the White Sea, down the Norwegian coast to the Oslo-fjord, and from there to Hedeby and on to England.

He began the first voyage by sailing north for three days to the limit reached by whalers and then on for another three days until the coast turned to the east. I have elsewhere given reasons for believing this to be Nordkyn or even Slettnes rather than North Cape. Six days for 260 miles suggests that he stopped each night. At Nordkyn he awaited a wind 'west and somewhat north'. I take this to be WNW or west by north, as the text uses 'west-north' for NW (Anglo-Saxon put the north or south last in such compounds, not first as we do). After four days' sail the land turned south, at the entrance to the White Sea, and here he says he *had* to wait for a due N wind, to sail for five days along the coast until he came to a great river (probably the R. Varzuga) the far bank of which was settled, so that he did not dare to go any further. This river still, according to the Admiralty Pilot, marks a division in the vegetation cover on this desolate coast.

It will be evident that there are some problems in this voyage. Perhaps the most obvious is that the courses 6 days north, 4 days east and 5 days south imply a finishing point north of the start after a rectangular course, whilst a glance at the chart shows that the true track was 6 days NE, 4 days SE and 5 days S, SW and then W, finishing well south of the starting point. Some have proposed, following Mediterranean usage, a forty-five-degree clockwise shift in the cardinal points, so that north actually meant northeast, east meant southeast and so on. Evidence for any general use of this system in either England or Scandinavia, outside translations from Mediterranean texts, is very weak. I think it more likely that the Norwegian cost was conventionally assumed to run north–south, which is reasonable enough in the most populated parts of the country. The Old Norse term for northwest was 'ut north' or 'north and out to sea' and southeast was 'land suth' or 'south and in towards land'. These terms were so firmly established in the language that they were even used out in Iceland, where they made no sense, particularly on the East coast where southeast was actually south and out to sea! Language usage is determined by the majority of speakers, and it is not surprising that a Norwegian who, as he tells us, lived further north than any other, should follow the ordinary usage even though it was not accurate in his part of the coast. He could scarcely have used 'land north' for a course parallel to the coast, and if he had, there could be no certainty that an Anglo-Saxon whose ordinary term was 'east-north' would have understood him.

The chart may seem to suggest another discrepancy, the disparity in speed to Nordkyn, 260 miles in six days, and on from there to the White Sea entrance, 330 miles in four days. There is however a strong east-going current, as much as two knots, to the east of North Cape, and that would be worth 25 miles in every twelve hours, so the figures really check quite well and are I think reliable. The total time for the whole voyage is credible, because Ohthere got exactly the wind shifts he needed: the only ones in fact with which the voyage could be made, as the normal summer weather around North Cape would have given constant headwinds with the outflow from the polar high-pressure area. The voyage back may have been a good deal less impressive and it is noticeable that he says nothing about it. How did he come to embark on the outward voyage in the only weather system in which it was practicable? Perhaps he was just very lucky, and no more needs to be said, but I think the account includes some valuable hints about the voyage strategy involved.

We notice that at Nordkyn he *awaits* the shift to WNW, but later *has* to wait for the due north wind. The sequence of winds is that round a depression travelling roughly northeast, and eventually passing ahead of the ship, probably eventually moving east as it meets the polar high. Only so is the sequence of winds south, westnorthwest, north intelligible. I find it striking that the tactic of waiting at North Cape for the wind to go to the north of west is immediately recognisable to present-day trawler skippers. It ensures that the centre of the depression has passed ahead and the wind can be relied on to moderate and blow itself out, not increase, as might happen if the centre was still approaching. It appears from the chart that Ohthere could easily have laid the course down to the White Sea once the wind had veered to southwest. He did not *need* to wait for it to shift further and (unlike the later occasion) does not say that he had to. The word he uses meant 'to wait for something one expects to happen' and has this implication even more strongly in Old Norse than Old English. Later on, to overcome the strong adverse current out of the White Sea (whose overfalls have been said to be the origin of the name), he *did* need to head straight into it with a true following wind, and here he says he *had* to wait. There is nothing to be said for the view, enshrined in many standard works, that Ohthere could only blow dead downwind. He was probably a good deal more skilful sailing-master than any modern critic can hope to be.

This view requires not only that Ohthere knew that the winds flow anti-clockwise (he presumably would have said 'against the sun') round a depression, but also that in his coastal home he could recognise an oncoming depression, and make a rough estimate of its speed of advance, and this may seem rather a lot to believe of the late ninth century. It could be done by noticing the increasing swell which soon outruns the depression which caused it, and often changes the sound of the surf on the beaches, in the outer isles of Scotland as well as Norway. The time elapsed between this and the first sight of the clouds on the western horizon which herald the approaching depression gives an indication of the speed. This sensitivity to wave pattern has been noted by David Lewis as an important part of the equipment of traditional Pacific island navigators, and some such wind strategy must have been required for the voyages from Norway to Iceland and Greenland, easy and rapid with the right wind, difficult and dangerous with any other, and lasting for a long enough time for the weather on departure to change radically. Ohthere's 500-mile voyage evidently required him to set sail in the path of an approaching depression to secure the right wind shifts: the implications of this for his confidence in his ability to forecast them, and react alertly to signs of them, are obvious, and indicate a mental attitude important outside the realm of navigation alone.

His next account, of the voyage the length of Norway from his home in the far north to the trading town of Kaupang (perhaps an annual event, though he does not say so), is no less interesting. The Old Norse name of the port was Skiringssalr, and Alfred's form 'Scirincges heal' shows the usual substitution of the softer 'sh' sound for the harder Scandinavian 'sk'. Modern English 'shirt' and 'skirt' show both pronunciations of what was originally the same word. The English form may well have been the commonly used international name, which would explain the place 'Shishuna' in the south of 'Norbega' opposite 'Darmarga' with its port of 'Selesbuli'. The names are taken from the Arabic geographer Idris, and the identification of Shishuna has been resisted by Scandinavians because the palatised soft sound is not found in Old Norse. There is general agreement that Selesbuli is an Arabic version of Slesvik near Hedeby, Ohthere's destination. The anglicisation of Skiringssalr in King Alfred is taken so far that the ordinary prose word for 'hall' has been substituted for Norse 'salr' which in the corresponding English form 'sele' was only used in poetry. It seems more likely to be the result of familiarity with the place than a one-off translation specially produced for Ohthere's account. One might compare such English forms for foreign ports as Gothenburg (Göteborg) or Copenhagen (København): they are usually fairly close with a strong English trade.

Ohthere gives the distance from Senja to Kaupang by saying 'You would not do it in a month if you stopped every night and had a usable wind every day'. The word here translated 'usable' is usually said to mean favourable, but it is rare and uncertain (perhaps a half translation from Norse) and not even the most sanguine North Sea skipper has ever taken seriously the idea of truly favourable winds for thirty successive days, whatever happens in favoured trade-wind areas. The limit of the ambition is to avoid foul ones, and the

clear sense is that one must allow a month under the most favourable circumstances imaginable, or be ready to keep going overnight
occasionally. The implication that it is normal to stop overnight, at
any rate in the Leads (the passages between the coastal islands), not
only suggests a vessel easily able to find a suitable small beach or
sheltered anchorage, but also perhaps that he thought of the voyage
as starting well before midsummer, with its non-existent nights.

The way in which he measures progress southward is not
latitude. It resembles the method used by Wulfstan, whose voyage
ends this chapter, and to some extent that of the modern primitive
Pacific navigators described by David Lewis in his fascinating *We,
the Navigators*. Ohthere tells us that for the first part of the journey
we have Iceland to starboard. The manuscript says Ireland, which is
untrue, but this was the period when Iceland was being settled from
west Norway, and it is inconceivable that Ohthere did not know of
its existence, even if an Anglo-Saxon scribe did not. The letters 'r'
and 's' are in any case very similar in O.E. manuscripts. The 'islands
between Iceland and this land' are to starboard for the next stretch,
presumably the Faeroes and Shetland whether you take 'this land'
to refer to England (most likely) or to Norway. Then 'this land'
(evidently England) is to starboard until arrival in Kaupang, in the
south of Vestfold, the west side of the Oslofjord. He clearly regards
the headlands passed in the first part of the voyage as departure
points only for an Iceland voyage until about the south end of
Hiteren (see *Odin's Raven* chart p. 95). From there until about
Stavanger the departure points are for Faeroe and Shetland, and
south of Stavanger for Britain direct. Evidently Ohthere and many
others had craft for which such oversea voyages were normal
enough to be used as reference points on a coastal voyage south.

From Kaupang he sailed to the great port of Hedeby (Haithabu)
called 'Aet Haethum', on the heath, in Old English. For the first
three days he had to port Denmark (i.e., south Sweden which then
formed part of Denmark) and open sea to starboard, but two days
before he came to Hedeby he had Jutland, Sillende, and many
islands to starboard. Most recent editors have taken Sillende to be a
part, obscure and speculative, of the east coast of south Jutland,
though Jutland is named just before. In the context of the voyage I
much prefer the older interpretation of it as Sjaelland. Ohthere can
scarcely have been unaware that the direct route to Hedeby was

blocked by the Danish archipelago. Sjaelland was the centre of the Danish kingdom, and it is inconceivable that coming down the east shore of the Sound as he clearly did (open sea to starboard for three days) he should not have named it when it was the first land he would actually sight to starboard. To follow its coast round to the SW, passing north of 'the islands belonging to Denmark' (Moen, Falster, Laaland) would be a very sensible route to Hedeby. It might, depending on wind and current, be a little longer than the Great Belt route leaving Sjaelland to port, but it is navigationally more straightforward, and a Norwegian from the far north without local knowledge might very well have felt happier on it.

King Alfred at this point, Hedeby, uses a different informant. The next voyage description comes from Wulfstan, probably a northern Englishman, with a different way of speaking and sailing, and perhaps a different type of craft. The opening sentence reveals the differences immediately. There is no reference to 'His lord, King Alfred'. 'Wulfstan said that he left Hedeby and was in Truso in seven days and nights, the ship running under sail the whole way'. Truso was a site near Elbing, south of the Frisches Haff in Dantzig Bay, perhaps Druzno where excavations suggest some such settlement. Wulfstan does not at all present it as an emporium like Hedeby or Skiringssalr ('no beer is brewed among the Ests but they do have mead'), and does not mention any trade products that made the voyage worthwhile, except perhaps the honey, the only sweetener of the day. The distance sailed is at the shortest just over 400 miles. We have seen that Ohthere averaged forty miles a day if he stopped at night and eighty if he did not. Wulfstan, not stopping at night, averages only sixty miles a day, evidently in a heavier and slower craft, perhaps of what Alfred elsewhere calls 'the Frisian shape'. Just as Ohthere instead of latitude uses the concept of what faraway land he is now 'level' with, Wulfstan measures his progress eastward along the south coast of the Baltic, Wendland, by reference to the successive places he is south of. The first are Langeland, Laaland and Falster: the projecting south point of the latter (present day Gedser, the ferry station to Germany) would be an important stage on the voyage, probably on the second day. He probably sighted all these, but his next marks to port are Skane, far out of sight fifty miles north of his track, and Blekinge-Möre, Öland and Gotland, up to a hundred miles north. That he knew they were there suggests he had sailed to Birka, a common voyage from Hedeby, for they are the coasts one would pass along on the way there. David Lewis reports that the Pacific island navigators use a traditional system of 'etaks' or moving islands, on long voyages dividing the stages by reference to many such, all far out of sight to one side of the course line. To measure movement across the open sea they think of this island reference point as at first lying under one star seen from their position. As they advance it will come to lie under a different star as if it had moved backwards relative to them as they sail past it. Hence the term moving island: they were at pains to explain to him that they knew of course that the islands did not really move, but that was the way they systematised their concept of the voyage. Wulfstan's seven points (if we count the adjacent Blekinge and Möre as one seen from this angle) perhaps coincide roughly with the seven days of the voyage, for at Elbing he would be about south of Gotland, so that it lay between him and the Pole star. When south of Bornholm he perhaps thought of Öland as northeast of him (between him and the summer sunrise) and when he had moved far enough east to put it between him and the Pole star its place as the next point to the northeast was taken by Gotland. It is not the same as the Pacific system, but reminds me of it: the system suitable in the equatorial and clear skies there could not in any case develop in the cloudy high latitudes of viking navigation. But some coherent way of thinking of the relationship to one another of widely separated places, without compass, chronometer or sextant was indispensable in the ocean voyages to Faeroe, Iceland and Greenland discussed in the next chapter. It is unlikely to have had much in common with our concepts of latitude and longitude, and that is why I think it important to try to win some hint of it from the only two voyagers of the viking age whose words were written down by a contemporary and perhaps in answer to his elucidatory questions. There is of course in these voyages, as in the Old English poems, very much which this approach does not exhaust.

4

The Tenth Century

The end of the ninth century saw the end of the mass seaborne invasions of the British coasts of the North Sea. The Old English Chronicle tells us of the dissolving of the Great Army to settle down to plough their lands. 'Those without any money got ships and went south over the sea to the River Seine.' Evidently in 896 in England surplus warships were a drug on the market, and the voyage was the impecunious vikings' way out. The Rollo who founded the Scandinavian colony of Normandy landed there in 900 and was granted it in 911, and features of the material from there suggest that some of his followers and settlers came from the Scandinavian areas in England. Some of the finds from the Atlantic coast of the Continent, such as the ship burial on the Ile de Groix off Brittany show very well the widely spread but very mixed culture that resulted from a generation of long-range voyaging. Under a mound as high as those at Gokstad and Oseberg, whose edges were crumbling under the inroads of the sea its owner had used so well, were found the remains of a forty-foot ship, built of oak with pine mast and oars and therefore probably built in Norway. A metal dragon tail ornament (reproduced on *Odin's Raven*) had survived the burning of the vessel, which probably had a wooden dragon head as well. Burning the burial ship, though a favourite scene in films and novels, was in fact unusual among overseas vikings, and might suggest that the man still firmly adhered to the older heathen practices of Norway and Sweden where the rite is found. A girl accompanied him into the grave as sacrifice, as we find in the Isle of Man ship burial at Balladoole and as is reported from the Swedish vikings in Russia by Arabic writers. Similar instances are known from both Norway and Sweden, and it seems that the man had very conservative views on religion. Of his material equipment, however, only the spears were Scandinavian in type, and one of those was English. In all his finery nothing else was at all reminiscent of his homeland: all the decorative and conspicuous ornaments such as sword and shield-boss had evidently been acquired on his voyaging, and in external appearance he must have been indistinguishable from any other west European chieftain of comparable wealth. As, to judge from the sources, his band probably included some English, French or German speaking followers, it cannot even be excluded that, after twenty years or so, his own command of Norse was somewhat faded. The very rapid and empiric acclimatisation to local culture was even more marked among those vikings who settled on the Continent than among those in England. Only in the remote islands where they were not in close contact with a culture of greater material wealth and comfort did they retain unchanged their traditional language and way of life.

In the tenth century raiding in Ireland and land-taking on the Continent continued, but not for three-quarters of a century were there further widespread descents on the English coast, from Cheshire to Thanet and Southampton in the generation after 880, which saw a revival of the large voyages of conquest of the ninth century, culminating in the arrival in the Humber in 1013 of King Sweyn of Denmark. From the Humber his ships could reach almost the whole of Scandinavian England by way of the Trent, Ouse and their tributaries. On this, as on the previous voyages of Sweyn's fleet, the route was not the obvious one directly across the North Sea, though that could sometimes be used by warships (e.g. voyage J, from Ribe to England, in diagram p. 91) but the older southern circular route down the coast to the shortest crossing point, across to Sandwich and then north again coasting round East Anglia. I think the most likely explanation for this return to the easier but longer coastal route is that a different and less seaworthy type of ship was involved. There are two possibilities. One is that large royal fleets were already built round, if they did not entirely consist

of, very fast long highly specialised warships propelled by as many
as forty pairs of oars. These ships because of their length, which was
more than their low freeboard and narrow beam were really strong
enough to carry, were vulnerable at sea to breaking up or swamp-
ing. The account in *Flateyjarbok* of such a ship with forty rowing
benches and 170 ft long has been dismissed as incredible by many.
But if the famous *Long Serpent* built just before AD 1000 really had
74 ells of keel on the ground (111 ft) then she must have been about
140 ft overall, as the curving stem was not scarfed direct to the keel
in a viking ship, there was a transitional piece, the *undirhlutr*
(bottom bit) recorded in Middle English, in between. We are told
that the *Long Serpent* had thirty-four rowing benches, so the low
straight midships portion over or through which they rowed must
have been about 120 ft long unless the benches were unusually
spaced. It is legitimate to doubt an account first written two hundred years later, but there are entries in the Old English Chronicle
which point the same way. Manuscripts differ, but I follow Garmonsway in thinking that the entry for AD 1008 required three
hundred hides to provide a ship and ten a 'scegth'. If we take the
hide as being roughly enough land to support a family then the ship
referred to might very well be a highly specialised warship of some
size by comparison with the 'scegth' which I take to be something
like a sixareen or femboring. I cannot see that the term was
restricted in Old English to large ships as the confused Latin render-
ing of the Cotton Domitian MS implies. The entry for AD 1048
speaks of a payment of eight marks for each rowlock of a ship: for
62 ships the sum works out at 324 pounds per ship and on a later
occasion for 32 ships it seems to be 345 pounds per ship; a reasonable agreement, suggesting that the average ship in the royal fleet by
1040 had eighty or eighty-six oars (or at any rate was paid as if it
had). Not only the hull, but the large number of men on board with
their requirements for food and water must have made coastal
voyaging preferable for such ships.

Another reason for choosing the short crossing might have been
the mixed nature of the fleet. We see from runic gravestones all over
Scandinavia that the immense sums to be collected as Danegeld in
England attracted warriors from everywhere. Thorkell the Tall,
brother of Sigvald the leader of the famous Jomsborg vikings,
campaigned in England with notable impartiality, fighting for both

sides alternately, with the fleet he brought to Sandwich at the beginning of August in 1009. His ships were presumably of a type meant for warfare in the Baltic where Jomsborg, though its precise site is not known, certainly lay. It is not surprising that the fleet took a cautious route if the developed seaworthy North Sea and Irish Sea raiding vessels of the previous century were now in a minority. It is particularly striking that even on hurried departures from the Humber for Denmark it was evidently necessary to go down to the Thames again to cross to the Rhine mouth before coasting back, in spite of the increased danger of being attacked. The voyages thus have very little in common with the open ocean voyages which were still being made from Norway to the Irish Sea by way of Shetland and Orkney.

Kings from Dublin frequently crossed to assert their power in northern England, and ruled from time to time in York. One of them, Gudröd, was honourably entertained at Aethelstan's court, where there were many Scandinavians including the future King Haakon of Norway. He soon became bored in the unusual sur-roundings, as a later chronicler tells us: 'the old pirate, accustomed to living in the water like a fish'. Pirate may be more affectionate than it sounds to us: Anglo-Saxons writing in Latin used *archipiratus* to mean the captain of an armed fleet, even one given such legitimacy as the service of one of these sea-kings could confer. Gudröd (later Godred, King Orry) was not necessarily more (or less!) piratical than Chaucer's shipman.

The rapid seesaws in fortune of the Scandinavian invaders in the Irish Sea area at this time show how mobile they must have been. When defeated in Ireland or England they could sail away to England or Ireland, and if under pressure in both could retire to the Isle of Man or the Scottish Isles, to return next year. At its most powerful the viking Irish Sea kingdom united the Scottish Isles, Ireland, Man and the East and West coasts of Northern England. It could be crossed from east to west in a day and a night, but at its largest extended from north to south over ten degrees of latitude, almost comparable to the thirteen degrees Norway covers. These periods of unity were often interrupted, and never lasted more than ten years or so. The pure longship type which was developing during this century was quite unsuitable for the open sea voyages from Norway, and presumably the ships which exercised this dominion over the Irish Sea, and occasionally raided the Continent as well, must have been the general-purpose compromise type of which Gokstad is an elaborated example. I suppose it is possible that some longships were built locally, but there is no record of them and it is difficult to see much role for them. The English reconquest of the five boroughs and the Kingdom of York was essentially a land-based affair. Only in AD 1000, when the viking fleet had sailed away to Normandy, did Aethelred's English fleet devastate the Isle of Man whilst he laid waste Cumberland. The west coast of Scotland is very similar to the Norwegian coast and remained the haunt of galleys as long as did the homelands. The distribution of foreign, particularly Arabic, coins shows at least two routes home from the viking kingdom. One crossed the north of England from Morecambe Bay to the Humber and there took ship again probably to Ribe and Hedeby. The other route went up the western isles and then via Shetland to Norway or the Faeroes to Iceland. Both Danish and Norwegian ships voyaged to Ireland, Man, Anglesey and Wales, but there was no love lost between them. The voyage from Denmark is as likely to have rounded John of Groats as Land's End. Both routes involved exposure to Atlantic seas before reaching the landlocked Irish Sea.

This seems to me the distinctive feature of the viking voyages of the tenth century. There had of course been ocean voyages, to Iceland, before AD 900. And coasting raids, never out of sight of land for months, did not stop after AD 900: after AD 1000 the large fleets of relatively unseaworthy warships replace the small group of long-distance voyagers as the typical viking activity. But the tenth century is pre-eminently that of the open sea voyaging to Faeroe, Iceland, Greenland and the shores even further distant usually unfortunately lumped together as Vinland. This is unfortunate because the important and identifiable coasts in North America reached by viking navigators before AD 1000 are Markland and Helluland, and contact with them seems to have been kept up until the end of the Greenland colony in the fifteenth century.

Voyages such as these required different ships and navigation from the familiar North Sea routes which rarely involved more than two nights at sea between Norway and Shetland, Shetland and Faeroe, Faeroe and Iceland. The raiding ships propelled by sail and oar could carry their crew of thirty or so armed men for surprising distances, even through the Mediterranean to Alexandria or Constantinople, and return with their booty, but they were not well adapted to carry heavy weights and farm animals across the open sea. The Ile de Groix ship was probably about the same length as *Ofeigur* (diagram p. 93) but much narrower, shallower and more lightly built. These raiding ships were very seaworthy for their low freeboard (necessary for rowing) partly because of their high ends but mainly because their light weight enabled them to rise buoyantly to a dangerous sea. To carry heavy weights required a higher freeboard, and that made it more difficult and less efficient to row, increasing the dependence on sail alone. This made it more important to be able to use a wide range of winds, and to have a more efficient sail, needed to shift the heavier weight, but also made possible by the greater displacement to carry it. It is my view, for the reasons discussed at length in part two, that the permanently raised mast of the trading ship was so because it was so tall, rather than because it could not be raised by a small crew. Peter Foote has pointed out that the straightforward interpretation of a verse about the ship of King Magnus Bareleg in AD 1100 is that its mast was seventy feet high. On such a mast an efficient sail-plan, twice as high as it is wide, could have been set to great advantage. If this aspect-ratio seems surprising (it is close to the optimum for this type of sail) it should be remembered that the Humber Keel, the Femboring, the Sixareen, the Coble, all vessels for which Scandinavian ancestry is certain, all have sail-plans like this, which are required if the ship is to have much ability to windward. They may all have developed them separately and independently, just as they may all have independently adopted a trapezoid shape, but I prefer to believe there is a common origin.

This seagoing weight-carrier was called the *knarr* and its general character was known from many references in the sources, before the discovery of planking from a 70 ft knarr in the Bergen harbour excavations of 1947; but it was the discovery at Skuldelev, now magnificently re-assembled for exhibition in the museum at Roskilde which confirmed and gave real shape to the earlier ideas. Though found in Denmark, Skuldelev 1, like the Ile de Groix ship, was built in Norway. Though nothing survived of her rig the hull looks most seaworthy, with a full swelling bow very different from that of Gokstad, so that one can understand the Old Norse adjective

'knarr-breasted' applied to certain favoured Icelandic girls. Skuldelev 1 is not however as big as Gokstad, only two-thirds of the
length, and not much over two-thirds of the tonnage of the heavy
Magnus Andersen version, but she has the same moulded depth,
which shows how much greater are the freeboard and draught
relative to the size of the ship. We must remember that 'knarr'
means a type of ship, not a size or employment: the sources refer to
little knarrs as well as large ones, and employment in war as well as
peaceful trading. In the same way it seems that the earliest cogs were
used on occasion as fighting ships, small and manoeuvrable enough
to be used in rivers, and only later did the term become restricted to
large and heavy merchantmen.

The only knarr for which the sources give any indication of size is
later. It was wrecked in 1118 near Eyjafell in Iceland and is usually
reckoned to have been about seventy feet long, the same size as the
Bergen one, as two accounts tell us it had 27 spaces between frames
and the knarr was closer framed than ships of Gokstad type. The
Äskekärr ship for example is fifty feet long but has twenty-three
frames as compared with the fifteen which a hull of that length built
to the Gokstad type (e.g. *Odin's Raven*) has. The knarr wrecked in
1118 must have been about the size of the Hull, Bristol and King's
Lynn ships which continued to fish, whale and trade round the
coast of Iceland, often in considerable numbers, until the eighteenth
century.

Tuxen, in his pioneer work on the Norse longships writes in 1886
of the craft which settled Iceland as carrying forty people and being
about the size of the 'jagt of forty tons, which is at present the
smallest size regularly trading between Denmark and Iceland'.
These were just over fifty feet in length with a beam of sixteen feet,
very close to Skuldelev 1, which is fifty-four feet by fifteen. They
had no charts and no reliable compass: many Hull whalers do not
seem to have used them because of the rapidly changing deviation
up at Greenland, and we can see how little change or progress there
had been for this class of ship in the intervening thousand years
(almost). That was because so much development had been
achieved in the previous five hundred. At its beginning vessels were
only paddled, and in sheltered waters, and by its end direct passages
were being made between Norway and Greenland and back with
substantial and rewarding cargo in both directions.

These superb vessels were not only different from those of the preceding century, but also more specialised, and they probably required more specialised masters and crews. They can never have paid their way as the general purpose vehicle of an estate owner who was not engaged in deep-water voyaging and international trade. They had presumably developed out of the earlier ship-type as the great trading towns developed, but were not really needed until the tenth-century transoceanic voyages began. If engaged in the carriage of farm stock to Iceland they probably preferred the old route by way of the islands which would simplify the provision of fodder and drinking-water for the animals. We know from the sources that the first planned voyage to Iceland, that of Floki, went by way of Shetland and Faeroe. The diagram (p. 91) shows how journey time increases disproportionately the longer one is at sea, presumably because more contrary winds are met with, so one can well understand settlement voyages travelling a route which could be divided into short stages between which animals and men could recuperate whilst awaiting the next favourable wind.

How many of these specialised vessels were available in the early tenth century to lift people and stock to Iceland? There is no satisfactory basis for calculation, but it would fit the estimates of many historians if we assumed (at 70 people per voyage) about thirty voyages a year between west Norway and Iceland. As we only know of one man who ever completed two round voyages in the same year, and he became famous for that feat alone, it seems that between thirty and forty knarrs must have been engaged in this trade, apart from those running to England and to the Continent and those, probably smaller, running to the Baltic. The population is believed to have been increasing, and we hear, though in later sources, of bulky cargoes imported from England and the Continent. The treaty provision of AD 991 between Olaf Tryggvason and Aethelred provides that any merchant ship of any country, even if wrecked, is immune from pillage in an English estuary, and an English ship and its cargo are immune in foreign waters if the cargo is still afloat, or has been landed onto the beach but is still the ship's property. Once it had passed into the consignee's or purchaser's hands the ship had no further interest. In any harbour one might evidently meet foreign cargo ships.

A number of these knarrs were presumably owned in west

Norway, the jumping-off place for voyages to Britain, and they would thus be available for emigrants to Iceland or Scotland.

Greenland is traditionally said to have been first sighted at the beginning of the century, but it was not until 986 that a real attempt at settlement was made. Twenty-five ships set out from Iceland and fourteen completed the voyage. The others were not all lost, some turned back, having either lost their way or lost heart for the voyage after reaching the limit of their endurance.

What sort of ships made this voyage? Most historians seem to assume that these too were knarrs, though some of the earlier ones, as you might expect, took it for granted that they were Gokstad ships taking a rest from the Russian swamps, the White Sea, the North Sea, the Irish Sea, the Mediterranean and every other field of viking activity to which they despatched that ubiquitous factotum. But neither knarrs nor Gokstad ships seem very likely to have been in the possession of not very prosperous peasant farmers in west Iceland in that sort of numbers. A knarr would certainly be required for direct voyaging between Norway and Greenland of which we learn later in *Landnamabok*, and the exploration ship in which three voyages of discovery were made to north America must have been a knarr. Evidently there were examples in Greenland hands fairly soon afterwards. But scarcely so soon, and scarcely twenty-five.

Two alternative craft should be considered, those surviving from the original voyages which had carried the settlers from Norway to Iceland, which were not all knarrs, and those subsequently built in Iceland. A fair number of the latter are mentioned in the sources, occasionally claimed to have been built from native oak, which certainly never grew in Iceland. *Ofeigur* (p. 93) was built entirely of driftwood, and the efficient exploitation of the resources of the many islands of western Iceland must have required the building of general purpose craft very like the boats of the pre-viking age but more seaworthy as they were more exposed to sudden storms. Such vessels, able to manoeuvre to some extent under oars in a way a knarr could not, would be more suitable for an exploratory voyage round an icebound coast.

Survivors from the end of the age of settlement fifty years earlier would not be very different, though probably larger and faster, and perhaps originally better built from choicer timber. The twenty-five ships which sailed to Greenland may have been of at least three different types, and it cannot be assumed that it was the knarrs which won through and the others which turned back. We often hear of knarrs leaving Iceland for Norway, drifting about for a month and then either coming into an Icelandic fjord again or being wrecked on a headland in the attempt. With a smaller crew and more or less unlimited stowage for drinking water in a full hull which probably profited from ballast for its fairly high rig, the knarr had a very long endurance at sea, but all the evidence is that it needed it. The earlier vessels were well adapted to the voyages which they made, but I doubt if many of them spent more than a night or two·at sea. The knarr could cheerfully contemplate a month: it retained the single square sail and relatively small and ineffective side rudder, though the latter's advantages for beaching were less important for the knarr. With a much heavier hull it was less manoeuvrable, and was in one way the end of the road for Scandinavian ship development, just as, in a different way, the eleventh century long ship was. Both had in different ways reached the limit of the scaling-up process applied to the originally light-weight Scandinavian open boat, in order to cope with the increasing demands the expansion of the viking age had given rise to. Any further advance would have to make fundamental changes in essential features, and it seems that this did not happen. The viking ship types were replaced by more successful foreign models. Their success is not necessarily entirely because they were superior as ships: it may be partly because the countries for whom they were familiar native ship types outgrew the Scandinavian countries. But a really large hull carrying heavy weights in heavy seas has in the end to be built on different principles from a light and buoyant descendant of earlier skin boats, and the more southern types were more capable of development than the viking hull which had early reached perfection but had limits on its possible size. The regular reference to the towing astern of a large boat which could be used for loading cargo, itself suggests that the basic advantages of shallow draft and ease of beaching had been given up in exchange for increased seaworthiness, and the trenailing of the planks to the frames suggests that the flexibility and lightness had been lost as well. We cannot really wonder that the knarr was replaced in the medieval carrying trade by the cog, though it left descendants in north Norway and in the early clinker-built keels on the Humber.

It is impossible to close the chapter without reference to the voyages to Vinland, cited whenever the long distance voyaging of the vikings is concerned, but often in a narrative conflated from various sources of differing ages and varying reliability. That version is produced by taking pieces from all the medieval works, choosing the parts which seem to fit together, and then reassembling them into an apparently consistent account without allowing for the authors' widely varying aims, skills and beliefs, or such contradictions as the assembly of all one version's different crews in a single voyage in another. It may be this sort of enthusiasm which causes the confusion about the Vinland voyages and the well-merited scepticism with which such accounts are sometimes received.

There is no doubt that many voyages were made from Greenland to various places in North America, probably starting about AD 990 and continuing into the fourteenth century, for 350 years. It is impossible in a single chapter to try to go deeply into the textual criticism of the sources about Vinland. The dates of authorship now accepted are Adam of Bremen 1075, Ari's *Islendingabok* 1127, *Graenlendinga saga* about 1175, *Erik the Red's saga* (sometimes called *Thorfinn's saga*) about 1275. The last is based only on the others, and its author's imagination, and mistaken belief that the geographical 'knowledge' of his day (that Greenland must be joined at the top to Russia, and America at the bottom to Africa!) enabled him to improve on them. He conscientiously remodelled the accounts to harmonise with what he believed to be the truth about geography and Christianity and the good name of the leading families of Greenland, but his work is safe evidence for nothing: except that the phrases he used were current in his day.

One great source of difficulty is that Vinland was for the eleventh century a myth as well as a reality. The idea of a glorious land to the west, flowing with milk and honey (or, more attractively to thirsty Scandinavian seamen, wine) was an old one, and when the new lands to the west were discovered the temptation to identify the best of them, such a contrast to Greenland, with this promised land must have been irresistible. Gwyn Jones observes that in land-naming Leif Eriksson was his father's son: Erik had deliberately chosen the lush-sounding 'Greenland' to lure settlers thither, and it is probable that Leif would do the same.

The importance of Adam of Bremen and Ari in this connection is that they are both serious historians with no axe to grind, who whilst they do not add to our knowledge of the Vinland voyages, do show that they know of a real land called Vinland, beyond Greenland but inhabited by people like those who live there. Adam emphasises that his account is not a repetition of old fables about self-sown corn and wild grapes yielding excellent wine, but is derived from trustworthy informants among the Danes. Bjarni, the first voyager to sight North America, had visited Norway before his death, and given to Earl Erik an account so modest that he was blamed for his lack of enterprise: an interesting sidelight on the thirst for adventurous exploration which still characterised Scandinavia in AD 1000. And Herman Palsson suggests that Authun, who is said to have brought a polar bear from Greenland as a gift to King Sweyn of Denmark, may have been one of those reliable informants whom Adam met. This is a good example of one of the difficulties of using saga evidence: a judicious opinion requires some knowledge of Icelandic humour and imagination, and it would be difficult to have too high an estimate of either. The story of Authun is certainly, as Herman Palsson says, 'one of the most delightful short stories in world literature', but there is perhaps enough fiction in the matter of Vinland already, without bringing in Authun.

It seems best to confine this discussion to the details of the six voyages (five successful) recorded in *Graenlendinga saga*, the earliest and most reliable source to mention them. It may well have been written for Brand Saemundarson who was Bishop of Holar in Iceland at the time it was composed, and was himself the great-grandson of Snorri, the first Scandinavian to be born in North America. The style is simple and seems early, and with one exception referred to later, nothing in the language tells against it being an unsophisticated report not much changed in the century and a half it was transmitted by reminiscent story-telling out in Greenland. The first voyage, the discovery, was an impromptu one by Bjarni Herjolfsson, an Icelander and evidently one of the specialists of this ocean-going age to whom I referred earlier. Eager to go to sea from his youth, he had his own ship, trading between Iceland and Europe, spending the winters alternately abroad and in Iceland with

his father. In the summer after Erik the Red's settlement of Greenland Bjarni returned to Iceland only to find that his father had
accompanied Erik. He decided to carry on to find him in his new
home, even though, as he said, the voyage must seem foolish as no
one on board knew anything of those waters.

The voyage did not go very well. It took three days to get out of
sight of land, which even remembering the height of Snaefellsjokull
is slow going, and also suggests Bjarni was determined to pass well
to the south of Cape Farewell. After this the fair wind died
altogether, to be followed by north winds and fog so that for days
they had no idea where they were going. Evidently they lowered the
sail during this time for when they next saw the sun and could
establish directions again the saga tells us that they hoisted it, or
winched it up, with a word implying the use of a windlass. This is
perhaps because that was the ordinary word in the author's day, a
century and a half later, though the Seaman's Law already cited
calls the compartment immediately forward of the mast the
'windlass-space'. Heavy gear and small crews must have made a
winch very desirable in these merchant ships, and the knarr
Skuldelev 1, though it has no signs of a winch mounting such as we
find in the Kalmar wrecks or the Bremer cog, could certainly have
used one. As Bjarni's *hafskip* on a later voyage of exploration
carried a crew of thirty it may have been appreciably bigger than
Skuldelev 1, and perhaps had some arrangement by then (like
eighteenth-century whalers) to be propelled by sweeps like Skuldelev 3, so that the large crew could help to manoeuvre the ship in
calms.

After the weather had cleared and Bjarni and his men were under
way again (presumably northwards?) they sighted next day a
well-wooded coast with low hills evidently not Greenland, and
leaving it on the port quarter continued on their way. Two days
later they sighted a flat land, also lacking the glaciers characteristic
of Greenland, and the wind left them again. The crew wished to go
ashore to replenish with drinking-water and firewood, which suggests that a knarr, as one might expect from its long voyages, had
some sort of arrangement for a cooking fire on board. The Gokstad
ship was buried with a huge cauldron which would have held stew
for sixty, but the bonfire necessary to boil it would have endangered
the ship, and the earlier viking ships did not I think usually cook at

sea. Bjarni refused to land, and sailed on before a south-west wind for three days before sighting a high ice-capped island. After that they sailed a further four days in a gale in which Bjarni had to caution the crew not to push the ship more than it or the rig would stand. Then they sighted Greenland, making their landfall at the very headland, Herjolfsness, where Bjarni's father lived.

The second Vinland voyage was in the same ship, after Leif Eriksson had bought it from Bjarni. He sailed with thirty-five men, including one German, Tyrkir from Thuringia, and was evidently able to retrace Bjarni's voyage from the dead reckoning Bjarni had kept: obviously such voyages could not be made without agreed measures of course and distance, and some way in which illiterate navigators could record them, but that is part of the last chapter. Leif called his first landfall (Bjarni's last) 'Helluland' because of the huge stone slabs (*hellir*) which formed its coast between the glaciers and the sea. The next land he called 'Markland' because of the forests which lay behind its white sands. At both these places we notice that they anchored off and went ashore in the boat, presumably because the knarr, unlike the earlier viking ships, was not easily beached and unbeached. Helluland was probably the south-east part of Baffin land, and Markland either Labrador or Newfoundland (depending on whether you want to reserve the latter for Vinland, against the evidence, in my opinion). After a further two days' sail with a north-easterly wind (not of course necessarily dead before it) they came to a point with an off-lying island, and in sailing through the sound between went aground and dried out at low water. They were able to run ashore where a river flowed out of a lake, and when their ship floated again rowed out to it in the boat. Here they settled for the winter, and the buildings they raised were used by every subsequent voyage, so it must have been an extremely prominent site. The saga tells us that on the shortest day of the year the sun rose at south-east and set at south-west. The old Norse terms are directions, not times (though the direction was used to establish time) and it is important to keep the distinction in mind. There can be little doubt that the saga writer intended to give at least a rough indication of how much further south than Iceland Leif's houses were. Some scholars have treated this as if it were a sun amplitude for navigational purposes (even correcting for refraction, and lower or upper limb!) and then assumed from the resulting

Before the wind, with the sail boomed-out by spars

Crew with H.M. King Olaf of Norway

Unloading *Odin's Raven* in Trondheim

Loading *Odin's Raven* on to M/S *Sletter* in Oslo

Hammering the 'god nails' or 'mighty nails' into the dragon head
before sailing from Trondheim

Departure from Trondheim; the beginning of the voyage

latitude (in one case 36° 54′ North, not 37°!) that it cannot have been made by Leif but must come from one of the obviously longer voyages of *Erik's saga*. This raises the whole question of the sun in viking navigation and I return to it in the last chapter, but on any interpretation Leif is most likely to have been south of 50° N, and of Newfoundland. By the present-day distribution of the wild grapes Tyrkir found and made himself drunk on (without any intervening fermentation!) he must have been considerably further south, in New England. Leif called the place Vinland and filled the ship's boat with grapes and the ship with a cargo of timber. It was on the homeward voyage that by steering closer to the wind than his crew approved of (because of the danger of backing the mainsail) he rescued a shipwrecked crew and earned his nickname 'the Lucky'.

The third voyage too was in the same ship, this time under Leif's brother Thorvald with a crew of thirty. They reached Leif's houses without incident (or any report of intervening landfalls) and explored the islands to the westward in the ship's boat. The next summer, in the ship, they sailed east and then north but were driven ashore in a gale and smashed the keel. It took a long time to repair the ship. Thorvald was killed in a fight with the natives after the vikings had callously murdered some they found sleeping under upturned canoes. We must be careful not to import prejudices about nineteenth-century colonialism into *Graenlendinga saga* but it cannot be denied that the firm hand with the natives and the ludicrously advantageous trade and profitable homeward cargoes of luxuries do strike a chord. After Thorvald's death the expedition is said to have returned to Greenland with a cargo of grapes and vines, though it is difficult to believe that they can have hoped to root the latter (how about a nice Greenland hock from a south-facing slope, ice-wine with a vengeance?).

The fourth voyage was also in the same by now battered ship, a marvellous testimonial to the craftsmen of whichever Norwegian fjord in which she first took the water. She was perhaps the only knarr in Greenland. The master this time was Thorsteinn Eriksson, going to recover his brother's body, and he took a crew of only twenty-five: we notice that either, as in our own day, owners were evidently keen to cut down manning costs, or the voyage was not attractive. In the event they spent the whole summer drifting about with no idea where they were and only returned to Greenland a week before winter having accomplished nothing.

The fifth voyage was by Thorfinn Karlsefni in his own ship in which he had arrived in Greenland from Norway. He intended to establish a permanent settlement and sailed with sixty men, five women and farm livestock including a bull. That must have required a large vessel, and perhaps Bjarni's old ship as well as being past her best was not big enough: we do not hear of her again. Thorfinn spent two winters at Leif's old site, but had trouble (deserved) with the natives and returned to Greenland the next spring with a good cargo of grapes, vines, and furs traded from the natives.

The sixth voyage (the fifth to reach Vinland) was made by Erik's daughter Freydis in one ship and two brothers Helgi and Finnbogi in another in which they had sailed to Greenland from Norway on the route described in the last chapter. There seems to have been some sort of formal contract. Each was to take thirty able-bodied men as well as women, but Freydis cheated and took five extra men, which one hopes sufficed. Both ships were to stay in company: this meant, as we know from the Seaman's Law, that they were not to sail further away from the other than the range at which the yard could still be seen. The brothers arrived in Vinland far enough ahead of Freydis to have all their cargo unloaded and stowed in her brother's old houses when she arrived, and she made them shift it. Relations went from bad to worse and eventually Freydis brought about the murder of all Helgi and Finnbogi's men, and herself killed the women when no one else would do so. On the return to Greenland with the brothers' ship the story in the end came out, in spite of her threats, and she was 'ill thought of' which seems a moderate enough penalty.

The superstitious accounts of the supernatural and the dead in *Graenlendinga saga* which I have omitted do not affect the credibility of its account of the voyages, which is confident and consistent, though we cannot know how far it represents a tradition coming from Bjarni, Leif and Thorfinn, and how far it is the knowledge of the author's own day. Evidently the position of all three lands was satisfactorily determined with relation to Greenland, so that it was not thought harder to reach them than to sail the route between Greenland and Norway which these ships were otherwise engaged on. Complete information about distances is given only for Bjarni's first voyage, it seems to be taken for granted after that. Helluland was four days (of 12 or 24 hours? Probably the former) south-west of Greenland, Markland three days south-west of Helluland and Vinland two days south-west of Markland. It is tempting to incorporate hints from the later sources to modify this obviously over-schematised picture but we must remember that this had to pass from mouth to mouth for a century and a half. The distances are all comparable with those covered in voyaging between Iceland, England and Norway, and even Greenland to Vinland direct with cattle on board was no longer than the similar voyage from Norway to Iceland. In 1347 the Icelandic annals report that seventeen men on a Greenland ship, smaller than those that usually trade between Iceland and Greenland, were blown under Snaefellsness, driven there by the wind as they were returning home from Markland. Evidently the route was still trafficked and a knarr was not necessary: the eternal Scandinavian fifty-footer with sixteen or seventeen men was still in business after flourishing for six hundred years, and still had another six hundred to come.

The voyage from Norway to Greenland direct, using Faeroe and Iceland only as navigational marks to check the parallel of latitude, not as stopping places, shows on the other hand the great development in ship-type and long-range voyaging which had taken place in little more than two centuries. The vikings repairing their knarr's damaged keel on the coast of Newfoundland in AD 1000 had indeed come a very long way, in every sense, from their original small craft.

5

The Eleventh Century

It is natural for English historians to feel that 1066 marks a great dividing line. It evidently does so in political, institutional and language history, but its events did not make any great change in the viking voyaging of either the Irish Sea area or the North Sea until the following century. In the twelfth century there were many other factors changing the nature of the voyages anyway, as well as the Norman dominance of Britain (or most of it). Towards the end of the century we have to reckon with the possible use of compass, chart, astronomical determination of latitude, in ships with stern rudders, rigid and heavy build with watertight continuous decks and weatherproof fore and stern castles. This is not to say at all that the normal twelfth-century craft was so sophisticated, but that the possibility of all these has to be taken into account for that century in a way which can be excluded for the eleventh.

In some ways the eleventh-century viking voyages seem to show a return to older patterns, as the last chapter tried to show. The late-tenth-century wide-ranging raids whose impact on Britain led up to Sweyn's invasion were followed by a period in which the voyaging was consistently by the southern circular route, even when the intention was to enter England by the Humber. Sweyn's reign in Britain, and even more that of his son, almost created a North Sea kingdom, which however loosely knit must have depended on more frequent and rapid communication between its parts than had been usual when they were under separate rule, and these voyages did not necessarily all go by the longer southern route. Some hint of the sort of ship involved may be derived from the way in which Gainsborough on the Trent seems occasionally to have functioned almost as an alternative capital for this dynasty. The York viking kingdom of the mid tenth century was at risk as soon as its access to the sea was no longer secure on either coast, but Sweyn and Cnut were welcomed by Scandinavian England, unlike Harald Hardrada and Tostig in 1066.

It may be that Gainsborough is so prominent because of tidal and other navigational considerations. It is at the present day the limit of navigation for coasters and perhaps also then was as far as sea-going skippers wished to go. Even from there, as from York, two ebb tides on two succeeding days would be needed to get down to the sea, as presumably the night tides could not be used. There were probably many quite un-royal ships involved as well, and some of the evidently secondary Scandinavian settlements in the midland Danelaw, which reinforced the descendants of the Great Army of 867, may well be one consequence of the voyages of these ships. It seems that a large number of the coastal populations on both sides of the North Sea had craft capable of making the crossing and in the habit of doing so. As thirty-foot fishing vessels regularly did this in the nineteenth century, there seems no reason to doubt that similar vessels did so in the eleventh, even if the nineteenth-century motives (different rates of duty, different prices of industrial products) did not apply.

Even after the Norman Conquest it appears from the Latin life of St Cnut written by the Englishman Aelnoth that he was used to meeting in Denmark many visitors from England, some of whom wanted Cnut to intervene. Aelnoth's Latin is florid in the extreme, but we get some useful hints from him about the voyages of his day. One of his ambitious metaphors reflects the ships these visitors used: 'having worked along the coast under oars, safely in the lee of friendly lands, it is time to turn our prow to the open sea and hoist sail'.

The whole history of claim and counterclaim by various monarchs to the North Sea kingdoms shows that all had fleets which, if not as large as those of the previous century, and more addicted to coasting, could be readily committed to action, often successful, on the other side of the sea, and more than a hint of a distinction between permanent, professional and very expensive warships, which a king had to have though they ruined him, and simpler levied ships, is found in the sources.

Only two years after he had been accepted as king in succession to his father Sweyn, Cnut with a fleet of forty ships defeated in 1018 a viking fleet of thirty. The following year he crossed to Denmark with only nine ships (all presumably large royal ones) and returned the following year. With such a small and homogenous fleet he may have sailed from East Anglia to the Texel. We do not know, but on his next visit in 1022 his fleet assembled off the Isle of Wight, which obviously suggests a very short crossing followed by a correspondingly long coastal voyage up the continental coast of the North Sea. When Cnut's brother-in-law Eilaf left his earldom in England to joint Cnut's enemies from Norway and Sweden at the battle of the Holy River in Skane in 1026, he presumably took care not to travel by way of Denmark. But we do not know whether he sailed direct from England to Norway or went via Shetland. We do know that Earl Haakon, established in Trondheim as Norway's ruler after its submission to Cnut, travelled on the island route by way of Shetland and Orkney, for he was drowned in the Pentland Firth in 1030.

The fifty English ships full of thanes which Cnut took with him to help his conquest of Norway are one of the rare examples of a hostile fleet from England successfully attacking Scandinavia in the viking period, but even though they ended up in Trondheim, we know that they did not follow the route through the Northern Isles. They joined a Danish fleet in the Limfjord, whether they crossed direct or coasted round. When Harthacnut sailed from Denmark with 62 ships in 1039 to take England (where he arrived in 1040) he coasted so far south that he spent the winter in Bruges. He had what was for the century a fairly large fleet (few of those whose numbers are known are much smaller or larger than fifty) and there were political reasons as well as economic for the attractiveness of Flanders to the viking fleets of the time, but the sea crossing from there was only six hours.

The defence against the expected invasion from Norway by Magnus in 1045 was the stationing of the English fleet at Sandwich, which suggests that the direct North Sea crossing could be ruled out for a fleet of any size. No doubt the fleet's main concern was to protect southern England, but even a Norwegian landfall in East Anglia from Frisia would have enabled Magnus to enter either the Wash or the Thames before the English ships could intervene, and the clear implication is that any serious invasion fleet would have to (not just 'would probably') come well into the southern North Sea before beginning its crossing. The fleet was not there when in 1048 twenty-five viking ships under Yrling and Lothen (who reminds me of the knarr skipper in *Harald's saga Hardrada*) raided the Isle of Wight, Sandwich and Essex before crossing to Flanders. It looks as if they had either come down the Irish Sea or from southern Ireland.

The following year, 1049, Sweyn Godwinsson returned from Denmark with eight ships and kidnapped Earl Beorn off a becalmed royal ship and killed him, and there was further raiding in the West from Irish Sea vikings. The many islands of that region provided secure bases for old style piratical bands, so that alongside the formal royal fleets maintaining large-scale national interests we still find voyages more typical of an earlier day.

All the kings of England in this century having come to power by means of a large fleet immediately reduced it. The permanent financing of these specialised craft, useless in peacetime and immobile without a multitude of paid oarsmen, was evidently more than the economy could bear in taxation. The crews of the earlier viking ship fleets had foraged for themselves, and at the expense of foreign victims: to saddle one's own subjects with their upkeep was impossible. Eleventh-century navies on their rare and leisurely but massive excursions were very different from earlier viking fleets. If they had to be kept concentrated against the threat of similar hostile navies they were not going to be much use for coast defence against viking raids, and we never hear in the sources of them being so used. The motives for the reduction of the royal fleets were mainly financial and tell us nothing about the frequency of viking activity at sea.

Some of this raiding in the fifties of the eleventh century was the work of expelled English leaders of the house of Godwin with friends in Flanders. In 1052 the royal fleet, described unusually as forty *small*ships (evidently a limited service levy), was at Sandwich when Earl Godwin himself made a raid on Dungeness in a rising midsummer gale. The fleet sailed to intercept him but the weather was so bad they could not find him, and he returned to Bruges. On the fleet's return to Sandwich the crews dispersed, and Godwin on hearing of this set off again. One wonders whether he got the information from a shadowing reconnaissance ship, landing and picking up beach parties to collect local news, or whether there was such a steady commercial trade between Sandwich and Bruges that the information was easily derived from questioning merchant skippers. Godwin's first stop was Dungeness again, and then the Isle of Wight and Portland, both prominent headlands to be rounded in sailing along the south coast, and places where it would not be surprising if there were some sort of royal information-gathering lookout: both had royal manors. The Old English Chronicle tells us that he took care to seize all the serviceable ships he found, but doesn't make clear whether this was to incorporate them in his fleet or to deny them to any pursuing force. His son Harald came from Ireland with nine ships to join him, and they then sailed east again, along the South Coast and round into the Thames, without opposition. They anchored below London Bridge on September 14th to wait for the flood tide (a very large spring rise) and when it came weighed anchor and moved through the bridge 'veering towards the north bank as if to surround the king's ships'. It appears from all this that these Anglo-Saxon ships were very similar to the general purpose viking ships of the previous century rather than the very long and mainly oared vessels of the contemporary royal fleets.

There are other references to a pirate host from Norway in 1058, and to various small fleets raiding in the Irish Sea, but the next voyages of significance are those of 1066. William's cross-channel landing of cavalry, fodder, armoured knights, portable castles, has nothing in common with the usual run of viking voyages, and to lift the weights involved in one lift viking ships would scarcely be the preferred choice, particularly over such a relatively short distance between relatively developed facilities. The Bayeux tapestry no doubt gives a reasonable though conventionalised representation of William's ships, at least those of the leaders, in spite of such eccentricities as putting a figurehead described as on the bow into the stern. But he must have had a large train of transports which were of a different type, though given a similar representation in the tapestry. To go so far as to use the tapestry as evidence of asymmetrical hulls, goose-winged sails, and other interesting speculations about the detail of viking ships in the north seems to me to go far beyond what such a document deserves or will support. In any case the whole conduct of the operation, a concentrated, short-range, centrally directed descent, where those out of touch anchor and wait for others to catch up, is like no account of any viking voyage we know of or can deduce.

On the other hand the activities attributed to Tostig in the same year do seem to belong to the traditional type of viking voyage. He is said to have sought out support from every country with a North Sea coast, and to have harried the east coast of England with a fleet which waxed and waned in size depending on its success. He started in May with a raid on the Isle of Wight, moved on to Sandwich where he gathered more men, some willing, some unwilling, and on arrival in the Humber had sixty ships. He had been joined by seventeen from the Orkney earldom, probably the most stable viking state established in the British Isles. After Tostig's defeat in north Lincolnshire some ships were lost and others went home so that he had only twelve with which to sail north to meet Harald Hardrada's 300. They had sailed from Norway in early September on the northerly winds which were to delay William the Conqueror in Normandy until September 27th. We know from the sources that the weather that month continued warm and dry, though with some fog as one would expect from the high pressure area to be associated with such winds, but it still seems very late in the year for such large numbers of ships to be at sea so far from home. It lends added point to the cry of the Norwegians at Stamford Bridge that they would either conquer England or remain there dead. Some of the Norwegian ships, including Harald's own, sailed by way of Shetland and filled Bressay Sound, others went direct to Orkney whether by accident or by design to avoid over-burdening the resources in Shetland.

The combined fleet after various brief attacks on the north-east coast entered the Humber about September 20th, and the English ships withdrew before them up the Ouse and then, shrewdly, up the Wharfe to Tadcaster, apparently opening the way to York. The viking fleet could scarcely afford to leave an undefeated adversary behind them to cut them off from the sea and the river route to the midland Danelaw, so it had to stop at Riccal, below the confluence of Wharfe and Ouse, with fatal consequences. Not only were the viking forces necessarily divided, part advancing to York, part guarding the ships, but the advance guard were increasingly remote from their supplies and armour still in the ships. If the English defeat at Fulford was part of the price of the ships withdrawing away from them it was in the end worth paying for the destruction of the viking threat at Stamford Bridge. The English ships at Tadcaster not only prevented the viking fleet going past Riccal but assured control of the river crossing at Tadcaster for Harald Godwinsson, so that hastening up the Roman road from the south he could move unhindered through York to defeat Harald Hardrada's host one-third at a time as it slowly got into action at Stamford Bridge on September 25th.

The detail of this disastrous viking incursion into the Humber is important, because the Danish ships that made the last viking voyages, campaigning over the same area against the Normans in the next ten years, seem to have studied the events of 1066 and perfected their very successful different tactics in consequence. The later campaigns show very well how the essential advantages of the shallow-draught old-style viking ship could be exploited to make even the invincible William the Conqueror appear clumsy and helpless, and it was no doubt in revenge for this that he carried out the harrying of the north with such ferocity. Such fleets represented the only real, and unreachable, threat to Norman rule.

The 240 ships despatched by Sweyn Estridson in 1069 came partly in response to English prayers and partly on payment. The crews were a mixture of English and Danes and attacked Sandwich first before moving on to Ipswich and Norwich. They entered the Humber between August 15th and September 8th, again suggesting that the collection of these large fleets was not possible before midsummer. The informality of the organisation is shown by the very narrow escape of the man who was certainly their most important English ally and figurehead, Edgar the Aetheling. He was one of only three survivors when a solitary ship on a foraging expedition in north Lincolnshire was surprised by a patrol from the Norman garrison of Lincoln. The ship was captured and broken up.

The fleet moved on up the narrowing river to York, which was sacked on September 20th with the massacre of its Norman garrison. On William's arrival the Danes withdrew to their ships without risking battle against the armoured knights, and crossed over to the south, or Lincolnshire side of the Humber again. When William and his army after an exhausting march round the extensive marshes of the Humber-Ouse-Trent confluence arrived at Axholme on the Lincolnshire side, the Danish ships went back across to the north, Yorkshire side. At this point William, perhaps to preserve his conquering image untarnished, departed to quell less resourceful opponents in the south, leaving Robert to pursue the Danes among the marshes that winter. He was occasionally able to surprise some crews sharing the feasts of the local population and chase them back to their ships, but at Christmas the Danes moved on York again. William, hastening from the south as Harald had done in 1066 was not so well served by an intelligent fleet, and found himself delayed and sidetracked at the Pontefract river crossing which he did not control. By the time his outflanking force reached York the Danes had gone again. According to one account they eventually, like their predecessors, accepted money to depart.

There were other raiding voyages after the conquest, but none so successful. The one on the Tees in 1070 by Danes seems likely to have been a direct crossing, and Sweyn himself came into the Humber in the same year and after a brief campaign made an even peace with William. It is possible that he was examining at first hand on the spot the possibility of a reconquest of Scandinavian Britain, but William had only been successfully eluded, not defeated, in the previous venture. As Sweyn waited two days in the Thames before returning to Denmark, instead of sailing from the Humber, I conclude that he had some of the large royal ships with him. The two days presumably allowed stragglers to catch up, and gives some idea of what a large area was covered by a viking fleet, or army, on the move. Quite apart from the blanketing effect on the sail of another ship close to windward the individuality of the captains and the limited control at low speed afforded by the side rudder was such that one probably did not welcome any other ship within quarter of a mile.

In 1075 two hundred ships under Cnut, Sweyn's son, entered the Humber together with Earl Haakon. Once again they moved to repeat their triumph at York. But this time they lost all the men who went on the raid, including Haakon's son. This sort of raid was now only profitable in areas the Normans had not yet brought within their system of fortification. In Britain this meant the Irish Sea, and raiding there continued with undiminished intensity. In 1079 Godred Crovan invaded Man, and later the Northern Isles, where he ruled in Islay until his death at the end of the century. On his death the Chronicle of Man and the Isles tells us Ingemund arrived from Norway to take over the kingdom, and later King Magnus himself with 160 ships by way of Orkney to Man.

The defeat of 1075 was the last time a viking fleet landed in England. According to Aelnoth and to *Cnytlinga saga* the next ten years saw a stream of messengers inviting Cnut to avenge his kinsman Harald and restore their ancient liberties, but the fleet which he collected with some difficulty in 1085 never sailed, and the Norman conquest could be steadily consolidated by castle building. Shipborne violence continued in the Northern Isles and Scandinavia throughout the Middle Ages but the characteristically viking voyages were over.

Aelnoth's ambitious Latin in his life of Cnut provides an appropriate epilogue: I have received much help with it from my colleague Pat Simcock, but *any* attempt on Aelnoth is fraught with difficulty.

> The coasts passed with oars ready for sea, and the neighbourhood sufficiently scanned, let us, making for the high seas, skilfully caulk the leaks in our ship, lest an inrush of the hostile and deceptive sea carry off the voyagers prematurely. The beam of our Lord's cross raised aloft, let the sails of courage rise to it, so that running speedily before a south-east wind we may carry the merits of our Hero to the bay with our wished-for port, and fix the anchor of our hope in the divine mercy with our ears deaf to the songs of charming sirens, lest disaster on the rocks destroy our cargo of spiritual stock in trade, leaving luxuries brought from afar scattered and floating on the waves in which we mix our tears

The word translated 'luxuries' is 'gazis', from Persian, extremely rare in medieval Latin and a nice reminder of the very far-flung culture which the voyages behind this muddled metaphor had produced.

6

Navigation

Perhaps this chapter should be called 'Pilotage'. From that it will be apparent that I think some of the 'mystery' of the skilled long-distance voyaging of the viking age is the product of controversy among later historians. The argument between those who assert that regular transatlantic voyages were made by dead reckoning only, and those who assert that this is impossible, and some other method of latitude sailing must have been used, has a somewhat adventitious appearance. I suppose few people familiar with the sources, and with the practice of navigation, would be very happy to join either party. Most, like me, would choose the former if they had to choose, but enthusiasts who feel that the navigational triumphs of the viking age positively require some further explanation have obligingly produced a very long list of devices to provide it. There is absolutely no evidence from any worthwhile source that a single one of any of these ever existed in the viking age, though they are now to be found illustrated in coffee-table books, reproduced in maritime museums, and taken seriously in otherwise authoritative articles and reference books, so anyone writing on viking voyaging has a duty to deal with them. This is not easy.

It may be best to begin with what is, as yet, an imaginary case. How could one set about proving that the vikings did not use the sextant, if it was asserted that they must have done? That none has survived cannot prove the negative that none ever existed, and the absence of any reference to them in any text is no insuperable objection either. The texts are two centuries later than the voyages, and come from a clerkly background, not a seafaring one: the instrument and its use would obviously confer such advantage that it might be a jealously guarded professional secret. The sailing directions for Norway to Iceland and Norway to Greenland indicate that the vikings did sail along parallels of latitude on ocean crossings, and the obvious way to stay in a given latitude, or recover it if it is lost, is by noon altitude sights of the sun, and twilight sights of Polaris, giving a check on the position about every eight hours or forty miles. Exact measurement by sextant would require one to make allowance for changing declinations, but Stjornu-Oddi's table of sunrise and sunset bearings could be argued to involve the expression of declination in units of the sun's semi-diameter, and to represent an older tradition. So once one had taught the skipper to read (or to memorise a declination table) and do simple proportion sums in Roman numerals, latitude could be maintained on a month's crossing.

All the assertions in the previous paragraph are, if not demonstrably true, at any rate not provably false, and are to me reminiscent of the enthusiasts for arcane 'viking navigation', but of course they do not establish a case for the use of the sextant in the tenth century. What they do show is the characteristically modern ideas of quantifiable measurement by delicate instrument, and tabulated information available for unthinking use, typical of literate and mechanical societies. But it is almost impossible to *prove* the negative.

One can only ask why, if sextants were available, the height of the Faeroese peaks above the horizon on the right course to Greenland was not given angular expression instead of something as difficult to determine as 'the sea halfway up the mountains'. This term is used again as a measure of the correct distance off for passages up and down the Norwegian coast, though the two distances seem very unlikely to be the same. Why measure latitude on northern exploration by lying across the boat and noting where the shadow cuts your body, without noting what sort of boat and whereabouts in it you were? Why measure latitude on exploration south by saying that on the shortest day of winter the sun rose somewhere (unspecified) north of south-east, and set somewhere (unspecified) north of south-west, or possibly of southeast by east and southwest by west? Why say of a latitude within the Arctic Circle that the sun at midnight bearing north was as high as it is at home when it bears northwest (on some unspecified day: presumably midsummer)?

These are the references, none earlier than the twelfth century, and the last from the end of the thirteenth, which are usually brought forward to support instrumental navigation in the viking age. All these expressions are sensible attempts to give the best approximation possible for a feature recognised as indicating the position of the place. By the year AD 1000 those most concerned seem to have had a tolerably clear idea of the relationship between the sun's altitude at noon and at two other times, its azimuth at sunrise and sunset, five occasions in all, the declination on the day, and the latitude of the place, of the observation. One could scarcely cover fifteen degrees of latitude in just over a month, as Ohthere did, without noticing that, and the sun's height at noon, or the amount north of east at which it rose were presumably part of the total impression formed of a place, then as now. But if men who perceived these things had to express them in such varying and inconsistent ways as those set out, it suggests that they did not measure them with any instrument, did not use standard quantities and did not possess any standard terminology: these are all features of the seventeenth-century scientific advance which affected the languages of Europe by providing generally available and agreed words for the exchange of such information. It also suggests that the work of Stjornu-Oddi which is the first step in that direction was not based on the earlier practice of practical navigators as is sometimes implied.

Having thus established at least the improbability of the use of the sextant (it is impossible to establish its impossibility) it is time to turn to the other devices really proposed by enthusiasts, and see if a similarly negative attitude to them can be justified. The first navigational resource to be considered must be Floki's ravens. They are in *Landnamabok*, the early account of the settlement of Iceland, and are therefore more respectable in the eyes of Norse historians than more apparently scientific devices recorded only in late romantic sagas or, even worse, nineteenth-century oral tradition recorded by eager folklorists in Faeroe. Floki took three ravens with him on his voyage of discovery. The first one he released flew back over the stern the way they had come, the second rose straight up and then alighted on the ship again, but the third flew forward in the direction in which he found Iceland. If Floki could get the birds to leave the ship at all once the crew had fed them he was luckier than most modern masters, but perhaps he starved them. The use of birds in this way is so widespread, from Noah's ark to the Indian and Pacific oceans, that there is no reason to doubt that they were occasionally used by viking voyagers. One should remember however that the great majority of these were not seeking new lands across unknown seas, and therefore didn't need ravens. Floki could not know the distances on his first voyage, but the subsequent voyagers did, and in fact you do not need to be out of sight of land for much more than eighty miles, say fourteen hours' sail, on the passage to Iceland. The direct route apparently took 84 hours, and of that 72 or so would be out of sight of land.

I owe to one of Uwe Schnall's formidably learned footnotes the information that the Floki story was interpreted in the Archive for Natural Science and Technology in 1912, in the light of the difference in speed between an enthusiastic raven and a viking ship, as requiring thirty ravens for the average passage from Norway to Shetland. The picture of a viking ship flying off a fresh raven every two hours or so, as the helmsman loses sight of the last one on splash-down is affecting rather than convincing, and gives new depths to Odin's ravens. But at any rate the ravens are within the possible technology of the age, which I do not think can be said for the other suggestions.

The most obvious way to keep a steady course across the open ocean is the magnetic compass used today, and it has been claimed that its use in the viking period was not only necessary to explain the voyages performed, but can be established from Faeroese oral tradition recorded in the early nineteenth century by Pastor J. H. Schrøter. A regrettable reconstruction by C. Sølver of such a viking compass, complete with runic lettering and shadow pin for azimuths is exhibited in Kronborg Maritime Museum in Denmark but has not, fortunately, won such wide acceptance as the equally misleading sun compass and sunstone reconstructions which greet one in most Scandinavian shipping museums, often with no indication of their completely speculative character. The use of the magnetic compass in the viking period could scarcely be proved by appeal to the beliefs of Faeroese fishermen in 1810 even if there were no doubt that those beliefs were correctly recorded. Unfortunately the most authoritative discussion of Pastor Schrøter's work by Christian Matras, the greatest scholar of the Faeroes, concludes sadly that 'Schrøter's lively imagination so misled him that his recordings of historical tradition have to be regarded as distorted or counterfeit'. If the vikings *had* had compasses it is an amusing consequence of the fluctuation in position of the earth's magnetic poles that Ohthere's northeast course which he calls north would in fact have been about north magnetic in his day, when the magnetic pole was about 80°N, 85°E. But no one, fortunately, has yet launched that as an alternative explanation for his use of north.

The next device to be examined is also one of Schrøter's, a handy appliance to enable the viking navigator to add a reliable longitude to the knowledge of latitude which Schrøter took it for granted the vikings had. In this variety of the clepsydra or water clock, water drips through a hole in one bowl into another, taking exactly twenty-four hours to empty. If, on an east-west voyage, it is started exactly at noon on one day it is clear (particularly to anyone familiar with the classic nineteenth-century longitude by chronometer method) that comparison of this accurately measured twenty-four hours elapsed, with local noon at the ship's new position, will give the difference of longitude. It would be unkind to ask how one is supposed to transform the remaining water at noon into minutes of time and then of arc to apply to the original longitude, or how one rates the decreasing drip rate from sinking level or a clogged up hole. I have never succeeded in completing the exposition of this method to a practical navigator without being interrupted by laughter, and it is another classic instance of our talent for foisting our approach to a problem onto past ages. It seems fairly unlikely that before the acceptance of *some* standard meridian (not necessarily that mysteriously defined as 2° 15′W of Paris) position-finding was thought of as a comparison of time difference between the ship and that standard, particularly in a society that completely lacked time reckoning apart from the sun. This obviously nineteenth-century method is rejected even by those who hanker after some sort of viking sextant, but its folklore dressing is not bad: the verse associated with it by Schrøter may well be genuine and old (it does not refer to time measurement) and we are told that *jagt* skippers in the north Norwegian coastal trade at the beginning of the century used a traditional water-clock. The accounts I have seen seem to refer to an alternative version of the hourglass, no doubt because the sand would have become clogged with damp, used to keep track of time on one tack in bad visibility, and not to anything like Schrøter's method.

Much the most important of these devices is the bearing-dial or sun-compass developed by Sølver on the basis of a roughly semi-circular wooden fragment with a hole in its centre which was excavated in Greenland by C. L. Vebaek. It was later further refined by Ramskou's suggestion of a sun stone which would enable it to be used as a sun compass for course-setting even when the sun was not visible. Facsimiles of it are found in Scandinavian museums, all closely resembling a modern pelorus. The theory is that it was orientated with reference to the point covered by the shadow of the central pin (the sun's bearing being known of course from azimuth tables derived from those of Stjornu-Oddi) and then any other point required could be read off and the ship steered accordingly. It is quite true that it seems that if the fragment were completed it would have 32 points, but we should remember that there is no evidence that the thirty-two points of the modern mariner's compass were in use in the viking age. I think there were at least sixteen, because I take 'west and hwon northan' to be either WNW or W×N but some give it a merely general meaning, and the learned division of the horizon was into twelve. In any case the lines on the Greenland dial, as it is often called, do not radiate accurately from its centre and the divisions are not equal. It is far too small to be practical, far smaller than the modern sun compasses used, briefly, on land, in deserts with unbroken sunshine, during the last war to overcome deviation problems in tanks. As its last defender observes desperately that it might perhaps be a *toy* bearing dial for a child, it has evidently passed its peak. In any case it will be apparent that to orientate it using azimuth tables requires some source of time, whether starting with local time or 'Greenwich' time, which is independent of the sun's azimuth. You cannot use the sun's bearing (from what?) to establish that it is three p.m. and then enter the azimuth table with the time three p.m. to find out which point of the sun compass card to put under the shadow! In any case if you know that the sun bears SW (roughly) at three p.m., and you know independently

(Schrøter's water-clock run on from noon?) that it is three p.m., why bother with the sun-compass? Why not bring the sun to one point off the port bow if you wish to steer WSW, and so on? Without independent time the sun-compass is useless, and with it it is unnecessary.

The *solskuggjafjol* or 'sun shadow wood' lacks any archaeological foundation, and has not even the doubtful authority of Schrøter's lost transcripts of folk-lore behind it, as it is first mentioned (as 'old', but without any earlier reference) by Winther in 1875. It is said to be a piece of wood floating in a bowl of water to keep it steady (!) so that from the length of the shadow cast by a central pin one can read off the latitude. Declination is taken care of by fixing the pin in different notches to give a length appropriate to the date. Later improvements, incorporated by its supporters, include having the latitude of Bergen or Cape Farewell marked on the base, so that you simply steered the ship to get the end of the shadow to fall on the right mark at noon and then kept it there for the next month (varying the length of pin as above, in accordance with Stjornu-Oddi tables, this time of declination not azimuth). This reminds me of the custom in some regular traders of keeping the safe clearance courses round obstructions permanently marked on the chart with their radar ranges written in, so that the watch-keeper is relieved of chartwork and simply keeps the ship on the tramlines. The system is as old as Lecky, and I think it was probably in this viking age context derived from him! The *solskuggjafjol* observation has to be taken at noon. I have never seen anyone advocate its use for ex-Meridians but it could I suppose easily be refined to permit this by incorporating another series of notches. The same problem of ascertaining the correct time for the observation remains as with the sun compass: it is difficult to believe that the variation of a shadow no more than six inches long would enable one to get noon from the greatest altitude as can be done with a sextant, or permit double equal altitudes.

A variant of this device sometimes found (in picture books of course, not in reality) is the 'sun-board', a device for measuring the sun's altitude depicted either as held out at arm's length like an Arab navigator's *k'amal*, or installed on the ship's rail like an anti-aircraft sight. 'Sunboard' is a genuine Old Norse word, which I take leave to doubt about *solskuggjafjol*, and means a strake of plank-

ing. Falk surmised that the name derived from the practice, referred
to above, of estimating the sun's height from the shadow cast by the
boat's gunwale or upper edge. Reuter went further and assumed it
was a separate piece of wood with gradations specially intended for
this observation, for which there is no warrant in the contexts in the
Bishops' sagas which Falk is discussing.

The last of these inventions is the sunstone, another genuine
word, mentioned in some late romantic sagas and some church
inventories from the Icelandic Middle Ages. Peter Foote's speculation that it was used, following the example of the Celtic church, to
concentrate the sun's rays to ignite the Easter fire, and was in fact a
burning glass, is certainly the most sensible and best researched
approach yet, though we do not have any explicit references to such
a custom in Iceland. Thorkild Ramskou sees in it a piece of Icelandic
felspar whose polarising properties enable an observer to tell the
position of the sun (and therefore set a sun-compass) even when it
was covered by cloud, by detecting the plane of polarisation of the
sun's light. This would extend the usefulness of a sun compass,
though one should remember the fact, naturally not given prominence in Ramskou's book, that this only works if the observer's
zenith is free of cloud, a condition always satisfied for the airliners
which use a modern polarising sun compass as heading reference on
the transpolar section of their flights, but much less usual at sea level
off Iceland. The point previously made about sun-locating devices
applies to this one as well. Without access to some time information
not derived from the sun's bearing, the sun's bearing cannot be used
as a directional reference. As Rosencrantz says to Guildernstern in
Tom Stoppard's play: 'The position of the sun if it is out would give
you a rough idea of the time: alternatively, the clock, if it is going,
would give you a rough idea of the position of the sun. I forget
which you're trying to establish.'

A friend of mine in the film business can date historical feature
films with great accuracy. I do not mean by this that he can tell
whether the action of the film is supposed to take place in the viking
age, the Middle Ages, or the sixteenth century (though that is not
always very easy) but that he can tell whether a film about the
Middle Ages was made in 1966 or 1968. He does it by the leading
lady's gowns and hair-styles, which inevitably project back into the
Middle Ages the fashion points which were highly valued by

designers in 1966 or 1968.

I hope it will now be evident that the vast range of pseudo-viking, pseudo-scientific navigational apparatus which scholars have provided for the vikings' voyages is an example of the same kind of fundamentally unhistoric imagination, coming between us and the proper object of attention. The profit and pleasure in the study of a past age is not to see it as an unimproved version of our own, which shared our aspirations and approaches, though it lacked our refined techniques, and though it is probably true that Bergen and Roskilde were the first European towns to have their latitude accurately determined, it happened long after the viking age. It is not coincidence that in the period when longitude by chronometer was new technology, an essentially superstitious ancestor-worship presented the vikings with a chronometer method for longitude, and when the polarisation plane aircraft compass was new technology we were too generous to deny our ancestors that too. In both cases of course it had, like the leading lady's dress, to be re-created in medieval terms, but that has never been harder for historians than for film studios. But there is no archaeological or written evidence from the viking age or the next eight centuries for the use in navigation of ships at sea of any of these devices. The compass is the exception. Its introduction, after the end of the viking age, so significantly altered the presentation of voyaging in the north from that we find in the sagas, that it is inconceivable there can have been any concealed use of it before.

Rather than seek to interpret earlier navigation in terms of our own it seems better to listen to what its exponents have to tell us. It is in this respect that David Lewis's work with living informants in the Pacific is so epoch-making for the study of ancient voyages, as he is able to reveal the fundamentally different thought-processes of a primitive navigator (the 'moving islands' for example) in carrying out impressive voyages which we naturally seek to explain in terms of the latitude and longitude which to him are exotic newfangled concepts of doubtful practical utility. For the viking age the only contemporary accounts are in Old English. If we are prepared to take in the twelfth-century unsophisticated *Graenlendinga* saga as well, because of the interest and irreplaceable nature of its material, that should complete the corpus, and it is to that that this book is devoted. The huge mass of later saga literature is tempting in its detail, and its superb conviction, but one might as well use Chaucer's shipman as evidence for the viking age:

> But of his craft to rekene wel his tydes,
> His stremes and his daungers him bisydes,
> His herberwe and his mone, his lode-menage,
> Ther nas noon swich, from Hull to Carthage.

The voyages described in the later sagas are the projection back into a romantic past of men living in an age in which compass, chart, and possibly some device for measuring the sun's altitude were known to intellectuals if not on every ship. If we examine the descriptions in *Beowulf*, Ohthere, Wulfstan, it is apparent that of latitude or sun height, longitude or time difference there is not the slightest trace. All think primarily of time sailed on a certain course, followed by visual identification of some coastal feature, followed by another carefully recorded length of time on another course. Wulfstan from time to time relates this to his framework of reference for the Baltic as a whole, by reminding us that he was now 'abeam' (in imagination) of some other well-known feature of a different voyage. This concentration on course and distance is, it cannot be denied, the classic dead reckoning navigation, but I cannot see that it is inconsistent with, or exclusive of, the use of other signs to confirm or question it in practice. Ohthere and Wulfstan were after all reporting voyages they had made, not telling exactly how they had done it, and they cast their information into the form that would enable their hearer to relate the new information to his own model. Ohthere is slightly more the coaster, carefully detailing each change in the trend of the coastline, ticking off the inlets where one departs from the coast to cross them. Wulfstan is more concerned to establish a sea position with reference to known places than to trace a coast. His system resembles ours more than Ohthere's does, but it would be misleading to suppose that it worked in our terms.

During the last war the liner *Queen Elizabeth*, independently routed, and zigzagging all over the Atlantic, carried, among other less experienced passengers, a group of trawler skippers going to the United States to ferry back minesweepers and landing-craft. After over a week at sea, a group of highly specialised navigators peering anxiously northward from her bridge were comforted by one of the skippers: 'If it's Cape Farewell you're looking for, it'll be another hour or two yet'. He was right, and without any access to navigational equipment or any great interest, had by a combination of dead reckoning, swell, sea colour and temperature, accurately located a very fast ship of a type quite unfamiliar to him. All three of his companions, from whom I had the story, regarded it as a triumph but not in any way as mysterious. He had, they said, been round there a lot, on and off. In many ways the accumulated experience of these pre-electronic navigators is as important as the true primitives collected by David Lewis, and a better guide to what is probable for viking voyages than much academic speculation.

Rather than rely on early nineteenth-century tradition re-vamped by unreliable informants one might do worse than re-read the Reverend William Scoresby, Fellow of the Royal Society of Edinburgh, Curate of Bessingby, and formerly the most successful English whaling skipper. On p. 369 of volume two of his *Account of the Arctic Regions* published in 1820 he describes the course home from Spitzbergen as he and hundreds of his fellows had followed it for hundreds of years, and at once shows in their proper light, longitude-giving water-clocks:

> It is not unusual for a ship to bear away, without the navigators having first obtained any certain knowledge as to their situation in longitude. Not having perhaps seen any land for some weeks or even months: having neither a chronometer on board, nor the means of taking a lunar observation: they set out ignorant of the meridian on which they sail, and sensible of their being liable to an error of 5 or 6 degrees of longitude. If the homeward bound steer too far to the eastward they make the coast of Norway, and if too far to the westward they probably make Faeroe. The appearance of certain birds, seaweeds and medusae – sudden alterations in the swell, and the examination of the depth of the water, are the principal intimations which give them a knowledge of their situation. The appearance of seaweeds and medusae in the water, and of solan geese, skua gulls and land birds on the wing denote their proximity to land. A westerly swell generally prevailing between the latitudes of 60° and 65° its sudden cessation indicates

shelter from some land. If in the 62nd or 63rd degree of latitude the westerly swell be suddenly obstructed, it is evident that the Feroe islands are not far distant to the westward: but if the same effect takes place in the 61st degree it denotes the proximity of Shetland to the westward.

There speaks the most scientific and experienced navigator of these waters in 1820, and the relationship to the course descriptions of *Landnamabok* is unmistakable. Apart from the use of a compass on which in these latitudes he did not put too much reliance, Scoresby navigated on this voyage in a way possible to the viking age and suggested by the sources. This is the more important because in other circumstances he used every resource of his day, including longitudes by lunar distance, and carried out important research on the deviation of the compass.

Until the last twenty years many small ships sailed these waters without the means, ability, inclination or time to make any use of astro-navigation. One voyage to Newfoundland by a ninety-foot Humber oil barge which lost its wheelhouse and compass three days out was recounted to me by its master, the late Capt. A. Storey. He explained to me that in the 1928 Depression newly qualified masters had to take what jobs they could get, and that when they could not see the sun they steered by the run of the sea until they could see something, quite often another ship going their way, which they tried to keep up with as long as possible. The problems of the viking age voyage from Norway to Greenland were not very different, and the first trawlers to visit Greenland soon learnt not to use their magnetic compass for course-setting.

This brings us back to the use of the sun for direction, the only alternative, with the Pole star, but that is so high and so difficult to see in the summer twilight that it can never have been very important at sea in the far north. We have already seen that a time independent of the sun's direction is required. For dead reckoning in an illiterate age some way is required of keeping it during different watches in such a way that the skipper can work it up later. If apparatus we must have, and I think that the essence of viking navigation is that it depended very little on apparatus, it seems best to concentrate on apparatus which serves these two essential ends and actually exists in finds from the viking age. Two such objects exist, but it cannot be proved that they were ever used in the way I suggest.

Finds of the boards and pieces for a board game like draughts are not uncommon from the viking age, and in at least one example, from Ireland, the board has holes in it, probably to fit it for use on shipboard so the pieces did not slide. I have myself seen an ordinary cribbage board used in an English trawler to keep a very complicated reckoning involving towing and hauling the trawl near the two known sea-bed obstructions, and wonder whether the very rectangular courses described by Ohthere may have been influenced by being recorded on a rectangular model to keep the reckoning. I suppose that after a week at sea some device was needed to keep track of days' sailings. The advantage of a wide board with many rows of holes like the 'gaming' board is that a record can be kept of course as well as distance: the schematised picture of the Vinland voyages for instance goes onto (or comes from?) such a board very easily.

In the later traverse boards, still in use in the 1920's on small Norwegian traders, from one of which, stranded at Blakeney, an example is still preserved in that village, some fairly subtle operations were possible. In this, the usual type, the holes radiate from the centre in lines corresponding to the points of the compass. At the end of the watch it is possible by moving the pins one place in towards the centre of the sector they cover, alternately one from the left-hand edge and one from the right, to end up with all on the same line which is the course steered during the watch as an average of all the different headings a sailing vessel may have been forced to adopt. This makes it possible to keep a good dead reckoning without pencil and paper and calculation, and whilst I emphasise that there is no contemporary evidence that the 'gaming' boards were used in this way on viking ships, they must have had some way of keeping the reckoning over a month.

To tell the time from the sun without using its direction (south means midday) may seem a more difficult problem, but it had been solved by AD 1000 in England. The Canterbury portable sundial hangs from a chain, using gravity as its reference, not south, and measures the sun's angle from the vertical, not from south. This means that it can be used anywhere without prior knowledge of where south is, and measures time by the sun's altitude at noon, not its direction. This altitude depends on the latitude of the observer, and the sun's declination, which is different in different months. The Canterbury instrument copes with this by having a different column for each pair of months equidistant each side of the solstice, and is calculated for the mid-latitude of Britain (or the North Sea). Later instruments of the type have means of adjustment for different latitudes, but the Canterbury one is, with the exception of a slightly different one from Pompeii, the earliest of its kind. It was found at the same level as a tenth-century brooch in the cloister garth of Canterbury by an old and respected groundsman digging in the course of his job, and it fits a date about the year AD 1000.

It is constructed with great finesse. The tip of the shadow of a pin which project horizontally from the face moves downwards as the sun rises higher, and at noon covers a small jewel, extinguishing its glow and giving a very accurate determination of the instant when that happens. As a time-teller it is not very accurate: it is at its best in the summer months and would certainly enable you to orientate a sun compass if you had one, and bothered to use it. The many interesting problems it raises are peripheral here. What matters is that it reduces the complex interaction of time, declination and latitude to a simple incremental formula easily remembered so that one can reconstruct it anywhere, at any size, once the principle is known. If the projection of the shadow pin is one unit, then the distance below it of the spots required for noon the year round will be one-quarter, one-half, three-quarters, one, one and a quarter and one and a half units. This simplified relationship only works for latitudes round about 55°N and thus seems most likely to have been worked out there. I cannot see a useless formula being developed in the Mediterranean where it would not work and then exported to the North Sea where it would.

So we can safely assume that some men round about the year AD 1000 could reduce declination and latitude to such a handy rule of thumb. We cannot of course assume that they were to be found on board a knarr lost in the North Atlantic: they may have been the atomic scientists of their day, only to be found in the most distinguished intellectual circles of Jarrow or Canterbury.

It will be remembered that when the fog lifted and Bjarni, lost in the North Atlantic south of Greenland could again see the sun 'he could sort out directions again'. No reference to any perception that he was south of the latitude of Greenland or Iceland: yet after some days' uncertainty he must surely have used the sun's altitude when it first broke through to decide whether he should assume it was SE or SSE? Or did he conclude that without knowledge of his latitude he must wait until the sun started to drop again, and take that as south?

Questions like this perhaps interest us because they represent the only point at which the navigational worlds of then and now touch one another. If you were the owner of the cargo and responsible to no one for its delivery to any particular port at any particular time, but merely wished to sell it somewhere for enough to buy another which you could hope to sell somewhere, with enough cash, beer or honey in the deal to keep you and the crew happy, then exact navigation was perhaps the least of your worries. Our anxious concern to put reliable tools for it into the hands of viking age voyagers is perhaps misplaced. I have seen the navigational resources of one convenience flag ship of our decade: a general chart of the Atlantic, the North Sea, the Mediterranean, the Baltic, an almanac and a list of Radio signals. It is not perhaps as funny as the traditional story about a road map of Europe, but it shows that it is possible to get around with effectively no access to post-viking age improvements except radio bearings.

Many viking age navigators were engaged on voyages on which any error of course up to 90° would not, in the very long run, affect matters much. The track chart for *Odin's Raven* (p. 95) is specially drawn to get away from our hackneyed Mercator North-up assumptions. A glance at it will show that if the initial course from south Norway is well chosen, an unnoticed error of 90° to the southward will prolong the voyage but not fetch up anywhere other than Britain. As the great majority of viking voyages were made in company there is a reasonable hope that one's companions, particularly if the alteration was across their bows, or pushed them off the wind, would enquire solicitously about one's intentions. One should not joke about serious matters and it is perfectly possible that a backing wind might insensibly push a whole fleet off to the southward, but after twenty-four hours with the voyage half over someone would surely notice that sunrise was not where it was yesterday? We must in other words not exaggerate the requirement for exactness in the voyaging of the viking age, and certainly not assume that the quite exceptional special requirements of the direct voyage to Greenland were the norm for ordinary North Sea traffic. If our imaginary navigator with the 90° course error after twenty-four hours were to reform, and decide on a passage down the Irish Sea by way of Shetland or Orkney he would now have to keep his course within a sector of 45° between SW and W approximately, perhaps for as much as four hours between the disappearance of the afterglow in the NW and the reappearance of dawn in the NE. He would have to be extremely unlucky for those four hours to coincide with a sudden wind-shift and the absence of any planet he could see (not necessarily recognise) or any bright star visible in the darker part of the sky.

I do not wish at all to minimise the very real new ground won for human self-confidence against its environment by the viking Atlantic voyages, but they were the exceptions built by outstandingly capable and enterprising men on the basis of a practice developed for voyages which either coasted or made hops of no more than 200 miles or so. The range of visibility of high land is about one and a tenth miles times the square root of the height in feet. I find it difficult to believe that the average viking navigator, if there was such a person, could work out a square root, but I feel fairly certain he had a good idea how far off you could expect to see Iceland, Faeroe or Shetland. Most viking voyages were made between points with very high peaks, and when to this range (forty miles for Shetland, fifty for Faeroe) you add what David Lewis calls the 'expanded target' by the use of the birds, seaweed, etc, described by Scoresby and *Landnama* it will be apparent that the great majority of the recorded viking voyages require no sixth sense or lost apparatus, but only sensible pilotage by eye and a good ship. Concentration on the relatively few transatlantic voyages and the *Landnama* course description of a route west from Hernum in Norway due west to Hvarf in Greenland, passing north of and barely in sight of Shetland, south of Faeroe with the sea halfway up the mountains, and south of Iceland so that one has birds and whales from it, has I think distorted our picture of viking voyaging. The south tip of Greenland, Cape Farewell, is approximately 60°N, and this parallel would take one south of Shetland, not one whole degree north of it. A course to take one barely in sight of Shetland and north of it and then thirty miles or so south of Faeroe must be

appreciably south of west, and will never make Greenland. As
Schnall points out this course to Greenland involves three appreci-
able course alterations, and I think that the desire to establish the
existence in the viking age of the constant-latitude sailing which
later periods practised has led writers to ignore these difficulties.
We know that these later navigators did have devices such as the
backstaff which enabled them to keep a constant latitude. We do
not know of such devices from the viking age, and only this
ungrounded assertion that viking voyages were based on latitude
sailing can be adduced to support the various invented devices for
doing so in the viking age. The argument is completely circular. It
seems much more natural to conclude that this route, like all other
viking ones we know, was based on looking for one fixed point after
another, and not at all on the astronomical maintaining of a constant latitude. In any case, the trans-ocean voyages were only a tiny
proportion of the whole, and the majority of viking routes were
much more SW–NE than E–W. The old suggestion that the flight
paths of migrating birds in spring and autumn across the North Sea,
provided a rough indication in the absence of the sun, though not
often mentioned by recent writers, seems to have more to be said for
it. The *Landnamabok* course, like all the other apparently 'modern
astro-navigation' methods proves to be simply a rough indication
requiring an experienced pilot to interpret it flexibly. Even the
apparently precise determination in the Greenland observation of
the sun on the meridian both north and south carried out at Kroks-
fjartharheith in 1266, long after the viking age, proves on detailed
investigation by Almar Naess to be inconsistent. From Gardar in
Greenland the sun bearing NW on midsummer day had an altitude
of 3° 42'. If its altitude bearing N on July 25th was the same, as the
text says, then the latitude must have been 75° 47'N. It follows that
on that day the sun's altitude bearing south at noon must have been
32° 8'. Unhappily it is impossible to produce a plausible cross-
section for any type of boat of which we know which will then cast
the shadow of the rail across the face of a man with his feet against
the ship's side. That the vessel is said to be a sixareen (the ancestor
of *Waterwitch*, see p. 93) only makes matters worse. It is clear
that the author of this fascinating passage had a clear idea of the
relationship of sun altitude on the meridian to latitude, but it seems
equally clear that he had neither accurate instrument nor agreed

terminology to express the idea.

One very important element in the planning and execution of less ambitious and interesting voyages within the North Sea is some agreed measure of distance. This aspect has fortunately attracted less ingenious speculation, though it must have played a much more important part in the development of the historically important voyages. It has been well dealt with by Roald Morcken in the *Mariner's Mirror* (Vol. 54, p. 393) and his account may be summarised as follows:

One day's sailing = 2 *tylftar* = 24 *vikur sjovar* = 144 nautical miles. From this we see that one *vikur* = 36,000 ft. If this is done in one hour, then the speed is 10 ft per second, or one minute for a sixty-foot ship to pass a floating object thrown from the bow as a Dutchman's log. This speed of 1 *vikur* in an hour corresponds to the *doegrsigling* or day's sail. The distances check well enough with the following given in the sources:

> Stad in Norway to Iceland $3\frac{1}{2}$ days = 504 miles, actually 525.
> Reykjanes (Iceland) to Ireland, 5 days = 720 miles, actually 690.
> Kvalsund to Lindesnes (Norway) 2 tylftar = 144 miles, actually 150.
> Bergen to Trondheimsfjord 4 tylftar = 288 miles, actually 286.
> Baffinland to Herjolfsnes, 4 days = 576 miles, actually 590.

It does not check at all with either Ohthere's or Wulfstan's voyages, and though the latter was very likely using a different ship type, the discrepancy in Ohthere's case is explained by Morcken as a specifically Norwegian measure of 6 *vikur* to the day, a day's rowing, used even by sailing vessels in later periods. One can well understand that on such a deeply intersected coast the actual distance made good was less than on the open sea, and the distance, 36 miles in twelve hours at three knots, was certainly the most economical long distance speed for *Odin's Raven* under oars, but the discrepancy does require explanation. It may be that Wulfstan, as an Englishman, simply reports the length of time he actually took on his voyage, and is not using the Norse unit of the day's sailing, or day's rowing, as Ohthere may be when he says, as a generalisation, 'you would not do it in a month', though he does also refer to favourable or usable winds as being involved. But the other cases Morcken cites seem convincing and again suggest that the basis of viking age navigation was still, as it had been for Beowulf, the expected time of arrival on the second day.

The Duke of Wellington observed that there is no substitute for personal reconnaissance upon the spot, and my ideas about the realities of the navigation of a viking ship have been much affected by the rewarding experience of fitting out, sailing and helping to navigate one. That is dealt with in detail in part two. The main lesson is that as in most sailing vessels one makes the best course one can, and the intellect is concentrated much more upon that, than upon the great circle course. 'The fool's eyes are upon the ends of the earth', but anyone conducting a single squaresail vessel does well to focus his eyes distinctly nearer home, and concentrate on the best course for the next three hours, or three minutes.

Frames being fitted to cleats in fully planked-up hull

Fitting-out at the jetty at Rød

Running battle with femboring

Into a head sea off Stad

Not hay, but fish drying

Rowing down the fjords

Rowing into Lerwick

Facing Approaching an oil rig in the Ninian Field

Crew in Lerwick Galley Shed

Maps and Plans

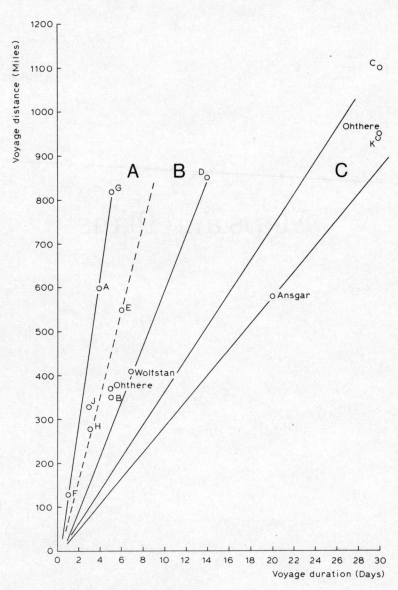

Distance and Duration of Viking Voyages.

A.	Stadland to Iceland
B.	Skane to Birka
C.	Denmark to Novgorod
D.	Wollin to Novgorod
E.	Birka to Novgorod
F.	Aalborg to Oslofjord
G.	Oslofjord to Trondheim
H.	Helgoland to England
J.	Ribe to England
K.	Aalborg to Iceland

The first is from St Olaf's saga, the rest from Adam of Bremen, cited by Dettlev Ellmers.

Sector C on the diagram presents no problem: all are trading vessels on long voyages. There is little difference in speed whether coasting from Hedeby to Birka (Ansgar), down the Norwegian coast to Kaupang (Ohthere), where the ship stopped each night, or sailing out to Iceland from Aalborg where at any rate the last two-thirds of the voyage must have been continuous sailing like Wulfstan's. The centre of this type would be 500 miles in 16 days, four days to cover 125 miles (which the Raven did in twenty-four hours). It may seem reasonable to produce a figure of thirty miles in a twenty-four-hour day from this, but it would probably be quite misleading as a guide to the way in which the voyage was carried out. Such a distance with a good favourable wind would take little over three hours, and scarcely more than six with any wind worth sailing with. But long voyages naturally often involved more days with unfavourable winds on which the ship had to remain in harbour, as it could not be rowed. The desire to keep these to a minimum might explain the permanently fixed – perhaps therefore too tall to be easily lowered and raised – masts of the merchant ships, which would allow of a higher aspect rig more able to work to windward.

The question is whether the sector AB is one, contrasting with C, or two. Ellmers assumes that there were three types of voyage, merchantman stopping at night, merchantman continuous, warship continuous. He lists all the voyages of sector A as warships. The longest is from Oslofjord to Trondheim, average speed of 7 knots, which must have involved relays of oarsmen (possible in a coastal voyage) or steady southerly winds, but the next longest is from Stad to Iceland, so different that it is difficult to believe it was the same type of ship. The average speed of 6 knots must have been under sail, and this continued surpassing of the doegr sigling (average 5 knots) agrees with the unusually favourable winds specifically mentioned in the account. Ohthere and Wulfstan lie so close to these performances, or at any rate to the slower side of this sector, and so far from the best of sector C as to suggest that differences within AB may be simply a matter of luck with weather. The centre line of AB actually has two 'warship' voyages on it, and as these are only doing sixteen miles better than Ohthere noon to noon, there seems no ground for assuming any great difference of type. Yet it is noticeable that Wulfstan in a week's continuous sailing is only averaging half the doegr sigling speed, presumably because during the week he had some weak winds and perhaps some calms: it would be impossible to predict favourable wind for a week at a time.

My view is that many of the AB voyages were made in general-purpose craft, not unlike Odin's Raven, or Skuldelev 3 with more oars.

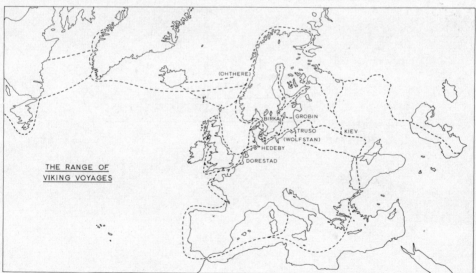

THE RANGE OF VIKING VOYAGES

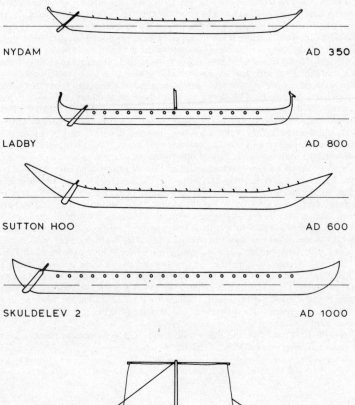

NYDAM   AD 350

LADBY   AD 800

SUTTON HOO   AD 600

SKULDELEV 2   AD 1000

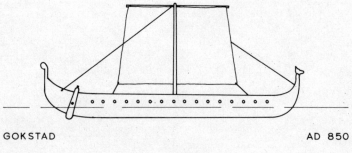

GOKSTAD   AD 850

A.L.B.   1:150   D.A.W.

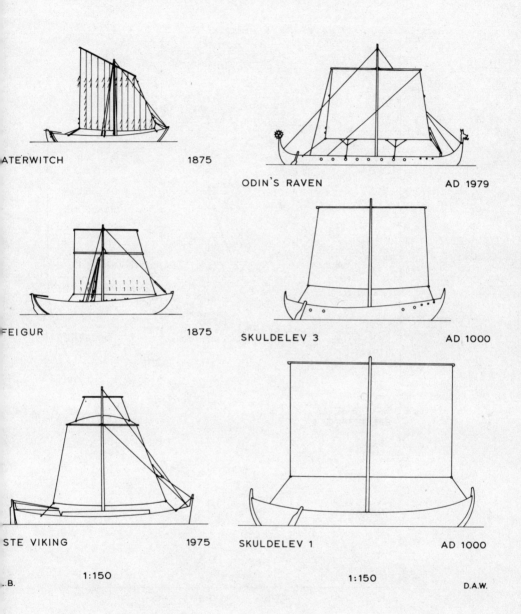

ATERWITCH   1875

ODIN'S RAVEN   AD 1979

FEIGUR   1875

SKULDELEV 3   AD 1000

STE VIKING   1975

SKULDELEV 1   AD 1000

1:150   1:150

.B.   D.A.W.

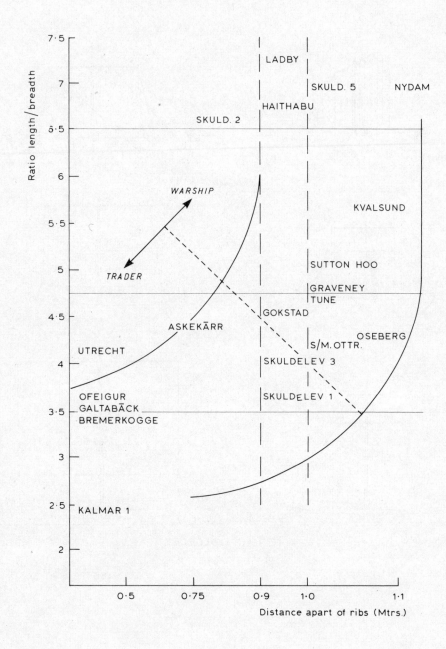

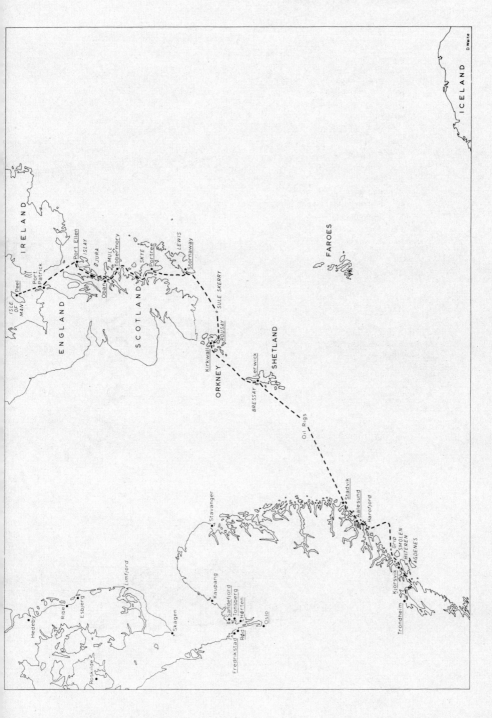

D.Waite

ICELAND

IRELAND

ISLE OF MAN • Peel
Port Patrick
Port Ellen
ISLAY
JURA
Oban MULL Tobermory
SKYE Portree
LEWIS
Stornoway

ENGLAND

SCOTLAND

SULE SKERRY
ROUSAY
Kirkwall
ORKNEY
Lerwick
BRESSAY SHETLAND

FAROES

Oil Rigs

Stavanger

Stadvik
Aalesund
Hardfjord

SMOLEN
HITTEREN
VAAGENES
Kjorsvik

Trondheim

Limfjord

Kaupang
Sandefjord
Tonsberg
Hutten
Oslo
Rod
Fredrikstad
Skagen
Esbjerg
Ribe
Hedeby

THE HULL

1 Dragon head prow
2 Dragon tail stern
3 Sloping frames (4)
4 Vertical frames (11)
5 Deck beams (11)
6 Oar ports (16)
7 Engine
8 Propeller (Folded)
9 Rudder
10 Tiller
11 Rudder strap (Leather)
12 Rudder pivot (Rope)
13 Seachests (17)
14 Chart locker
15 Compass

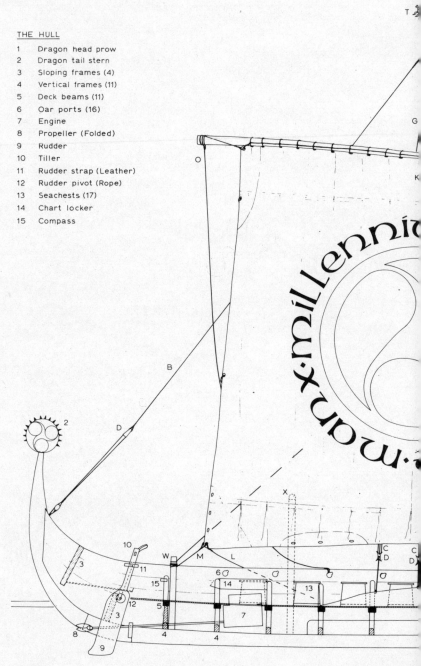

A L BINNS

THE RIG

A   Forestay
B   Backstay
C   Shrouds
D   Jomfru purchase
E   Anchor pendant

F   Main halyard
G   Spare halyard
H   Halyard sheaves
J   Rakke line
K   Rakke downhall

L   Tack
M   Sheet
N   Port brace
O   Starboard brace
P   Bowline
Q   Duva, Signat
R   Priare

S   Mast
T   Weathervane
U   Yard
V   Bearing-out spar
W   Fixed support for yard
X   Removable supports for yard
Y   Seglstikke
Z   Reef bands

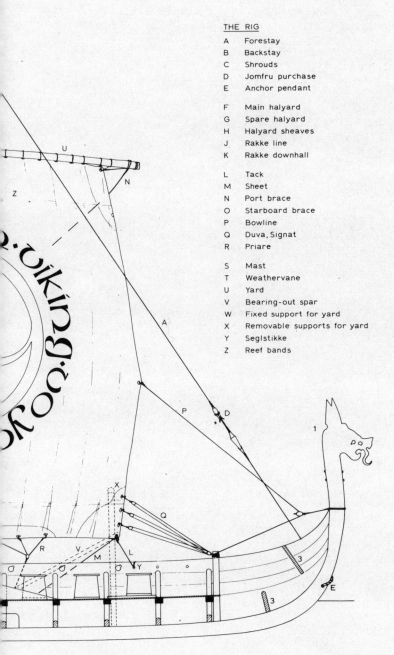

D.A. WAITE

PART TWO

ODIN'S RAVEN

1

Birth of the Idea

It was July 5th, the morning of Tynwald day in the Manx Millennium year of 1979, and I was sitting in the dark but brass-gleaming bar of a quiet pub in Peel, away from the waterfront but the haunt of herring-workers. I had just come from the ship and was listening to one of them voicing some scepticism about the 'thousand years of history'. 'Someone was telling me', he told the landlord, 'they've got the wrong year altogether, anyway.'

'Is that so?' said the landlord. He didn't say it in a challenging way, he combined a sense of wonder with gratefulness for the enlightenment he'd been given that was flattering to the speaker, with a hint of cautious awareness that there is much to be said on both sides of every question, typical of landlords the world over, particularly when they know that it will infallibly be said, at length, by some customers for the next hour. 'Is that so?' Just a shade more wondering surprise this time, and a hint of stage-management about the pause. Then he evidently made his mind up to reject the attractive gambit, and delivered his reply in practised landlord deadpan style, turning to ring up the till. 'I thought everyone knew there was no special significance to the actual date at all.'

He was quite right, of course. Even a twenty-year-old Manx fisherman can project more world-weary cynicism than a Roman emperor, and an outsider soon finds that knowledge of Viking history in the tenth century isn't the first thing needed to understand the Manx Millennium. There is a lordly and generous attitude to time in the Island: no one is small-minded enough to fuss about an hour or two, and everyone is ready to spend an hour or two on a friend met by chance on a busy corner. Over a thousand years, from a whole population – that obviously amounts to a lot of time, certainly enough to cover any margin of uncertainty.

Once the Millennium had been proclaimed it was certain that the traditional symbol of the viking ship would be at the heart of it, on everything from ties to teatowels. Some historians think that the viking ship motif found along the coast of North-West Europe shows the deep impression left in the popular mind by the terror of the original Viking raids. I doubt this. From Shetland to Brittany, not to speak of Scandinavia, the viking ship theme, and all that goes along with it in festivals of varying sobriety, looks to me more like a positive affirmation of a past of glorious disreputability by people who feel themselve its heirs. The point about viking ship festivals, none very old, is not at all continuity, but its opposite, an attempt to cross a gap which is very well known to all to exist, and is really regretted by some. Looking at the whole range, from Shetland to the Isle of Man, from Up-Helly-Aa to the Peel Vikings, from Lerwick Galley-shed to Peel Longhouse, it is not difficult for a mainlander to see the point. It is understandable if once a year islanders living way outside the mainstream, who once controlled what was once the highroad, feel inclined to celebrate their ancestry in a riot of half-serious horseplay. Particularly if their economy is still dependent on the great gamble of fishing in relatively small wooden craft. To proclaim the stark simplicity of a viking ship, one mast, one square sail, not unlike their grandfather's fishing boat, is in a way a defiant gesture against the industrial society which buys their fish, and perhaps against the expensive and mortgaged complexity of their own modern craft. No wonder that the viking ship makes for them a symbol of a golden past as well as an identity with which to confront the visitor. It manifests the difference between their ancient culture and that continental one which produced Europe's cities, castles and cathedrals. An Englishman's home may be his castle, but the Islander's castle was his boat, and you need to remember this when you face the sad multiplication of viking ship ashtrays, salt-cellars and tulip-vases.

Though the symbol certainly has a history, it wasn't much used in that way in the viking age itself. Vikings were collectors of coinage rather than minters of it, but early piratical kings like Eric Bloodaxe in York for example did not put the viking ship on their coins. Swords and Raven banners were the chosen symbols and it may be very significant that those coins from the viking age which do show a viking ship belong to a very commercial series from Hedeby, the great market port where Scandinavian products were exchanged with Europe, and the other coins in the series all show merchant-ship types. No one nowadays has festivals dedicated to them, the keels and hulks which steadily traded with smaller crews across the seas infested with viking ships, but it may be some consolation to reflect that they probably showed a better return on the capital invested in their long-lived heavy hulls than did those expensive works of art, the viking ships. They were lucky to get on to the coinage in their own day, for few since have claimed them as ancestors and made ashtrays in their shape, and a modern Norwegian or Manxman, even if he works on a huge and ugly super-tanker, still thinks of the graceful viking ship as the emblem of his forefathers.

Where the viking age did put its ship as symbol was in or over its graves, and we can feel that this was fitting without necessarily understanding the reasons. Some hold that it was a continuation of earlier beliefs in a voyage after death which can be traced as far back as the Bronze age, and which take classic form in Charon ferrying the dead over a river of forgetfulness. The shipshaped arrangements of stones around a grave, less time-consuming and more lasting than a real wooden ship, are found down to the immediately pre-viking period in grave-fields such as Lindholm, overlooking the Limfjord in north Jutland.

Others say that the presence of evidently royal ships in such otherwise lavishly furnished graves as Sutton Hoo, Oseberg or Gokstad simply shows that the idea of the next world was one even older and more materialist, so that a king packing for the next world took care to take with him everything for which he had use in this. And certainly the skaldic poems celebrating the arrival in Valhalla of such kings as Harald Hardrada or Erik Bloodaxe suggest that they will be recognised in the next world as much by their splendid retinue as by the ravens and wolves which evidence their slaughterous victories. This attitude to some sort of life after death was not the monopoly of royalty, though we should beware of thinking that the beliefs of peasant or fisherman were necessarily very like those celebrated by the court poets. The viking buried at Balladoole in Man took with him not only his thirty-foot boat and best clothes and horse, but was accompanied in his mound by a girl whose skull had been split by a sword-blow.

For others, the ships carved on the Gotland stones or on fragments from the Isle of Man represent the biography for an illiterate age of the man who lay beneath the stone or had in some cases been drowned abroad, 'west over the sea'. It is not difficult to detect a narrative purpose in some of these stones, but they are more easily interpreted as versions of recognisable heroic stories such as that of Sigurd the dragon-slayer, and though ships do not figure largely in his story it is not surprising if they appear regularly in the life of other heroes. Dr Johnson observed that a man is not upon oath in an epitaph, but it seems unlikely that even in the viking age so many of the deceased had quite such heroic lives as an over-literal interpretation of these stones would suggest, and it is probably better to compare them with the scenes from sacred story common in later Christian art: though that doesn't mean that the stories of sea expeditions told in these pictures formed some sort of holy writ. Perhaps no more was involved than the sort of general assertion common in eighteenth-century epitaphs that the dead man had achieved in every aspect of life a perfection in which we have ceased to believe. The reference may have been more specific. We can see from the court poetry (and from the Old English poem *Beowulf*) that the commonest way of praising a chieftain was to compare him, to his advantage of course, with the great figures of legend, sometimes intertwining the story of their lives with that of his. It seems reasonable to assume that the pictorial equivalent of this in similar allusions could be made in carving the stones.

Various as are the reasons brought forward to explain the viking ships in viking graves, they are probably not more mixed than those which led to the revival of the viking ship as an emblem in nineteenth-century northern Europe. It is probably not accidental that the area in which it was most enthusiastically taken up, north of a line from the Isle of Man to Jutland, is one in which it was possible to feel that the nation's fishermen embodied the best of the national spirit, engaged in combat with the sea, and an area in which the boats they used were clearly descended from the viking ship, many of whose features they retained. So there was some real foundation for a romantic desire to see in them guardians of an old tradition.

It was certain then that when the Isle of Man decided to celebrate the Millennium of Tynwald in 1979 someone would say 'We should build a viking ship.' Given the composition of modern Manx society, its taxes and financial aspirations, the odds on the speaker being a man with the drive and means to make it more than a wistful joke were not bad. Even so, to make the idea stick and carry it through the wilderness of detailed planning of so many apparently unrelated necessities requires a personal involvement. Not many Manxmen or Shetlanders are so provably involved as Robin Bigland, whose family had come from Norway to Cark in Cartmel certainly by the twelfth century. There is no point in elaborating on the nature of the twentieth-century attempt to re-establish communication with the past on our own terms by re-enacting it on various levels from village pageant to Hollywood epic. The Manx Millennium Viking Voyage had some elements in common with both, but wasn't like either, as it really was a voyage and over the same waters which inevitably involved the same anxieties about wind, water, food and beer. Motives are always mixed, and those of the only begetter and others of the subsequent crew of *Odin's Raven* that I personally heard ranged from 'It was the obvious thing to do' to 'It sounded such a crazy thing to do I wanted to be on it' through 'I thought it would be a good booze-up round some of the places I've never been' and 'I wouldn't like the others going and me not'. It seems to me that this absence of self-conscious historical dedication was not the least authentic part of the voyage. Very similar things were probably said on the tenth-century voyages to Man, and the mixture of careless enthusiasm and cheerful realism was not the least Manx part of it. But if it had not been Robin Bigland who said, 'We should build a viking ship', *Odin's Raven* probably would not have been built. The decision to do so, and to aim, within the limits of common sense and prudence, at an authentic viking ship, proved fruitful for the study of an important aspect of the viking age. A large number of 'viking' ships have been built in our century, some purely for film use, some in intention archaeological reconstructions. The former have been built by professionals not hampered by lack of funds, but essentially restricted to appearance and entertainment as the aim. The latter, built by amateurs hampered by lack of funds, could never be pressed to find out their ultimate performance: they did not inspire confidence and occasionally involved tragedy for their crews. There was not one in the twentieth century that could match Magnus Andersen's *Viking* in the nineties of the last, and that famous Gokstad ship copy which crossed the Atlantic in 1893 has created its own fascination and folklore ever since.

The Gokstad ship has been the model for most replicas partly because of the seagoing reputation won for it by Andersen, partly because it is the only one, even at the present day, for which good constructional drawings, most recently by Arne Emil Christensen, are available. The Ladby ship is more typical of the true longship of the period, and a copy based on it in Denmark performed well among the islands there. But it only survives as a shadow in the earth like the Sutton Hoo ship, and neither it nor the Kvalsund boat could seriously be considered for the long deepwater voyage from Trondheim to the Isle of Man.

Once the decision to build a good replica was taken it was almost automatic that it should be of Gokstad. Limitations of space, time and money required it to be a two-thirds version, fifty feet long instead of seventy-five. This creates interesting problems of scale, for the obvious solution of making all dimensions two-thirds of the original is not available, as one cannot scale down proportionately either sea waves or men. The upright tee-pieces which hold the sail's yard clear of the oarsmen when sail is lowered (we called them yokes on board) have to remain their original height of two metres if there is to be room beneath them for the crew of full-size men to move about particularly when the tent is rigged at night. They are thus bound to seem disproportionately high and a little unsightly compared with the originals.

The Gokstad ship was rowed through oarholes in the third strake of planking down from the rail. This enabled the oarsmen to get a level swing with their oars entering the water at the best angle and gave them some cover from the weather and from enemies. If they had rowed from the rail not only would they have been more exposed but either their oars would have entered the water too steeply for efficient rowing at sea or they would have been too long and heavy for safe handling in bad weather. In *Odin's Raven* oarholes in the corresponding plank would barely have been above the waterline, and quite unusable at sea, so the oarholes had to be located in the uppermost plank, where we see them in many medieval illustrations, though not in Gokstad. This plank narrows fore and aft where the graceful upspringing sheer begins, and is no longer wide enough for oarholes, so that the rowing positions are relatively more concentrated amidships. This is important when the ship is being manoeuvred, for the turning power of oars near the bow is much greater. As the ship's beam is narrower there, the oars have to be shorter, a disadvantage as it means they enter the water more steeply, but an advantage when rowing the head round if tacking against the wind in choppy water, as the oars are so much handier than the longer main or midships ones. This shows some of the unexpected consequences of scaling-down and the matter does not end there. The plank through which the oars pass in the Gok-stad ship is close above one thicker than the rest, the *meginhufr*, which is fastened to the ends of the cross-frames. This is important for it transmits the drive of the oars to the hull just above the waterline and does not distort the extremely flexible hull which might happen if Gokstad were rowed through its very lightly sup-ported uppermost plank.

The frames in *Odin's Raven* were kept at the spacing of about three feet which seems to have been traditional in oared vessels of the viking age, and this means that they are, in relation to the length of the hull, further apart and fewer than in Gokstad. To have put them at two feet would have produced a stiff and close-framed hull whose behaviour at sea would not have resembled that of Gokstad.

Such unavoidable basic modifications in building real hulls for real waves suggest that whilst scaling is inevitable in tank testing it should be avoided as far as possible when building replica ships and one should use originals of the size one can manage to build and crew. They were not in this case as unacceptable as they may seem, as the *Raven* was not envisaged primarily as another Gokstad replica, but was intended to be representative of the type of viking ship that made the majority of viking voyages. It is now generally accepted that the traditional longships did not make the crossings to Scotland or Iceland, and the problems of carrying food and water for large crews of oarsmen on long voyages with uncertain landfalls may make it seem unlikely that many full-size Gokstads did either. But the dimensions of *Odin's Raven*, 50 ft × 11 ft 9 in × 4 ft 4 in deep from gunwale to keel, come fairly close to those of Skuldelev No. 3, the typical small trader in the Viking Ship Museum in Roskilde (43 ft × 10 ft 9 in × 4 ft 10 in deep). The *Raven*'s hull, 6 in shallower on a length 6 ft greater is less a sailing hull, and carries less on a given length, but is not less seaworthy, and it will be fascinating to compare her performance with that of the Skuldelev 3 replica now being built.

The most important distinction between the longship and the merchantman was, as the name for warship implies, the ratio of length to beam. In this Gokstad lies very near the borderline between typical longship and typical merchantman (see diagram, p. 92) and in the 50 ft version can carry a crew of twenty but be handled by one of six more or less indefinitely, carrying provisions for a month at a time. I think that the majority of the ships in most viking fleets were of this type, though they were led by ships of the full Gokstad size and in the eleventh century by very much larger vessels.

Those ships which came from Norway to Man *via* Shetland, Orkney and the Hebrides must presumably have had a sailing ability at least the equal of the ordinary merchantman, but carrying larger crews for raiding purposes could usefully use them to row when the wind did not serve. The hull best suited to this is one like Gokstad which gives up some sail and load-carrying ability to get a fast and easily driven hull, with freeboard kept down for easy rowing and lightness, but more beam and fuller waterlines than a true longship which did not have to make open sea crossings of a week or more. In this the agreement with the ships of the Bayeux tapestry, whose beam length ratio resemble *Odin's Raven* (Gokstad) at 1 to 4.5 rather than Ladby and the others at 1 to 7.5 is striking.

Not surprising then, that *Odin's Raven* was to be based on Gokstad: not surprising either that a committee was to be set up.

Once the scheme had been drawn up at the beginning of July '78 a preliminary discussion was held in Robin Bigland's offices in Derby House, Athol Street, the new financial quarter in Douglas, and on July 21st the meeting was told that the Lieutenant-Governor, Sir John Paul, had agreed to become patron. His support was the more appreciated when he later admitted to having had private doubts about whether the ship could ever be built. Before the meeting was a quotation from Rød shipyard to build a fifty-foot viking ship on the Gokstad model for fifty thousand pounds, and it was decided to go ahead, accept, and then try to raise enough money to build the hull, fit it out properly and sail it from Trondheim to the Isle of Man to arrive on the eve of Tynwald day, the Island's great historic festival. Whilst it was hoped that about ten thousand pounds might be raised in Norway, and that the Manx government's Millennium Committee might also contribute, it was clear that as well as public and private donations as much commercial sponsorship as possible would be required. The contract with the shipyard was signed on August 28th, but by the end of September, perhaps because many could not believe the ship would ever really accomplish the voyage, only twenty thousand pounds had been raised, and half that was already committed as first payment to the yard. Two thousand pounds of this had been raised in Norway. By the end of the year about twenty-five thousand pounds (half the cost of the bare hull) had been raised in the Isle of Man, and ten thousand in Norway, the latter almost entirely due to the generous participation of DNC Den Norsk Creditbank. Then the Manx Millennium Committee agreed to contribute another twenty thousand, and though some financial concern existed up to the end of the voyage, the basic solvency of the project seemed reasonably secure by Christmas '78.

It was fortunate that the original idea and leadership of the project had come from Robin Bigland and it was also a happy chance that Rød Boatbuilders had been brought to the attention of the project. The suggestion came from Arne Wisth, a Norwegian feature journalist interested in Manx-Norse relations who had taken part in the joke 're-occupation' of the Isle of Man in 1977, returning from a Ronaldsway airport renamed Hasraldsway with a tribute of Loghtan four-horned sheep. There are many places in Norway where the skills to build such traditional clinker craft exist, and many of them are very beautiful as well, but there can be few which fitted the bill so perfectly. Rød ('the clearing') lies at the head of Elingaardskilen, a long narrow inlet just north of Frederikstad on the eastern shore of the entrance to the Oslo fjord, almost opposite the Royal graves in Vestfold in which the Oseberg and Gokstad ships were found. It is not far from Hankø, whose annual regatta is the Cowes week or Newport of Norway, but is discreetly tucked away behind a headland which half hides the unmarked entrance. There is an even less visible second entrance behind an island to the north, which we did not find until half-way through the trials period, having sailed past it half a dozen times.

The approach to Rød from the landward side requires no less local knowledge. Coming north from Fredrikstad on the main road to Oslo, you turn off at the signpost for Hankø and pass innumerable signs to Onsoy church, where all the roads of Odin's Island seem to meet. It is natural to suppose that the church occupies the site of the earliest cult meeting-place at the most conspicuous and central position. Just past the church, a glimpse of the head of Elingaardskilen across the watermeadows heralds the communal meeting-place which has, in the remote Scandinavian countryside, replaced the heathen thing-place and the Christian church as the axle on which local social life revolves. It is one of those splendid rural Scandinavian garages which put in the shade our customary traffickers in ice-cream, road-maps and sweets. Its forecourt is a valiant attempt at a substitute for the village pub, and every time you pass it a group of teenagers will be discussing the last, or next, young farmers' club dance with a friend who has driven in on his father's tractor, much used as a sports car to attend the local hops. The shop part of the garage is like the best type of old-style village store if you can imagine one selling electric waffle-irons, garden furniture of cool French elegance, swimming-pools and all other requisites of the simple life of summertime Scandinavia. Perhaps every tenth caller buys oil or petrol: those seeking the boatyard do well to enquire here, as some yards past the garage two tracks take off into the woods to the left, unmarked save for two concrete litter boxes and an invitation, or command, to keep the area tidy.

If you take the right-hand track (the left leads only to a forestry clearing) and persist for a mile or so along it, turning when in doubt to keep a steady approach to the coast, you come eventually to a cluster of small wooden houses among the trees and rocky outcrops which surround their arable fields. This is 'The clearing' or rather 'THE clearing' and after careful search you should discover a highly temporary looking wooden sign all of ten inches long, unless someone has forgotten to put it up, as they do now and then after a century and a half. It says 'Rød Boatbuilders' and points down the steepening defile to the left. It is best to leave your car there, ignoring the helpful local assurances that there is room to park in the forest, room to turn round at the boatyard, or that alternatively it's probably best to reverse back up the cliff-road anyway. The descent is not always uneventful even on foot and on winter visits to the yard you sometimes find yourself helplessly overtaken by those whose galoshes have lost their grip. Fortunately the fjord at the bottom is usually quite firmly frozen by then. I have never seen a party roped together and using belays on the way down, but have often heard stops to admire the view recommended during the ascent in a breathless voice owing more to the steepness of the hill than reverence for Nature. You could not wish for a better demonstration that the water is the natural highway of Norway than the last hundred yards of the road to Rød boatyard, and of course much of its material arrives by sea even today.

The appropriateness of the place for the building of *Odin's Raven* is not a merely a matter of fancy. Sean McGrail observes in the context of the National Maritime Museum's more rigorously archaeological experiments that the choice of the place to build a replica boat 'is a most important point, for the environment can influence the boat builders probably to the detriment of authenticity. In addition it is only in similar surroundings that the modern worker can appreciate some of the problems faced by boatbuilders of long ago. . . . Wearing Viking age clothes is not essential for the builders of a replica of a ninth-century boat, but it is essential to work in the appropriate surroundings – probably on a hard, sloping down to a tidal creek and in sight of trees – there the various aspects of the experiment will interact naturally and authentically.' Building the *Raven* was not conceived as an experiment of this kind, it was rather the inevitable prelude to the voyage, but more than a sense of fitness is involved in feeling that Rød was the right place.

It may still not seem a very attractive location for a boatyard. Why isn't it on the level and easily accessible ground at the head of the fjord, why not where the two broad and shallow little side valleys slope down to it across the hayfield? The building-place has been there for a century and a half, and it is before that time that one must seek the answer.

An important part of the resources of the large farms in Norway has always been their timber, and for many remote farms without good natural facilities for selling it the obvious solution was to process it themselves by building it into a boat and thus exporting it on its own bottom so to speak. This was the genesis of the characteristically Norwegian tradition of the 'boatbuilder farm'. It provided occupation in forestry and carpentry for the workforce in seasons when little could be done on the farm, helped the fishing and enabled a meagre soil to support a population which could never have lived off it alone. In time some of these farms became famous for the quality of their boats and sent them very far afield so that boatbuilding took precedence over farming. It was nevertheless still done on whatever corner of the farm lay handiest to the sea, and examination of land boundaries of Onsoy shows that Rød boatyard is the extreme SE corner of the old Rød estate. Hence the surprising location of a thriving modern boatyard and hence too the sight of the manager's twin uncles tractor-ploughing the arable after a full day building a viking ship.

A perfect setting and a continuous tradition do not of themselves guarantee a good ship for deep-sea voyages. The other important aspect of the yard was a more modern one. It builds in light alloy as well as wood, and at the time the *Raven* was building, a large modern trawler was in to have a new aluminium bridge fitted. Skilled craftsmen went back and forth from a bit of axe-trimming on an oak frame to a bit of argon-arc cutting-out alloy plate with no apparent sense of incongruity, demarcation or urgency. Indeed it sometimes seemed to both us and the trawler skipper that the yard, out of a kindly consideration for the other's feelings, was determined not to let one of us get too far ahead of the other. Certainly there was no routine assembly-line attitude at Rød. Everyone seemed to do a bit of everything and for major jobs everyone in the yard would leave what they were doing and rally round, though it was at the same time accepted that in one specialism one would take the lead and in another another. Everyone seemed to enjoy working on the *Raven* and as she was built without blueprints the ship was to an unusual extent the creation of the men who worked on her. There were no drawings until she was more than half complete, when largely at our continued insistence that we needed one for fitting-out details, Magnar Hansen, the yard manager, produced a general arrangement drawing.

The actual work of building the hull was quite independent, and the drawing was evidently regarded as a harmless but superfluous fad of the customer. The reality was the timber taking shape in the shed, the traditional interpretation of a tradition by craftsmen who had grown up working within it, and certainly did not regard it as enough part of the past to have much to do with archaeology. There was nothing bigoted about their attitude to this tradition. I have never seen so many electric tools in a British boatyard, and alongside loving detailed work done *in situ* with a razor sharp axe that looked like something in the Bayeux tapestry would be holes drilled with an electric drill – I do not remember having seen a brace and bit in the yard. Even if a boat was afloat off the tiny jetty it was usual to run a cable out to it before starting work on board. This sensible approach made it possible to incorporate traditional features which might otherwise have been impossible, or far too expensive, such as the grooved line along the exposed edge of each oak plank. There has often been a slight aura of mystery about this groove and much discussion of its significance if any. It is not easy to produce, and when the National Maritime Museum built their replica of the twenty-foot faering from Gokstad they found it necessary to forge a special blade for a hand plane to do it. The moulding tool or profile iron made to the original pattern proved 'difficult to sharpen, and tended to tear the wood'. When I enquired at Rød whether the handsome line visible in all the right places had been produced by moulding tool or hand-plane it was with a certain shy amusement that they told me that, after similar difficulty with the hand-moulding tool, what they had actually made was a new cutting blade for an *electric* plane. This sort of empiricism will never please the amateur purist of course, but it sums up the Rød attitude, and I think the men there would be happy to be judged by your attitude to it. They were determined to produce a masterpiece of faithful detail, and nothing was omitted merely because it was time-consuming: nor was time to be wasted on trivial traditionalism at the expense of hull strength. If a thoroughly craftsmanlike piece of inventiveness could save spoilt planks in a limited stock of very expensive seasoned oak, they were not the men to refuse. This is perhaps one of the reasons why the tradition embodied in small Norwegian yards like Rød continues to flourish and one can still in Norway buy at a competitive price a handmade clinker hull of natural timber.

2

Hull and Rig

The raw material of the hull, the carefully varied dimensions at which it is finished into ribs and planking, the various ways in which they are joined together, the beautiful shape of the end product which is the aim and result of these careful choices, form an integrated work of art. As you take part in the building of such a hull you are forced to trace this interdependence, to see that the solution to the problems posed by wind and sea was a hull of a certain shape, weight and flexibility and that to create it satisfactorily required a certain repertory of techniques. Each of these contributes something indispensable to the solution, each imposes its own limits on other aspects of the ship. You have the impression of contact with the creative minds involved in a way which goes beyond the experience of hearing a symphony or a play: it is more like taking part in the performance of one, perhaps even the composition of one. A Gokstad hull is a statement of the harmonious relationship of necessities which is no less precise for being nonverbal, and in every part of it we see a proportion which has to be just so if the aim of the whole is to be achieved.

The growth of the hull towards its final shape is determined by a series of subtle changes in the width and the curvature in three dimensions of each successive plank, and these are decided by the builder as he fits each plank against the one before. The frames are not inserted until the planking is complete, they follow the shape of the hull, do not determine it. In building nowadays, moulds the shape of the ship's cross-section are usually used to hold battens which assume the shape of the finished hull and serve as a guide: it would be unheard-of to construct a fifty-foot hull without them. Whether they were used in the viking period we do not know, but it would have been difficult to ensure the striking symmetry and fairness of line of the large hulls without some such arrangement. The hull is so flexible and yielding that it is particularly important that its curves are symmetrical and therefore I, like most of those interested, think that moulds were used, but not of course that these, like ours, were derived from a line drawing. We do not know the way in which the imagined form was given its first expression. In traditional building in later periods half-models were much used, and this may have been true of the viking age as well. The only model viking ship from the period (from the Dublin excavation) is far too clumsy for a builder's model and was probably a toy. The process may have resembled that at present current in traditional coble building, where it seems that for the builder the vision translates itself immediately into terms of the planking of which it consists. He seeks perhaps to improve on a previous coble's speed in a head sea by preventing her head from being thrown up by every wave, and giving her a fine enough fore-foot to slice through instead. This means that he must reduce the excess buoyancy of the bow by making the water-line a hollow curve instead of a convex, but he perceives this concave curve as an accelerated drooping of the forward end of the planks as they are prepared in their flat state. The hollow of the bow is for him the downward curve of the plank end which he knows from experience determines it. It must be remembered that in this sort of building the plank is not marked out until the previous one is in place, so that it is the change in outline and angle between one plank and the next which is the form.

There are two traditional devices for recording these changes without recourse to writing or to drawings with numbered dimensions (both of which can be excluded for the viking age). One is the boatbuilder's ell, the other the boat level. Both require only a taut cord between the stems of the boat, a simple datum found all over the world wherever boats are built. Measuring from this line to the upper and lower edge of each plank at different stations back from the bow gives the angle of each plank at the different sections and defines the shape of the hull and the pattern of the planking by marks directly recorded on the measure rod. I have myself used the system when fitting a new frame in my coble and found it clearest to use a square section rod and mark the distances at station 1 on one face of it, those at 2 on the second face and so on. Because you are recording directly on the rod you do not need to measure in agreed units like inches or centimetres or write down figures (or even, I suppose, be able to count!).

The boat level is a sort of protractor provided with a plumb bob. If its base is placed against a plank in a ship's hull a line drawn along the plumb-line effectively records the inclination of the plank at that point, probably the position of a frame. Thus the changing angle of a plank along its length can be recorded: this is another way of recording the complex curves of a hull, most used I should think (I have never used one myself) to ensure that both sides of a vessel are being planked up symmetrically.

We cannot prove that either of these was used in the viking age as neither has been identified from any find: remember though that they are both no more than sticks or pieces of wood with scratches on them, so that once it was known that the scratches were not runic letters they would be of little interest. This must not be taken to mean that every scratched wood not a runic inscription must be a boat-ell, but it does suggest how difficult it would be to recognise one if it turned up (or when it turned up?). Eiler Sundt's account, in 1865, shows them being used in the traditional building in North Norway of hulls of an unbroken evolution from the viking ships, and the system is also known from Faeroe and Shetland whose boatbuilding shares common ancestry in the viking age. *Some* way of embodying the form of a hull in a way that makes it possible to refine on it is necessary to explain the evolution of such developed and efficient hulls as Gokstad, and it seems more likely than not that these two devices, whose distribution is what one would expect of a viking boatbuilder's device, *were* used.

What else was? The elaborate interlacing ornament of contemporary manuscripts in Europe was certainly not done purely by eye, but was laid out in advance with square and compass, and the very similar animal carving on the prow of the Oseberg ship so elegantly fits the curve and so symmetrically repeats with variation that it too must have been laid out in advance in much the same way as the manuscripts. Everything is against any possible use of working drawings, which after all assume a difference between designer and doer which we have good reason to doubt for this period, but some way of taking and transmitting measurements is as necessary to accurate scarf jointing as to the finest jewellery, and the relatively rapid evolution of the viking ship from Kvalsund to Gokstad suggests an intelligent identification of parameters affecting performance that can scarcely be imagined without systematic measurement and comparison.

I find the most natural explanation of the carving of a ship's bow on the underside of one of the Oseberg deck planks that it was scratched by a shipwright to explain a point about the staggering of scarf joints in the bow to avoid dangerous weakness if they were directly above one another. It is rather noticeable that perhaps because of the greater flexibility of the hulls the otherwise impressive craftsmanship of the builders of Nydam, Sutton Hoo, Gokstad and Oseberg seems less concerned than modern practice about having joints in adjacent planks close together. These joins in the Oseberg sketch are very carefully and regularly staggered in a way which suggests a quite different bow construction as well as shape, presented by the stepped stem from Skuldelev in the Roskilde museum. This copes with one of the weaknesses of the impressively curved bow of Gokstad or Oseberg, which is that a large number of narrow plank ends come together, mainly above the waterline. A bow section carved out of solid, extending far enough back from the stem to a point where the plank ends are wider, can be stepped so that they are not directly above one another, and obviously spreads this loading. The Oseberg sketch can scarcely be decoration (it is on the underside of the plank) nor aimless doodling, for not only is it alone, but it is rigorously restricted to the essential structural features of one part of a quite different ship. Interpreted as suggested here, it underlines that the same men built the purely sailing merchantmen and the royal ships, which makes understandable the extent to which the latter draw on both traditions, the sailing merchantman and the rowing warship.

However the ancient builders formulated to themselves the hull they were to build, it must seem obvious that for us it is the three-dimensional object we see in Oslo, Roskilde or Schleswig. Unfortunately, this is in some important respects not quite so. Ship hulls unlike most other museum objects – axe heads, brooches, pottery – actually change their shape as they age, and are still changing shape relatively rapidly as they sit in the museum. The intentional flexibility of hulls where the skin planking is lashed to the frames, not nailed, of course permits this process to go further than in the other ships of the viking period, in which it is nailed to more closely spaced frames as at Skuldelev.

Two things have changed the shape we see from that the builders built: deformation by pressure and shrinkage of the timber. Boats are built to resist in their natural element the sustaining pressure of the water all over the underbody and mainly upwards, to some extent inwards. On the beach their weight rests on the keel and probably on rollers placed under it and under the turn of the bilge where a plank thicker than the rest serves as a sort of chine stringer. But, in a burial mound, the weight of the accumulated earth on top presses downwards and outwards, flattening any curve the keel may have had, and splaying out the hull. Similar, though less marked, is the deformation caused by mud accumulating over and in a wreck or offering.

Later attempts to restore the hull to its original form by lining up the rivet holes in the planking and frames cannot usually be made to work unless the timber has been treated with very careful conservatory techniques not available in the late nineteenth century when the classic Scandinavian ship finds were made. The consequent, and still continuing, shrinkage of the timber means that it is not possible to get all the holes to match because the requisite length and breadth are no longer there in the planks themselves, which may in extreme cases have shrunk up to fifteen per cent! The shrinkage is different in different directions, that along the radius of the original tree trunk being only half that across it at a tangent, so that the ovality of holes originally bored as round is more likely to be a sign of differential shrinkage than wear. As most viking ship planking seems to have been split radially out of the logs, not sawn, the shrinkage across the width of the plank, which affects the hull shape most, was kept to a minimum. But it can still affect the cross sections of the restored hull and thus its buoyancy and sea-keeping qualities, and thus historians' ideas of ancient migrations, as the next paragraph will show. And it must be remembered how relatively light, by our standards, for this size of ship, all viking ship planking was. In the full size Gokstad the ordinary planks are only $\frac{3}{4}$ in thick though 9 in wide: the meginhufr at the level of the frame ends (the waterline) is twice as thick, and the plank through which the oars are worked is 1 in, but those above it are only $\frac{1}{2}$ in, and it will be apparent how subject to distortion a structure of these scantlings is when it is 70 ft long. The distortion happened during the ship's life every time it came off the top of a large wave, much more took place in a thousand years underground, and some has taken place since it emerged from the earth to take its place in the museum.

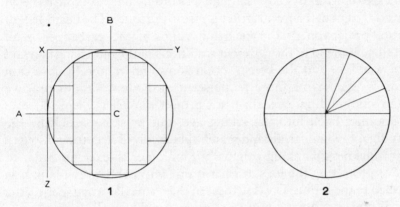

Shrinkage along AC, BC, radius of log, is only half shrinkage XY, XZ, tangent to log. So shrinkage is greatest across breadth, least across thickness in outer planks (bad), least across breadth, greatest across thickness (good) in middle planks. If planks are split radially, all are like middle planks (good).

It was inevitable that in restoring such a plastic object, particularly when the varying effects of shrinkage were not well understood, and techniques of excavation recording were not as developed as they are today, men should instinctively reassemble the hull in the light of contemporary taste. In the late nineteenth century the favoured hull shape was narrow and sharp sectioned, dependent on ballast for stability, and ancient hulls were accommodated unconsciously to this model. It may seem surprising to us that scholars were not struck by the implausibility of North Sea crossings by whole populations in vessels which required a ton of ballast to be stable even under oars alone, but so it was. Because of shrinkage there simply did not seem to be enough timber there to envisage a fuller (and of course less dramatic) hull form.

As the twentieth century progressed to a taste for beamier hulls each succeeding reconstruction became beamier, giving one an uncanny feeling that the old warriors were keeping abreast of fashion even from beyond the grave.

This problem fortunately affects Gokstad less than other hulls, though it has not escaped. The blue clay of the Gokstad mound made an almost airtight capsule for the hull and A. E. Christensen has been able by careful work to re-establish the original lines of the hull with a fair degree of certainty, though that is not quite the form you see today in Bygdoy. Though it is often taken as typical it is in fact different in form and structure from the usual. The beam-length ratio, projection of the keel and curve of the garboards is an intelligent blend of the different traditions of the merchantman and the warship, and the construction shows an elaborate obsession with weight saving more reminiscent of modern aircraft practice than shipbuilding. We must not project our ideas of production economics back into the viking age, but must be struck by the prodigality of materials and man hours involved in cutting down to $\frac{3}{4}$ in thickness planking originally four times thicker, in order to leave projecting the lugs at each frame with which the plank was lashed to the frame. The thickness of the frames is varied to meet the local stresses and to reduce surplus weight in the less stressed portions. Rough calculation suggests that the total weight saved by comparison with simpler structure cannot be as much as a ton, but absolutely requires maximum elasticity if none of it is to crack in a seaway. The impression is of a minimum weight and minimum resistance hull built regardless of expense and not particularly appropriate for commoner purposes. It represents the peak rather than the norm of the technology of its day, as will emerge from comparison with other survivals.

Any hull starts from its raw materials. The change from wood to iron shifted the centre of British shipbuilding from the South and its oak forests to Scotland and the North with their mines and furnaces. Now, after two centuries, the iron ore used is largely imported. Man in northern Europe has been using up shipbuilding oak at a faster rate than it grew itself for more than a thousand years, so that today it is a waste of time to look for shipbuilding timber anywhere in Europe within two hundred miles of the coast.

Pumping out after the capsize:
4.00 a.m. in Portree

Facing Arriving at Oban under sail

Arriving off Peel

The lonely sea and the sky

Entering Peel harbour

Timber originally meant 'building material' not necessarily wooden (belly timber was food), but wood, particularly oak, was particularly for ships, the building material par excellence. Already in 1893 Magnus Andersen had to get the oak for his keel from America because it was not to be had nearer home. Smaller parcels of timber can more easily be picked up, but good builders are reluctant to mix oak from different sources in a flexible hull whose integrity depends on a strictly proportionate deflection in different parts.

Our oak therefore came as a single batch from south Germany, so that stable ancients who had never known a sunset later than half past seven were to find themselves dipping and creaking in the broad sunshine of Atlantic midnight fifteen degrees of latitude further north. Before that, they lay for the winter in the forest at the top of the rocky track down to the boatyard. They lay on pine needles, cut into planks carefully sticked apart to allow air, and often snow, to circulate between the faces. On some of our winter visits to the yard they looked like a miniature of south Norway as we had seen it from the air, a little snow-covered plateau intersected by narrow steep-edged valleys whose vertical sides occasionally emerged blackly through the overall white. This wintering of the timber is very relevant to the building of a viking ship.

Some builders of viking ship facsimiles have found insuperable difficulty, which Magnus Andersen seems not to have had, in reproducing the same shape of hull elements with what were apparently the same materials. By no means the only example, but much the best recorded and published, is the National Maritime Museum version of the Gokstad faering, where in the end the curve of the bow had to be made from laminated timber to achieve a stable curve. It seems paradoxically likely that this may have been because the timber, too carefully selected, was too well seasoned and too well kept. Andersen, forced by shortage of time and funds to build with unseasoned wood out of doors through a Norwegian winter, was probably unwittingly more closely reproducing the conditions, necessary for success, under which the original viking ships were built. The builders of *Odin's Raven* did work under cover, in their largest, but unheated, shed, but brought the rough planks down to the yard only as they needed them for fitting. The timber was rarely under cover long before it went into the ship, and the curving prow remained true and the complicated reverse and concave curves of the garboard strakes were achieved with scarcely any steaming, though with copious use of the traditional long deep-jawed clamps which sometimes seemed scarcely to leave room to rivet the planks together.

If there is thus considerably more to the building of a really seaworthy viking hull than simply copying the present measurements of a museum exhibit in the same materials, the problems involved in rigging it to sail are compounded by the fact that none of the rig is present in the museums to be copied, with the insignificant exception of small wooden details, probably cleats and blocks. Such essential factors as height of mast, length of yard, and therefore sail area, are unrepresented by direct evidence and have to be deduced. It is probable that none of the ships from Oseberg, Gokstad or Skuldelev were properly fitted out for sailing on their last journey, and to the extent that they were, it was with gear a good deal more vulnerable, because of its materials and its position in the ship, than the hull itself.

Thus the century has seen a good deal more variation in ideas about the rig of viking ships than about hull form and construction. The absence of positive archaeological evidence has meant that imagined sail area is limited only by the hull's ability to carry it, which in turn depends upon its displacement and ballast ratio, the proportion of the total weight carried advantageously low in the hull to increase its stability. Different assumptions about these produce different sail-carrying ability, but the constants are the same today as they were then. The pressure on a sail varies as the square of the wind speed, so that in force 3 (10 m.p.h.) it is just over a quarter of a pound per square foot, and in force 6 (26 m.p.h.) it is two and a half pounds per square foot, ten times as much, and the waves, in force 3 not over three feet high will be in force 6 over twelve feet high. The weight of wind on a 70 sq m sail varies from about 190 lbs in force 3 to about a ton in force 6. A ton of salt water occupies 35 cu ft, so that every extra ton a ship carries requires the immersion of another 35 cu ft to support it by its buoyancy. The sideways thrust of the sail has the extra leverage of its height, which is greater than the width of the ship, so that the ship will heel until enough extra cubic feet have been immersed on the lee side to counteract by their buoyancy the pressure from the wind. These unchanging factors enable us to determine with a fair degree of confidence the limits of the possible for viking ship sails, but they tell us nothing about how far towards these limits of the possible the average viking mariner (if there was such a person) went. Static stability calculations under ideal conditions can be a very poor guide to the handling capabilities of a ship at sea and to judge that requires practical experience in similar craft. On the other hand it is valuable that we acquire our practical experience in wind and water whose characteristics have not changed since the viking age in the way in which every aspect of life on shore has done.

Within the fixed unchanging limits set by physics there are of course other restrictions on our imagined rig imposed by our view of what is historically plausible or probable. Even though Magnus Andersen carried a triangular jib on the forestay, and indeed asserted that it was impossible to control the ship without it (which needs to be borne in mind when his oft-cited praise of the side rudder is repeated) nobody at the present day believes that viking ships carried such sails. Nor, in spite of their presence in the femboring and the Humber Keel, does it seem likely that topsails were carried. They are essentially a means of making fairly high sail-plans more easily handled and quickly reducible, and the sail-plan of a viking ship is not likely to have been high enough to make them useful.

If you believe, as many do, that the mast of a viking ship did not project beyond the stern when it was lowered, then its maximum height was half the ship's length. This would give the Gokstad ship a mast 10 m long and *Odin's Raven* one only 7 m. A mast of this size does not need to be so thick as a longer one, and is handier to raise and lower at sea, and less liable to be damaged in harbour, but it is in my opinion too short. When you deduct the part of the mast below deck in the mast-step, the clearance above the yard at the mast head for hoisting the sail and the clearance below the foot of the sail for the heads of the crew and the shields along the rail, you are left with a sail not much more than 7 m deep for Gokstad, or 4 m for *Odin's Raven*. A small ship needs the same clearance under the sail to prevent it fouling as does a large one, but as this represents a larger proportion of the total mast length, a small ship needs a relatively longer mast if it is to have a reasonable sail, though this will also make it relatively less stable.

There are in Gokstad three uprights with crossbars sticking up

2 m above the deck: they are clearly to support something above the heads of the crew and out of the way and it is usually, I think correctly, thought that this is the yard on which the single squaresail was set, and that the distance between the two outer supports gives an indication of the length of the yard, which was presumably slightly longer. This suggests a 10 m yard for Gokstad, twice the maximum beam, or for *Odin's Raven* about 7 m. The area of the square sail, its height times breadth, is then 70 sq m for Gokstad and 28 sq m for *Odin's Raven*, which is quite inadequate. These sails, wider than they are high, are inefficient to windward or on a reach, and not easy to sheet running before the wind because they are so much wider than the hull. One can use spars to bear out the lower corners like a modern spinnaker-boom but this is scarcely reconcilable with the Old Norse term for these spars which connects them explicitly with beating to windward.

All this certainly does not mean that such a rig is historically inaccurate, only that it is not possible with it to give enough drive even to such an easily driven hull in anything less than a fresh wind. It saves so little rowing that one must wonder that the extra complexity of mast and sail can have seemed worthwhile, since a comparatively small angle of heel forces a reduction of sail because of the small freeboard. The rig is essentially a 'blow down-wind' one and it is understandable that nineteenth-century scholars, familiar as they were with working sailing craft, were not impressed. It is (barely) acceptable for a vessel with a large number of men on board anyway, who might as well row, but it is unlikely to be a reliable guide to the arrangements in vessels which mainly depended on sail, and is another instance of how misleading it may be to generalise too widely from Gokstad. The 70 sq m sail is a useful supplement, like the sails carried by the early steamships, but does not allow of serious regular reliable passagemaking over any distance. It was recognition of this which at one time led some scholars, particularly in Sweden, to advocate a much larger sail area, 90 or even 120 sq m. With a sail of this size Gokstad becomes a real sailing ship, capable of the voyages recounted in the sagas and Old English and Latin records, but we must remember that the records do not say that these voyages were made in Gokstad ships.

I do not find it a serious objection to this version of Gokstad that the lowered mast no longer lies within the boat. More serious are the unrealistic assumptions behind the stability calculations designed to show that this area is plausible for Gokstad, notably Haasum's assertion that even gross errors in them will not invalidate the conclusion that with 90 sq m Gokstad could sail unreefed in a wind of force 10, about fifty m.p.h. In this wind the wave height will be well over thirty feet, and to calculate the righting moment available at the maximum heel before the open ship fills is quite unrealistic, though the mathematical working of Haasum's examples is correct. The fluctuation in wind pressure also introduces an element of instability, and in practice a sail of the area suggested has to be reefed once the wind exceeds force 5, because a square sail with its yard across the top does not in fact spill the wind as it heels as quickly as a fore and aft sail, and the hull, having no watertight deck, cannot be allowed to heel more than about 12 degrees to the surface of the water, which even in force 5 is not very likely to be horizontal! It is evident that a vessel to make passages under sail will be better if it differs from Gokstad, as we see from the small Skuldelev merchantman which is about the size of *Odin's Raven*.

In it the sail area must have been greater per ton of displacement to permit reasonable progress in moderate and light winds, and the aspect ratio of sail's height to width would be better higher to enable side winds to be more efficiently used. It is the need to use a wide variety of winds, of different strengths and directions, that characterises the rig of a working sailing vessel. If the additional sail area is at the top and bottom and not at the sides, it makes the sail more efficient and easier to reduce in area by reefing. The drawback is that the heeling moment of one sq m of sail becomes greater as it is higher up the mast with greater leverage, and the Gokstad hull, with low freeboard amidships for the sake of efficient propulsion by oars, cannot heel more than fifteen degrees without putting the rail under. Merchantmen of the Skuldelev type with greater freeboard amidships can safely go to greater angles of heel, and their hull form permits them to carry more weight lower down which reduces the heel for a given weight of wind.

Another way to reduce the heeling moment in strong winds is to reduce the height of the sail's centre of effort, without reducing the area of the sail. This can be achieved by tapering the sail upwards so that it is no longer exactly square, but is narrower across the head than across the foot. As it is made of narrow cloths stitched together with vertical seams this is most conveniently done by tapering the outer cloth at each leech or edge of the sail, from its full width at the foot to nothing at the top. By this the height and efficiency of the sail can be made greater, and its centre of effort lower, than those of a perfectly square sail of the same area. It is quite impossible to prove that sails of this cut were used in the viking age, and the viking ship sails shown on memorial stones certainly look square, with no hint of taper, though it has not been exhaustively looked for. These drawings are not necessarily realistic in intention and in any case are not photographs. It is in fact not possible to tell from any photograph I have seen of *Odin's Raven* or a femboring that the sail is tapered, so the apparent clear square of these drawings should not influence us too much. Their conventionalised presentation of a square sail running fore and aft along the centre line enables the artist to show the most recognisable profile of sail and hull together, though a square sail in this unusually close-hauled position does not usually remain or appear square because of the pull of the sheets on the lower corners. The ships in question are obvious warships with plenty of men to row, and may very well have had the simple blow-along rig referred to above, and in that the advantage or need of the tapered sail is much less.

What can be said in favour of the belief (in which I am not alone) that the tapered sail, trapezoid rather than square, was used in the viking age? Most important is that all the modern vessels of this North Sea single squaresail type seem to have used the trapezoid sail as far back as we can follow them, and also to have used the same rigging to control it. I do not think it is taking the analogy with language too far to argue that it is most likely that the identity of form between north Norway, Shetland, Man and Yorkshire in the seventeenth century suggests a common Norse ancestry. Over hulls as different as the narrow lightweight North Norwegian boat, the fuller Shetland sixern and the heavy Humber keel the same advantageous shape of sail was set. All these manifest an unbroken tradition, and I can find nothing to suggest that the tapering took place separately in each separate development, but always before the date of our earliest evidence! This view that details of rig found in the pre-industrial tradition can indeed go back to the viking age receives some support from comparison of the priare with the interlacing pattern found between sail and hull on some Gotland picture stones, for example the Hejnum stone illustrated in Plate 1.

The priare is the key to the set of the sail as it controls the flow by pulling the foot of the sail down and to windward, doing for it what the bowline does for the luff. If the priare on the after half of the sail is hauled tight, the fullness in the sail is moved forward to where it should be for best effect, just behind the luff. The priare is rigged as a kind of crowsfoot to three attachment points on the footrope. Not only does this spread the load, but by moving the wooden block at the place where the three lines converge up and down the central line, or reeving through it the line which forms the right and left hand spans, the tension of all three can be varied. As is true of all sail-trimming devices more harm than good can easily be done by heavy-handed use of it, but it sometimes pays to harden in to a slight unfairness in the foot-rope with bagging just above it, in order to flatten the run of the sail higher up and avoid any tendency near the leech to curl back to windward. If we found this with modern Terylene sailcloth in *Odin's Raven* the effect was presumably even more marked with the less stable cloth of the viking age.

The pattern generated by these control lines or multiple sheets is to me very reminiscent of the interlace on the Gotland stones, though I don't think it could ever usefully become as elaborate as the most extreme examples. If they are indeed depicting a very fully developed priare system, then that establishes the existence in the viking age of a traditional device for this sail which we cannot otherwise trace back beyond the seventeenth century. The illustration was not staged but is an enlargement of a general deck view during trials, and its resemblance to the Gotland pattern is unmistakable.

All this should explain why it seemed reasonable to give *Odin's Raven* a mast 10 m long, with a yard of 7 m, on which was set a trapezoid sail 6 m across the head, 7 m across the foot, and 7 m deep, giving 45.5 sq m area, with a 1 m bonnet laced to the foot to give another 7 m, totalling 52.5 sq m for light weather. I do not think that this at all represents the rig of the original Gokstad ship, for which I think Christensen's low aspect ratio 70 sq m rig is still historically the most likely. But I think it must be truer to the rig of the majority of viking ships which made the crossing to Britain, and in practice the rig has proved itself very suitable to a Gokstad hull on a long summer voyage. In spite of earlier doubts that it was either too small or too big (mainly the former) I don't think any of us who sailed in the *Raven* would really want a very different rig. The hull resistance of a full-sized Gokstad hull at 5 knots is only 200 kg (Ship Research Institute of Norway) and whilst it is very difficult to scale this to the *Raven*'s two-thirds hull, she is capable of ghosting down a fjord with a quartering wind barely perceptible on the cheek, and with a 5 knot wind (the minimum registering reliably on our instruments) she would do a respectable 2 knots, at which she would answer the helm without hesitation. At the other end of the scale the full mainsail can just be carried in force 5, which would by calculation give a full size Gokstad 10 knots and on one dazzling (and independently measured) occasion with a gusting wind on the quarter and low wave height gave *Odin's Raven*, in spite of her shorter waterline, 12.5 knots. The great historical importance of this is that it suggests that boldly sailed vessels of this size with this rig, within the capacity of any large farm of the viking age to build and man, could cross under favourable circumstances from Denmark to Yorkshire in twenty-four hours and from Norway to Shetland in little more than half that, and even with an easterly of 5 knots for a whole week a crew of half a dozen men would complete the longer crossing within a week and the shorter in three days. In any less favourable wind they would presumably not set out: if surprised by a westerly gale underway these times might be much extended, but they compare quite favourably with those common up to the end of the nineteenth century and certainly explain the continuing strength of the Scandinavian element in the language and culture of the north of Britain.

This account of the sail is to some extent oversimplified, as no account has been given of the real art involved in cutting such a sail to be full or flat. The brute fact is that as we have no idea of the coefficient of stretch of vadmal, linen or linen wool mixture woven on viking age looms it is pointless to speculate. Some details from the sagas, like the throwing of buckets of water on a sail to improve its set, suggest that the cloth was not notable for its stability (though the trick was used well into the nineteenth century) and the *Raven* was given a sail of the best modern Terylene, cut full because of the multitude of devices for ensuring a good set which were built into the sail. It is in its way as much a work of art as the hull; it uses similarly obsolescent techniques not out of any sentimental obsession but insofar as they are operationally necessary.

The modern yacht sail is held rigidly vertical along its critical leading edge, the luff, by a mast usually nowadays of aluminium which not only interferes with the wind flow over the sail but also makes it virtually impossible to hoist or lower sail except head to wind. The foot is held straight and unvarying in length by the boom. This is the price of the superior windward performance (by which races are won or lost) of the modern yacht. But working craft could afford to wait for a wind, and the to modern eyes no doubt baggy sail of a viking ship was capable of being trimmed and flattened when necessary by devices whose effect was not at all inferior to the modern red-hot racer's Cunningham hole or clew outhaul and kicking-strap. Dr Johnson observed that the knowledge that he is to be hanged sharpens a man's mind wonderfully, and the knowledge that he might be drowned presumably had a similar effect on our ancestors. This is the importance of the surviving examples of working sail: the yacht is an avowedly competitive and luxury product, but the devices found on a Thames barge, Humber keel, North Norwegian femboring or viking ship reflect the painstaking exploitation of the only energy source available apart from man's own muscles, and reflect what was a matter of life or death for men as well as the societies of which they were a part, not merely the success of a Saturday afternoon racing round the buoys. In some ways the restriction of sail in our day to purely recreational usages has erected a bigger barrier between us and the viking age, spiritually and emotionally as well as technically, than existed for late nineteenth-century writers in spite of our technical superiority in understanding and evaluation of the material. It was quite natural for Tuxen, writing a hundred years ago about the old Norse longships to refer to the 'jagt of forty tons, the smallest at present sailing between Copenhagen and Iceland' but it must give any modern reader a sharp stab of envy at the irreplaceable immediately available to Tuxen and not to us which such casual references represent. The performance of *Odin's Raven* and replicas like her is an indispensable, though more artificial, way of giving the historians of our day the same material. It is evident that as its designer I have a vested interest, but her mainsail which together with the muscles of her crew and her small diesel when the flesh was weak drove her so many hundred miles represents a sail important to any understanding of our past, and worthy of much more attention than it commonly receives. Even those who sail with the form which supplanted it, the gaff sail, are commonly regarded as eccentric, and outside the Humber it would be difficult even in the most Norse regions of Britain today to find single squaresail vessels. And yet the possibilities for an intelligent skipper to adjust the sail to his taste and the prevailing wind and sea are greater in it than they are in the modern Bermuda rig with its fixed edges and sail wardrobe. For handiness and flexibility (as long as you are not racing to windward) the single squaresail has unsuspected depths and a considerable claim on our respect.

3

Keel-laying to Launch

In August 1978 the many problems raised by hull and rig still lay ahead but by the end of the month the Manx viking ship, still un-named, had at least a keel. We flew to Norway on Monday August 28th, arriving late in Oslo to make our difficult way through the rush-hour traffic to the hotel where we were to meet the yard's representatives to conclude the contract. The first rough calculations after our telephone talk suggested that, as usual, it might be a tight squeeze to fit the required quart into a pint-sized hull. Sixteen men and the necessary weight of the water and stores to allow a margin against hostile weather would not leave much freeboard in a two-thirds version of Gokstad. The total displacement available could scarcely be more than twelve tons at the outside. This is quite enough for the 8 hp available from sixteen oarsmen, or the sail area I thought could be reasonably carried, about fifty square metres. There would be $\frac{3}{4}$ hp per ton under oars, 4 sq m per ton under sail, both figures on the low side to promise acceptable speeds, so we certainly did not wish to increase the displacement. In any case all ships tend to increase in weight as 'improvements' are incorporated after the design stage.

The time-consuming weight saving of the original Gokstad suggested that they had faced the same problem who built her, and spent many man hours in the attempt to overcome it. Could a modern yard use its superior productivity to achieve an economically possible solution in our century? On a shorter waterline, and therefore lower speed threshholds and less volume in the water? The payload required to carry the weight of crew and stores was at least four tons, so there would only be eight tons available for the whole structure of a fifty-foot hull if she were immersed to the absolute minimum freeboard, which in a scaled-down ship was of course a scaled-down height above the sea surface, scarcely acceptable for an open sea crossing. Furthermore the Gokstad hull, unlike Skuldelev 1 or 3, was not built as a load-carrier and to immerse it too deeply, as well as making life wet and uncomfortable would make it intolerably sluggish and hard to handle as well as to propel.

The yard took it for granted that the essential structural features of Gokstad, the lashing of bottom plank to frame, and the extreme lightness of planking and framing were to be followed in the Manx ship. Indeed it was increasingly apparent that they had to be if the project was to succeed, for without them there could be no hope of building a ship that could carry out the voyage with any chance of success, It was late on Monday night after six hours of unbroken discussion that a new clause, guaranteeing a freeboard of 60 cm (2 ft) with a payload of four tons on board was inserted. It seems (and is) little enough, but marked another stage in the crystallisation of Robin Bigland's idea of the voyage into a reality. We now knew that we had to find ways of fitting what was needed into four tons: the yard knew that the planking of the hull could not be simply scaled from Gokstad, but that the ship, like any serious vessel, was built for a voyage and had to carry four tons at her marks for the voyage. And both the yard and ourselves were pleased with the sense of added definition and felt the long talk had been worthwhile. The rest of us chatted with a mildly festive air, not exactly like old friends but certainly with frankness very unusual in Norway after one evening: like relatives perhaps? Magnar Hansen signed the contract on behalf of the yard, and Robin Bigland signed as owner, accepting responsibility for the payment of all the sums specified, over fifty thousand pounds. At this time and indeed for some time afterwards, the contributions to hand did not even cover the initial payment due on laying the keel. In spite of that, his vision was in its way matched by that of Rød shipyard, who had already, without a contract, laid out for them a huge amount of time and money in acquiring the necessary oak. The keel was in fact already laid, and the proud stems raised, when we were making the contract in the nineteenth-century Turkish bath atmosphere of the Bristol's lounge.

At ten the following morning we drove down to Vikane, 'The place in the bay' to go on board the small fjord boat which was to take guests to the official keel-laying ceremony. It was a glorious autumn day, with enough heat in the sun to take the edge off the breeze which raised shining white wavelets chasing down the fjord, and it was a very Norwegian half-hour that we spent strolling round the wooden jetties critically admiring the many trim craft on view. The route by water to Rød might have been designed by a landscape artist: new views perpetually open round each corner of the channel, none as majestic as those further north, but each point enlivened by a summer-house, often with its own even smaller summer bathing hut down at the very water's edge. Most had a flagstaff, and the really enthusiastic had two, one for the bathing hut.

At Rød, at the head of the fjord, there was no breeze and the huge double doors of the building shed were open to the sun. As we jumped onto the jetty we exchanged the smell of warm diesel characteristic of the fjord boats for the nostalgic smell of stockholm tar and fresh cut pine which proclaims a Norwegian boatyard. Was it fanciful to detect something else? The wood chips lying in the thin and dusty soil outside the shed were not all white and smoothly curving pine: some showed the more angular deep-tanned honeycomb of new oak. Inside we could see, slewed at a slight angle across the launching ways, for it was just too long to fit in the shed lengthwise, an immensely long baulk of oak. Ships always seem larger out of the water than in it, and this keel seemed to dwarf even the heavy girders of the cradle across which it rested. The lighting, more dramatic than daylight had any right to be, had something to do with this. The doors faced due south and ran right up into the gable of the roof, so that the seaward end of the keel was warm to the touch in the dazzling almost vertical sunlight, whilst the uphill end lay in sharply contrasting mysterious shadow from which the prow rose up towards the loft that ran across that landward end of the shed. So steep was the slope of the track outside that this balcony gave on to it at ground level. So high was the prow that it rose well above even this balcony, but with a curve so smooth from keel to stem that if it were not for the carefully fitted scarf joints the eye could not have decided where keel ended and stem-post began.

We distributed ourselves silently and shyly along the walls of the building shed, perhaps more impressed than we had expected to be, or were prepared to admit, by this majestic visitor from the past who lay there waiting to be born. The ceremony might seem like the laying of a foundation stone, but that is a sort of burial, a firmly local prelude to a state predictable and permanent. What is raised on a keel has to adapt itself to different circumstances and thrive in them until one day it dissolves in decay: the associations are with birth and life.

The most enduring element from the viking age in Man is probably the constitutional one. Vigorous independent strength, as we see in many sagas, demanded careful control but accepted it only within rigid and narrowly interpreted limits. This is still manifested in the annual recitation of accepted laws from the mound in Tynwald. It was thus fitting that his honour Charles Kerruish, Speaker of the House of Keys, in Norway to return the parliamentary visit of Guttorm Hansen, Speaker of the Norwegian Storting, should join with him to perform the ceremony. It was a good example of the consistently and sincerely Anglo-Norse nature of the whole project. In his welcome to Norway, Guttorm Hansen had proposed a toast to 'our common past history and our present and future friendship'. Both the Speakers addressed the mixed gathering in their own language. Most of the Norwegians present, apart from the older generation of locals, spoke some English: only one of the English spoke any Norwegian. In that shed during the speeches it was fascinating to observe the technique of looking politely interested which the English have developed as a substitute for the ability to understand. Those Norwegians who did not follow a speech in English stood in detached dignity with no pretence of understanding. The rapt attention, and even occasional nods of judicious assent, which many of his English hearers produced for Guttorm Hansen cast an oblique light on those attentive English audiences we see on public occasions. It may be true as T. S. Eliot says, that great *poetry* can communicate before it is understood, but it was impossible to imagine that the practised English audience could possibly have looked more interested had they understood every word instead of every twentieth.

Perhaps because of consultation in advance, as well as agreement of views, both Speakers had a common theme. Charles Kerruish put the emphasis upon the way in which the ship would serve to draw attention to an existing and long-standing connection, but for Guttorm Hansen, a historian himself, it was a symbol of old continuity and modern change as well, since its voyages would, he hoped, be more peaceful than those of its predecessors. Both Speakers signed an oak tablet affixed to the stem to commemorate the joint keel-laying, and we all departed down the fjord to lunch at Hankö, where the walk up through the woods from the jetty was enlivened by vigorous speculation, almost disputation, about voyages past and future, how viking ships had sailed a thousand years ago and how this one would next year: whether we could improve on them if we tried, and whether we should do so if we could. After the excellent lunch the conversation grew more human and less technical. The ships to us represent pre-eminently past tradition, but in their own day were innovators of the most relentless sort. The small and self-reliant bands away for long periods from the traditional authority of their elders learnt how to exploit insuperable natural forces to advantage and found that in different countries different things were sacred, and there were different gods. As Sigurdur Nordal points out, the old burial mounds can never have seemed *quite* so impressive to widely experienced men who did not really expect, or perhaps wish, to rest in them. The ships that brought about all this must have had an impact like that of the railway or motor-car upon our village life. There were quotations from Old Norse poets, and their modern successors who still value impromptu doggerel after a banquet: all coming thick and fast and not always easy to translate without being too blunt for modern taste.

It was in some ways a relief to leave the hotel early next day and call upon a friend in the Norwegian Maritime Museum at Bygdoy just across from Oslo. I had last seen Jarle Björklund in the medieval monastery of Utstein, under the auspices of Stavanger museum, and knew that what I now needed more than anything else was help in locating rapidly in the unexhibited riches of the museum the answers to the many practical questions bound to arise in designing a practical sailing rig for a twelve-hundred-mile voyage. Like all such museums, not least our own, it contains much more than it has the funds to display, so that the clear and definite answer to many unsolved questions has perforce to lurk in scarcely visited storage cellars. A stranger, no matter how familiar with subject and language, will inevitably take weeks to get to the stage of familiarity with the material which the museum's own staff achieved years ago. So he does well to put his questions respectfully, and listen very carefully to the answers. And where the answers flatly contradict his own evidence from contemporary documents he will, if he is sensible, not raise yet another so-called conflict between archaeology and literature, but seek to find exactly what word corresponded to what thing, or what things were covered by the same word. Luckily Jarle Björklund, in charge of educational activities, is tactfully prepared to regard foreign colleagues as within the ambit of his job, and I was not disappointed. Within an hour I was facing with delight a table bearing almost every item I had requested: it seemed a pity that the plane left at tea-time, but I was able to catch it with all the essential documentation and reading-matter not only for the flight but for another two days. On the first of September it was possible to produce the first sketch of the rig with positions of sheets and tacks indicated, and it was with this rig that we sailed.

It was mainly based on Erik Andersen's 'Tack and sheet' (Hals og Skaut) in the Norwegian Maritime Museum's yearbook 1975, but in the museum I had been able to study details of the rig of various vessels (both full-size and model) from three centuries, and thus get a three-dimensional feeling for Andersen's thesis which it is more difficult, at any rate for me, to get from printed word and diagram alone. Words are the only way in which men of the past can communicate clear ideas to us, but few of the simple craftsmen of the past had the vocabulary or time to communicate with us in this way, and when we start to put their lives back into words there is always danger of misunderstanding: it's an odd thought that we probably understand the poets of the eighteenth century better than we do its fishermen! The rig given to the *Raven* was also modified by my own previous experience with various squaresails, and by two important British sources, Edgar March *Inshore Craft in the Days of Oar and Sail* and Sandison *The Shetland Sixern*, but when in March 1979 we saw in Fredrikstad the sketch Andersen himself sent to our friend Erik Rudström, there was surprisingly little difference between the two designs, considering our different views of the original Gokstad rig. He believes it to have been a fairly heavily ballasted craft carrying 140 sq. m, or about twice as much as A. E. Christensen or I believe probable.

With the construction of the hull well under way, the film record of the building process began. Jim Nelson and Odd Børstad, responsible for the provisioning of the ship, began to work out the weights and volumes required to provide various endurances. The decision of principle that it would be irresponsible not to have an engine of some sort, fiercely disputed to the end by many romantics, had to be embodied in practical suggestions: outboard, outdrive, saildrive with right-angle leg, conventional shaft drive? How would a flexible hull not intended to be driven straight off the top of a wave direct into the wind's eye behave with an engine? If the hull itself would not permit a course only possible under engine, what was the point of having an engine which could not be used to enable the ship to save herself on a course not possible under oar or sail?

But most important of all, and in the end decisive for the success of the project and the unforgettably happy memories we all have of it, was the selection of the crew. The main difficulty here was the large number of well-qualified applicants. The ballad of Sir Patrick Spens probably represents the last time anyone has expressed anxiety about getting anyone to sail a ship of theirs. Since then, in Britain and Norway at any rate, there have usually been more men looking for ships to sail than ships looking for men – and that, incredibly, continued to be true in two world wars. It is scarcely surprising then that for an unusual summer voyage in a viking ship it should have been possible already in August, only a month after the first mention of the voyage to raise three different crews in Man alone. In these early days serious consideration was given to the idea of having two crews relieving one another on alternate legs of the voyage. It is a good instance of how the appetite grows with what it feeds on that as the hardships of crew training progressed it became evident that those who were interested in crewing were certainly not interested in being relieved at each port, and the double crew scheme was dropped, though fortunately reserves were provided to replace crew forced to drop out by accident.

In Norway there are still many places where a dramatic foreign-going voyage is almost a passage rite to manhood, hence the crewing of the huge Norwegian merchant fleet from a relatively small population, and there were almost an incredible four hundred applicants for the four or five places available to Norwegians on the Manx viking ship. By the twentieth of September a shortlist of twenty-five Manxmen was established, from which the final dozen was to be chosen. Occupations ranged from harbourmaster to shaving-brush manufacturer by way of professional diver and brewery executive. It was in the view of some of them a distinctly mixed blessing that the number included a retired major fresh from training a Sultan's army in Arabia, who enthusiastically supervised crew training with an energy many Manxmen felt better reserved for Arabs, who as one observed were well known to have a lot of it – amounting to a crisis. At least one previous viking ship replica had lost ten per cent of her crew in the first seventy-two hours through seasickness, blisters and unfitness, and one more at least was lost with all her crew. It was sensibly determined that this was not to happen to the Manx ship, and with a crew of sixteen she could not afford any passengers. Throughout the winter of '78/79 those selected for crew training struggled up and down the steepest slopes of the island's hills two or three times running, on one occasion plunging naked into the ice-cold sea at the end. This baptism, tactfully photographed from behind, made most of the national newspapers beneath such captions as 'Shiver my timbers' or 'Hello cheeky'. As a change, King William's College cutter was borrowed and rowed out in the dark through the tide-race round the Calf of Man for people to discover how well they could pull an oar when sick and frightened. Those not frightened were adjudged lacking in proper sea-sense.

These, however they figured in the newspapers, were not mere stunts. The training followed carefully the recommendations of the Royal Canadian Air Force and the Royal Marines amphibious warfare school, and was certainly not intended to produce muscle-bound masochists. The Marines in particular put great stress on the idea of water-fitness, a familiarity and ability to feel at home in a small open boat. The idea was to provide a transition as painless as possible from the conditions to which twentieth-century office man is adapted, to the conditions a tenth-century emigrant must have regarded as normal. It would have been dangerous and possibly fatal to have in the crew people who could not survive the change with equanimity. It was not difficult to tell apart during the voyage those who were used by trade or service experience to working cold and wet in a biting wind, and those for whom it represented a special challenge which they had successfully, but recently, learnt to overcome. The feature all the final crew had in common was that they were capable of pulling their weight, either cheerfully or viciously, depending on temperament, in any hostile circumstance, whether professionally used to it or not. Even after the final selection had been made, several who knew they had not drawn a place in the crew or reserves continued to take a full part in the training. You could scarcely imagine a better testimonial to the morale of the crew and the quality of the training.

This naturally encouraged support for the project from the public in the Isle of Man and from various companies, and also from those concerned only with the technical side of things. A crew of this standard not only deserved a good ship but was worth producing one for. It was apparent that some striking performances in all sorts of ways could be looked for. This should be borne in mind in evaluating the trials reported in the next chapter. Some may seem at variance with what is usually believed. Things previously believed impossible or so difficult as to require complicated – and for the viking period rather implausible – apparatus were done regularly and easily by four or five crewmen. But they were all strong, fit, used to pulling together, and helped on not by commands from above but by common enthusiasm and good-humoured awareness of exactly what each meant by various gestures or, occasionally, oaths. The minute a rope was secured in tacking those who had done so would move to lend a hand to anyone still battling, and felt it as a reproach if he had time to call for help. The crew was probably as close to the characteristics of the original ones as has been assembled in this century (one must, as always, make exception in favour of Magnus Andersen's in 1893). We should not assume that the original crews were all professional seamen, which was rarely the case even in the most complex sailing ships. They were probably like many modern islanders, used to boats and fishing from childhood, but primarily farmers, craftsmen or merchants. The modern crew selected themselves from the shortlist by drawing ping-pong balls, the lucky ones marked with a cross, and showed a similar spread of occupation. They were:

Robin Bigland, underwriter; Colin Bowen, shaving-brush manufacturer; Odd Børstad, shipping agent; Brian Cousins, teacher; David Eames, fitter; Rolf Hansen, researcher; Knut Hoff, journalist; Michael Ingram, marine biologist; Eddie Kaighin, harbourmaster; George Kneale, welder; Shane Lucas, retired army officer; Knut Skogøy, architect; Rick Tomlinson, estate agent; Arne Wisth, journalist; Nigel Wood, accountant; Richard Young, transport manager.

A competition was held in Manx schools to name the ship, and at the end of January a quite independent panel adjudged the suggestion of Simon Galliver of Onchan to be the winning one. It was *Odin's Raven*, which was not immediately favoured by most crewmen, who instinctively thought of something more prosaic such as 'Norse-Mann' or 'Manx Viking'. To the end of the voyage it was unusual to hear anyone from the ship actually refer in conversation to 'Odin's Raven' though that was what was blazoned on their tee shirt (if it didn't say 'Bilge Rat' or 'Survivor' instead). The name was usually shortened to 'The Raven'.

As the ship was to be a two-thirds version of Gokstad, the building of the hull and the design of other features had to be subordinated to this. A sea-going hull of this size would not usually be built today of such thin planking on such widely spaced frames. To ensure that it truly followed the form of Gokstad it was necessary to use many more moulds to bend the planks round (one at each frame station) than would be usual today, or were probably used on the original Gokstad. Some *must* have been used, and the drawing of a viking ship being built in Almgren's *The Vikings*, often regarded as authoritative about the ships, seems to me more or less impossible. It shows no moulds at all, and only three clamps: it would not, I think, have been possible to plank a vessel in the way shown, and the photograph of *Odin's Raven* under construction presents an interesting comparison to this imaginative drawing.

The mast and yard were to be made at Rød as well as the hull, and their design presented interesting problems. No original mastheads survive but it seems most likely that they had a dumb hole with no sheave. The modern French word *hune* derives from Old Norse via Norman French, and a similar term is known from cobles and Humber keels. Our usual principle of 'the voyage rather than the ship' required rather more. We wanted to be able to display the legally necessary navigation lights, and to have the VHF aerial as high as possible to get a reasonable radio range. Very attractive bronze weathervanes have survived from the viking period, usually because they had been mounted on churches. They seem sometimes to have been mounted in the bow, where with a square sail they are usually invisible to the helmsman, which must induce queries about how they were actually used, but were often at the masthead, and we wanted to carry one there. We also felt it desirable to raise and lower the yard quickly and easily, as it has to be played up and down according to the wind strength if one is to keep the ship sailing to its limits. This required the halyard (unhistorically) to run over a sheave and have a purchase at its foot. The originals perhaps made use of the anti-friction quality of greased walrus skin rope not available to us. As we preferred not to have too much shiny Terylene rope visible, though we used it for purchases and sheets, the halyard was combination wire, covered in jute. A spare halyard for the stormsail in case the main halyard parted was also included. As cable had to run up inside the mast to avoid being trapped by the yard or rakke, the builders suggested a composite mast glued up of pine, much stronger for a given weight and much more predictable and shake free than a grown spar. This made it possible to avoid the jarring spectacle of a modern VHF aerial by building the aerial inside the masthead. The cables emerged at the foot in a position where they would not get trapped as the mast moved up and down in the mastfish. Although the masthead light always worked, the radio connections, as might have been expected, gave trouble, and we eventually mounted a reserve VHF aerial on the stern ornament when we were at sea.

To accommodate numerous details of this kind to the developing hull required several flying visits to Norway in the period between keel-laying and launch. One that lives in the memory was on October 17th when we flew from Humberside airport to Oslo in Robin Bigland's Piper Comanche which to one unused to light aircraft seemed at least as much the plaything of the elements as a viking ship. The clouds building along a front actually look worse seen from their own level as you fly round them than they do from down at sea level, and much worse through a light plane's icing windscreen than through the double-glazing of an airliner cabin's side window. The course was steered by a back-bearing on Ottring-ham radio beacon near my home village until we were more than

half-way across the North Sea. As we lost it and the read-out began
to waver we could see ahead, rising from the level, sea-like surface
of the rolling cloud, an archipelago of steeply rising cumulus, like
islands rising from the sea. Their grouping and distribution north
and south of our track corresponded exactly with those of the
oil-rigs in the Frigg field and these islands in the sky were produced
by the rising warm convection currents of heated air over the rigs. It
was an odd feeling to navigate between them as we were later to do
in the ship, and to get a position line from one island opening behind
another as if they were real islands. We had a headwind of forty
knots so that the computer which continually updated our position
from the beacon occasionally jumped and gave the impression (I
hoped devoutly it was wrong) that we were flying backwards and
further from the beacon than we had been thirty seconds earlier.
There was little fuel to spare as we settled gently down out of the
gloomy October twilight onto the golden lit runway at Oslo.

Not all the flights were so uncompromisingly direct, and the
route from Hull to Oslo sometimes rambled like Chesterton's rolling English road. I remember once going by way of the Isle of Man,
Dublin, Solway Firth, Aberdeen and Stavanger, almost a complete
tour of the Norse tenth century on the way. That was on December
9th when Ray Sutcliffe, a good friend to the project and the producer of a BBC TV series about the Vikings, was coming to see the
ship and arrange for its building to be recorded for his programme.
He was at that time in Dublin, hence the route.

It was on this visit that we first met Erik Rudström, an electrical
engineer and enthusiast for the old nineteenth-century north Norwegian fishing boat, the single squaresail femboring. He is no
fairweather yachtsman but takes his engineless craft, open except
for a small cuddy aft, up to the Lofoten winter cod fishery every
year. On one glorious occasion when the weather was bad enough
to discourage the modern motor boats from going to sea, he actually made the top day's landing of cod, all caught in the traditional
way from his thoroughly traditional sailing boat. He has also sailed
two femborings to Iceland and made his own film of the voyage. It
was a uniquely instructive experience to view this film in his
sitting-room, able to request stops so that we could examine a
particular frame in detail. There is no better substitute for actual
experience than this. Still photographs can be very hard to interpret.

Has the tack just begun? Is the bow rising or falling? Even the interpretation of carefully posed Victorian photographs of fishing smacks presents more difficulty than editors always realise; it requires a dramatic imagination akin to reading an old poem. But from a film you can follow the sequence of events and see how each adjustment of the rig fits in, particularly if you have the maker there to answer questions. Erik's hospitality is as brisk as his seamanship. He collected us from the pier where we had landed from the Oslo ferry in the most disreputable Mercedes any of us had ever seen. 'It has only two more days to live, the certificate cannot be renewed,' he observed, accelerating smartly over the packed snow up a steep hairpin between jagged rocks. Crammed in the back and watching the snow flash past beneath our feet we wondered how he had got the certificate last time, and more immediately, what the return downhill to the pier was going to be like. Once inside his house those who could gut were turned to with a large glass of home-made wine to gut some of his superb home-caught Lofoten cod. He has relatives near Rød and became a frequent and welcome visitor to the ship, though his presence on board usually meant there was never time to light a pipe. Like all great sail skippers in my experience, he was never really happy with a sail, saying 'Of course it may do more harm than good I know, to alter it, but if we do not try it we shall not find out'. He had sailed for Norway in the Olympic Finn dinghies, even beating the great Dane, Elveström, but eventually became bored by the inflexible limitations of modern bermudan rig and grew to prefer the superior freedom and challenge of the old loose-footed square sail – and the Arctic fishery.

In this period between keel-laying and launch when so much had to be decided the project seemed to bring together in a continuous and very fruitful exchange of ideas many people of very different specialism and backgrounds. Danish engineer Bent Tranberg, Bukh diesel technical service manager, was responsible for the brilliant solution of the technical problems of mounting a diesel with a long propeller shaft into a very flexible hull which was never intended to accommodate it. He brought the shaft out just to starboard of the keel but mounted the engine slightly to port of it so that the thrust was distributed to both sides of the hull producing the minimum distortion. As a young man during his naval service he had been an engineer in the Danish warship which escorted the first post-war copy of Gokstad, the *Hugin*, across the North Sea in 1949. He had often, he said, stood in the engine-room door and looked at it as they crossed the southern North Sea together or towed it upwind off a minefield, but never expected to find himself in charge of the installation in a similar ship. He was surprised that we were not to have an escort, though, of course, 'with one of *his* engines aboard we certainly didn't need one'. Though Knut Skogøy (who lives in Denmark) had been able to borrow a copy of *Vikingefaerd med Hugin* by Jørgen Røjel from which we had learnt much, Bent Tranberg was able to bring the voyage alive, and was a shrewd and reliable observer, not only of viking ships but of English poetry, as I found when we discussed 'McAndrew's Hymn' one lunch time in Fredrikstad. It was the first time I've had the chance of discussing Kipling's poem in a company that took it seriously and understood its imagined context better than any literary reader can.

Paul Graville wrote from Southampton University and allowed us to borrow his report on his tank testing of the Gokstad ship and its predicted performance. Some of his theoretical conclusions chimed very well with Erik Rudström's practical experience in femborings, and Michael Kiersgaard's 'Tanken omkring en Norlandsbaad' from Roskilde Museum. From the research department of the British Engine Insurance Company came, out of the blue, a detailed examination by one of their former engineers, G. A. Cottell, of the problems of raising the Gokstad mast at sea, which was in some respects much fuller than the version published by the Norwegian Maritime museum the previous year. So much that was new and valuable emerged from this gathering of completely non-literary approaches that we began to consider the production of this book to present some account of it: it will be obvious how much Part One depends upon it, rather than the usual saga quotations.

On each visit the hull had grown, and construction was well up to schedule at the end of January. Other important details had not kept pace with this for various reasons, and creating the bare hull is usually less than a third of the work and time involved in the finished vessel. With a modern fishing vessel it may well be less than a third of the cost but the *Raven* had a small engine generously given by Bukh and little electronic gear, and that mostly lent. By Easter it was reasonably certain that the launching date of April 28th could be met, though very unlikely that trials and training sailing could start immediately afterwards as had been planned. A fortnight before the launch I returned from Bremen to Fredrikstad to check that the engine was installed and runnable: the sails, rigging cut to length and spliced by Hall's Barton Ropery, and deadeyes were ready, and most of the sea chests on which the oarsmen were to sit and in which they were to stow their gear were finished. Other, not immediately necessary equipment had to be re-scheduled, so that some of it would be delivered to the ship before she was loaded in Oslo for the coast passage to Trondheim and some delivered alongside in Trondheim just before sailing for the U.K. Much of the time intended for trials and training would be needed to complete rigging and fitting out. To anyone unfamiliar with shipbuilding this may seem a criticism of the yard: anyone who knows the problem of building an unprecedented vessel where drawings are issued as the necessity for them is discovered will on the contrary be surprised that we still genuinely enjoyed talking about the ship and took pleasure in it.

On this last visit before the launch the figurehead carved from laminated oak by David Swinton was fitted under his direction. The coarse figurehead of *Hugin* in 1949 had been much criticised, and we were all duly happy that ours was regarded by all who wrote of it as an impressive piece of genuine craft. It was undeniably twentieth-century in feeling, but in a way the more genuine for that: certainly it was a straightforward and sincere interpretation of the conventional figurehead for our day. David made the rest of us feel somewhat guilty by the long hours into the night which he worked on finishing detail, carving nameboards and a superb version of the original Gokstad animal head on the tiller. The Norwegian craftsmen of the yard took to him immediately, recognising a kindred artist in their own favourite medium, whereas the rest of us were, I suspect, to them the usual run of ship murderers who would start mistreating their painstaking craftsmanship the minute we got it outside the fjord, by pushing it unsympathetically into a head sea or clumsily alongside a jetty. One had only to look at their own launch, much used by photographers during our trials, to see what a boat-builder expects a well-kept working boat to look like. They could not only recognise David's work for what it was, but recognised his aims and needs. It was fascinating to observe the accuracy with which artists, without any knowledge of one another's language, can not only communicate what they want but also discuss what they want to do. A humiliating experience for any interpreter.

The trials crew was to consist of Robin Bigland, owner, Eddie Kaighin, master, whose responsibility the vessel now became, Alan Binns as adviser for the trials period, and the three watch leaders Brian Cousins, David Eames and Rolf Hansen, with two crewmen, Nigel Wood and Rick Tomlinson. The two last were to sleep on board the ship each night as watchmen, whilst the rest enjoyed the comparative luxury of the factory canteen floor made available by the generosity of Mr Lilleby, a modern Manx-Norwegian industrialist. It was thought then that once fitting-out was completed we would move from Rød to Lilleby's jetty upriver from Fredrikstad and sail the trials from there. In the event we remained at Rød until we left for good, and commuted daily from the factory in a crew-bus until we did.

As soon as we arrived at the yard on the bright and breezy morning of Saturday, April 28th it was evident that the launch of *Odin's Raven* was a great day not only for us and the supporters from the Isle of Man but also for the population of Odin's Island and the whole district round Frederikstad. The ice on our last visit in the late and chilly spring still covered the fjord. We had visions of our newly launched ship skating straight across to the other side, but the ice had now melted. Egill Skallagrimsson in his head-ransom poem written in viking York calls a ship 'the ski of the sea' but we had no wish to take it literally, though we were happy to quote another of his lines, *Dro'k eik a flot vith isabrot*, 'I put my oaken ship afloat as the ice broke'.

Now the fjord was full of boats and the forest full of cars: in Norway it is often more difficult to find parking space for the former than the latter, and we had the usual crop of suicidal small boys who wanted to tie their dinghy up to the launching ways, and their fathers in motorcruisers lavishly equipped with whole cases of bottled beer who could not understand that a clear space at the foot of the slipway was intended for the Raven and not for the convenience of latecomers.

Norway is still a sparsely populated country, hence the tendency to add 'in proportion to the population' to all statistics, even those to do with rainfall or altitude. It takes something not only out of the ordinary, but attractive to the imagination, to raise a really large crowd. This was the first time we had seen how much public enthusiasm our light-hearted project could arouse. Though we later got used to it, it was slightly unnerving to see that there was standing room only on the quay, including many standing on the brink, and scarcely room for the local silver band, resplendent in uniform, to get a fair swing at the big drum or allow the drum majorette adequately to display her obvious talents. There was also a nasty piece of angle-iron sticking out of the water at the bottom of the launching ways. We could not shift it and it did nothing to ease the job of those on board for the launch. Robin was trapped on the platform where he was to speak, Alan and Rick were to pass the mooring ropes round the boats of the fjordship to drop the *Raven* alongside before she was towed off, but the rest were to go down, as they expressed it, with the ship.

The official party arrived on the fjordship from Vikane more punctually than we had dared to hope, the threatening weather gave way to fitful sunshine, and our luck continued to hold.

There were well over a thousand present, and they loved Robin Bigland's proud and happy assertion that even the builder of King Olaf's famous *Long Serpent* would not have been ashamed of *Odin's Raven*. They loved it even more when Lady Paul, after a speech in English which few followed, and a postscript in Manx followed by none, aimed a magnum of millennium champagne at the bow with such deadly effect that a TV camera crew positioned for a striking close-up were covered in champagne-bubbles and broken bottle. The lens blotted out by spray is a cliché of every sailing-ship film, but we were glad to see our friends getting it in thus early.

The *Raven* glided down the ways in a practised fashion and did not hit the angle iron. We got her alongside the fjordship without trouble, and greatest blessing of all, the skipper of the fishing-boat *Grundvig* which was to tow us down to Hankö was not one of those maniacs concerned to show what he can do with four hundred horsepower and a six-inch hawser. He could not have coaxed us towards him more gently had we been a net full of herring and at 1240 we were clear of the yard and making a modest three knots down the fjord to Hankö for the lunch, this time in the yacht-club. The Norwegian crew members were already in viking gear, the more reserved British in blue suits and white shirts. There has been considerable recent controversy about the effectiveness of side rudders and it was a relief to find that, at any rate under tow, the *Raven* was answering the helm well, though the rudder, over-balanced, had a tendency to slam across the midships position. We had a strong towing and mooring point through the bow at the waterline, as I knew from experience that it is almost impossible to get hulls of this type to lie quietly if the rope leads over the bow on one side of the high stem, when they tend to heel and swerve alarmingly. As we approached the yacht club, Eddie ordered the tow cast off, and took a well-judged wide sweep to drop us neatly along the floating pontoon under oars, making fast at 1330 in a position where she would be visible from the lunch tables. There were no draught marks carved, but the waterline was the top bolt of the stem scarf aft and the lower bolt forward. This indicated a trim aft of about a foot, very satisfactory without mast, fuel, stores or water, and indicating that the natural attitude of the ship in the water was exactly as we had wanted it. We therefore went happily up to the club to celebrate, leaving a Norwegian friend painstakingly altering our scruffy tugmen's hitches round the bitts to boy-scoutish clove-hitches guaranteed to jam if any weight came on them. The fjordboat had decently stood off until we had made fast, but now came in bearing the official party and we settled down to enjoy a magnificent west coast buffet of prawn, crab and lobster, with salad and icy akvavit. The poems were longer than they had been at the keel-laying but it was not so necessary to scribble feverish notes on the menu as this time a typed Norwegian text was available. Of the various presentations the ones that remain in the mind are Lady Paul's touching gift of the traditional Manx cross of hedgerow twig and wool, a croish kern, the copy of the Norwegian constitution that was a most appropriate commemoration of the link between Man and Norway, and Magnar Hansen's two-foot tall and incredibly ugly little viking. Robin Bigland presented to Lady Paul a beautiful silver model of the figurehead. After the celebratory poem declaimed by Knut Hoff as master of ceremonies, we were all at leisure to move from table to table meeting many of our friends and now and then strolling out onto the jetty to admire the ship. The time came for the official party to leave to return to Oslo. Those of us who were to go out to Lilleby's factory were to await the boat's return to ferry us over to Vikane where one of the crew buses had been left that morning. Rick, who was to do the driving, had conscientiously, out of respect for Norwegian law, refrained from touching any of the free-flowing liquor. The same could not be said of any other members of the crew though Eddie and I, as befitted our age and discretion, had borne in mind that we were on an island with no ferry service and had to find a remote and abandoned factory if we were to have anywhere to lay our weary heads. About seven it became apparent even to our younger colleagues that something was wrong and that the boat was clearly not coming back for us. Luckily a fishing-boat responded to our hail and came in to the pontoon, so we negotiated a passage to Vikane. There was general agreement that it would be prudent to treat ourselves to supper in Fredrikstad before finding the way out to Lilleby's, and it only slowly became apparent that it was not going to be easy, even on Saturday night, to find anywhere to eat after nine at night. Later, during the trials, we had developed such a good relation with the ex-merchant service owner of a Chinese restaurant on the quay that on our last night he sent a case of beer to our table, a considerable gift at Norwegian prices of about a pound a bottle. But this was our first evening in Fredrikstad and everyone we asked agreed that the only possibility was the Hawk Club. It was arranged that we would be admitted to their restaurant for a quick simple meal before leaving to find our quarters for the night. I have the bill before me as I write and observe that six of us spent thirty-four pounds before leaving, the rapid succession of coffees towards the end of the bill suggesting recognition of the work awaiting on the morrow. On leaving the restaurant I made the mistake of going downstairs to the entrance, noticing too late that everyone else had decided to take just a glance into the room where the disco was pounding out. An hour or so later, when I had become so much part of the scenery by the cloakroom that people were asking me to get them taxis, the unmistakable sound of a table going over under something heavier than a tray of glasses came out of the disco above the beat, followed in some haste by a bouncer to suggest I fetched the captain. I excused myself on the solid grounds that he was in there already and braced myself to interpret, insofar as they required interpretation, the management's intimations that the cause of continuing Anglo-Norwegian friendship would be best served by starting the voyage immediately, or at least vacating the Hawk Club. This proved easier said than done, but by a combination of bi-lingual persuasion and prising people's whitening knuckles off the banisters we eventually assembled the group outside and, leaving our producer to make a documentary, shot off to collect the crew bus from the carpark. The quest for Lilleby's was eventful, not least because some of the crew quite reasonably associated the wagon with being taken into custody and made occasional damaging attempts to escape. Eventually we stopped at any lighted window in the countryside to rouse unenthusiastic inhabitants to ask directions to a factory that was essentially a feature of their grandparents' day. Our luck changed when by smooth driving Rick managed to swing in front of a taxi, whose driver caused some coarse amusement by anxiously enquiring if I knew what a transformer looked like before giving very good directions with reference to a large one at the next corner. We thus got to within a mile of the factory and found a local sports club dance just breaking up, where we got directions to the house where the key was kept. It was after two when we got ourselves and two of the crew up to the canteen, leaving two who were too heavy to lift asleep in the back of the van. It says much for the standard of fitness of the crew that we were all awake and ready to go at eight next day, though some were stiffer than others, and others were more willing to reminisce about the highlights of the previous evening. All in all, a very traditional gathering of a British crew about to take over a new ship abroad. Sitting over coffee in Fredrikstad before going out to Vikane to join the ship we all agreed she was well and truly launched.

4

The Trials
and Cruise to Oslo

We found our way out to Vikane again, and found the same fishing boat which had brought us back the night before. He took us out to the Yacht Club jetty on Hankø, where we found our two hungry watchmen eating the last of yesterday's shrimps. The ship had already had several early morning visitors who had been startled to see them rising from their sleeping-bags. The only diesel oil on board was the few litres used to test run the engine before launching, and none of us felt bursting to row back to Rød, so when we left Hankø at 10 30 that Sunday morning our first call was back at Vikane. The man with the key to the fuelling point lived at the top of a white-painted wooden house on the north side of the harbour and had evidently seen us coming in, for by the time we found the way to the foot of his stairs he was ready for us, putting on his oilskins. The weather, good for the launch, had settled back into the cloudy westerly weather that was to remain with us until the next festive occasion, the visit to Oslo for May 17th, the Norwegian national day.

We took 300 litres to fill the tank, as the simplest way to discover whether the breather and overflow pipes were working properly, and, to get the initial running-in hours on the engine over as soon as possible, set off under power for Elingardskilen which we reached at 11 00. Here we stopped the engine and rowed up the fjord, practising turning under oars, and clearing our heads and throats by doing so. We were back at Rød shipyard at 11 30. Here we met those who had returned to a more staid official evening in Oslo after the launch, and all began to sort out the gear piled to the rafters of the storage shed the yard had put at our disposal. Those who had not yet been on board were of course eager to experience the ship under way, so we left again, still under engine, at 15 00. David Eames was engineer and checked round the engine in traditional fashion, discovering that the stern gland was running very hot, presumably because its oiling cup was bone dry and had never been filled. We returned to the yard at 15 30 to remedy this omission and left again at 16 30 to go outside the islands into the Oslofjord where a wind of 5–6 Beaufort (22 knots on our windgauge) was raising waves three metres high. It was from the SW so that we were heading straight into wind and sea, which viking ship hulls were certainly never intended to do, and found the ship on this first testing outing rather hard to control under these conditions. Any speed over about three knots led to considerable pounding, throwing sheets of spray over the bow. More seriously, if the bow was allowed to come more than two points (22°) out of the exact eye of the wind it fell rapidly further off until the ship was first rolling beam on and then, as the wind got inside the bow, turned almost on to a reverse, downwind course. The only way to recover was to come astern on the engine, as the turning moment from the rudder was not sufficient at any speed we dared to drive her to push the bow up into the wind. This was not surprising, as when the ship was before the wind we could see that the thick rope securing the centre of the rudder to the ship's side was stretching in and out two inches at a time, allowing the rudder to pull away from the ship's side and then dive back towards it (or into the propellor!) as the helm was put over.

It was very far from ideal weather for a trial trip, and the *Raven* needed careful coaxing round by Eddie on the tiller to begin the return to Rød, which we reached at 17 45 in thoughtful mood. The side rudder obviously had to be made to work much better, and the day's trial suggested that the only extra protection having an engine gave was the ability to go astern rapidly into a heavy sea, which is difficult for oarsmen. This first impression proved near the truth. An engine in a modern viking ship is well worth having for safety, but does not make possible long passages to windward you could

Off Grip. First attempted crossing; fishing vessel gives warning of impending gale.

Leaving Stadvik under storm sail

Dolphins

Dolphin doing a tail-stand

The Fortnum & Mason hamper

After the capsize

Brian and Colin on the capsized hull. Note sail in water.

not make without it. The positive side of the day's experience was that the buoyancy and sea-kindliness of the hull were such that even on such a really unpleasant day the deck had kept reasonably dry, very little baling had been necessary and water had come in only in two or three easily identifiable places, the only one meriting mention being near the bow scarf to the keel, not surprising after such a thrashing into a head sea, and easily caulked. It never gave any further trouble after the *Raven* was slipped the following Thursday.

On Monday the 30th we wanted to get the mast up and the sail bent on the yard. Our Norwegians in the crew, used to the light mast and yard of the femborings, regarded our mast and yard as far too heavy. They did not always allow for the fact that though the femboring length was about that of the *Raven*, the displacement was only a half and the sail area narrower and more divided. Our first attempts to pick up the mast where it lay suggested that they might be right, but Magnar Hansen professed himself very unwilling to see a ship with a fifty square metre sail leave his yard with a mast any thinner, and my own calculations suggested that one could not take more than half an inch off the radius, though that would have reduced the weight from 230 kg to 170 kg, saving one hundredweight, a quarter of the total. This would I think have been worth doing, but a mast weight of 4 cwt is by no means excessive for a hull displacing ten to twelve tons and not heeling more than fifteen degrees, so it was decided to try it as it was. At tea time we started to raise it. It soon became apparent that both mast foot and mast fish through which it went, required further finishing, but the yard's craftsmen were standing by with their razor-sharp hand axes to trim both, and an hour and a half later we had the mast up and the bilge full of shavings. With the spirit inspired by the training in the Isle of Man we then lowered it again just for the hell of it and found to our delight that as long as it was not allowed to fall below the forged hook fitted into the stern ornament to receive it (a most important proviso) the lead from the bottom block of the forestay purchase to the masthead was good enough, with an angle of about seventeen degrees, for four men to raise the mast alone. The pair of shrouds secured level with the point where the foot pivoted in the mast-fish cut out kept the mast over the centreline of the ship (we had of course a plumb-bob from the masthead) and were easily kept taut as the foot of the mast sank into the recess. The longer and heavier mast of a full-size Gokstad would be disproportionately more difficult to manage and would have needed more men, but they would have been available. How much mechanical advantage could have been derived from a purchase rove with the wood 'jomfru' (*see* pp. 96–7) found at Gokstad is impossible to say without knowing the friction of the rope involved, but if it was well-greased walrus hide, which we know from Ohthere's account was used for ship rope, I think the arrangement would work. This suggests to me that those early merchant ships of the viking age which had fixed masts without any arrangement for raising and lowering may well have had masts too long for this to be possible, because the angle of the hoisting tackle at the masthead was too narrow. That in turn would suggest that they (though not the ordinary 'viking' ship) carried quite high aspect ratio rigs of comparatively greater efficiency to windward, not unlike that of the modern femboring, which in this respect as in others might preserve features of the working vessels of the viking age. I have to admit though, that I known of no illustration from the viking age showing such a high aspect ratio squaresail: as the pictures are mainly of aristocratic warrior vessels this objection is not perhaps conclusive. We all believe that a fifteen-metre viking ship with our rig on a ten-metre mast could put the mast up and down without any problems under any reasonable conditions. The difficulty found in rowing to windward in some recent replicas (e.g. *Imme Gram*) is then not the objection it may seem, as the originals presumably lowered the mast before attempting to do so.

Some have argued that because there are no signs of fastenings for the shrouds in Gokstad, whereas there are in Skuldelev 3, the small trading ship, so called, from Roskilde, one should assume that Gokstad did not have any. It is true that for any credible sail area and wind strength they are not absolutely required, particularly if you assume a mast so short that when lowered with its foot still in the step amidships it did not project over the stern, i.e. only half the ship's length. Quite apart from the fact that what look like shrouds are shown on some Gotland stones, the conclusion is misleading. The upper strakes of planking in Gokstad are so light and have so little connection with the main structure of the ship that one would scarcely wish to attach the shrouds to them anyway. We made the lower deadeyes of the shrouds (copied from a timber detail from

Gokstad, though one cannot prove it was a deadeye) fast round the knees of the transverse frames in way of the mastfish which form the only rigid base from which the mast can be supported. This is the obvious way to stay the Gokstad mast and it leaves no traces visible on the excavated hull. The snag is that in a vessel the size of the *Raven* it reduces the clear deckspace in way of the mast, though it provides good stowage for oars between shrouds and ship's side. Those who had to live on board for longer than me preferred to lead the shrouds from the same point but out through holes in the rail and this worked very well though it obviously is not how it was done in Gokstad, or the holes would be there. We cannot claim to solve all the problems of rigging by our trials, but we do feel that the ship repays sailing so hard that shrouds are really necessary. Even a small movement of the masthead makes a considerable difference to the heeling moment and efficiency of the rig, which it is important to keep as far to weather as possible, and nothing suggests that our predecessors were too stupid to discover this. If there were no shrouds, one would perhaps have expected the cleats for the halyard to have enabled it to give some support to windward, as for instance is done in the Yorkshire coble's dipping lug. Traditionally in Norway the halyard leads aft, where all the cleats of Gokstad are, so there was evidently no particular need felt to use it for this purpose, as there presumably would have been, if there were no shrouds. The rings amidship in Ladby and Skuldelev 3 might just possibly be fairleads.

The horned deadeyes or 'jomfru' referred to above looked to Eddie's experienced eye as if they might allow the lanyards to spring off them as they came slack on the lee side, or even break across the grain at the thinnest part as we had not been able to get them all made of oak grown to this peculiar curve. He therefore devised a simple preventer lashing to restrain them if this happened, which I have not previously seen on the many reconstructions of rigs using these blocks. This is a typical example of the small insights gained in fitting-out with a Board of Trade eye and concern for a voyage rather than a museum ship.

Raising the mast, rigging it, bending on the mainsail, reeving off the sheets, braces and bowlines were clean, traditionally seamanlike and satisfying jobs. The same cannot be said about the application of the traditional pine tar distillate which gives so many Norwegian ships their beautiful golden tan. Its vapours catch the eyes and throat and it is more or less impossible to remove from skin or clothing. Every inch of the ship had to be treated with this stuff many times, and David Eames, distinguished both by the energy with which he applied it and the loudness with which he protested, soon acquired the nickname Trekkfast, the trade name of the version we were using.

The wiring for navigation lights, VHF, log and echo-sounder was also carried out, perhaps a little too rapidly. The deck planks, though they did occasionally jam, were only laid loosely across the beams, with no caulking, so all wiring was continuously exposed to salt water. I have found that unless twentieth-century electronics are provided with a twentieth-century citadel of dryness in which to work they soon stop working, and these were no exception. In my own boat I use RNLI type watertight fuse and switch board, and we would have done better to provide another built-in alloy box of the sort we used for the galley, which worked well, to shelter the electronics below the deck. In the original design for *Odin's Raven* they were housed beneath a small watertight poop deck or 'lypting' for which there is literary evidence.

A Spanish windlass of a twisted double strop, shortened by twisting it further with the spare tiller stuck through it, was arranged to tension the rudder tye against the boss on the ship's side. There has been much recent scientific discussion about these rudders, most notably in the National Maritime Museum's publication of the Gokstad faering and the subsequent observations on it. We found two problems. If both rudder and boss have flat bearing surfaces (which no one believes, but is one limiting case) and the rope is bar taut and has no stretch (another impossibility) then the rudder cannot be moved, and steering is impossible. If the rope is slack or elastic then the rudder can be moved, but much of its force will be wasted, taken up by the extension of the rope rather than applied to the stern.

The configuration of the inner surface of the rudder is critical, as well as the degree of rounding of the boss, and I now believe that the slight concavity observable on the inside of one or two side rudders is probably intentional and not accidental warping, as a flat rudder, even working on a rounded boss, exerts enough leverage at extreme angles to stretch the central rope. We found it impossible to find anything elastic which was strong enough to recover its elasticity, or to apply enough tension through the boss to any sort of rope natural or synthetic. It may be that walrus hide is the answer here as well, but we had to settle for a double loop of the combination wire we used for rigging, set up with a Spanish windlass. The first one was improvised on the spot, though Halls Barton Ropery later supplied (at a day's notice!) a purpose made one as reserve for the crossing. In fact, though it needed careful setting up, particularly after a down-hill run in heavy seas, the original lasted the whole voyage. We doubt whether the original's tree root would have done as well, but the whole steering system requires continual attention and renewal anyway.

The turning circle under power when we next tried was still very poor: the hull of course was not designed for it. Under oars, particu-larly with the bow oars on one side pulling and the after oars on the opposite side holding water she could be spun round, and after a week or so we found that a boldly backed mainsail, holding on to the bowline, would box her head round with a rapid sternboard. But the rudder, except under ideal conditions of smooth water and good headway of at least two and a half knots was not the first choice for anything more than a minor trimming of course, which it did well enough. It presumably owed its survival in viking ships to its convenience in a vessel which regularly beaches, where a stern rudder of equal length would require to be lifted at the critical moment (as is done in a coble). The difficulty of mounting a stern rudder on the curving stern of a flexible hull which you can ripple by shaking the stem also must have played a part. Where oar or sail were always available to manoeuvre with there was presumably little incentive to improve. The heavier and deeper cogs which replaced these ships were not so easily influenced by an oar for-ward, and had too much momentum to be easily sternboarded. They required a better rudder and got it. From continuous observa-tion in various sea conditions over a long period we formed the opinion that there were two basic difficulties in our side rudder installation even when we had altered its shape, pivoting point, and section, to trim it as well as we possibly could. Firstly, the inner surface of the rudder is often starved of water and more or less stalled, even at small rudder angles, creating a large drag and turbulence, interfering with the turning moment. Secondly, the water flow at this point in the afterbody is often not parallel to the waterlines but more or less vertical towards the surface. This is particularly marked on starboard tack when the hull is being pressed away to port and it is probably this, rather than the fact that the rudder is not so deeply immersed, which explains any difference in steering found in some replicas (e.g. those of the film *The Vikings*). In the *Raven* we found that the extra turbulence when the rudder *was* deeply immersed, on the port tack, generally outweighed the greater blade area in the water, so we would agree with Magnus Andersen that there was little difference. Our views in fact support his. His praise of the side rudder has been quoted from one book to the next, from the passages Haakon Shetelig first selected for quotation. In context he is only referring to the relatively lesser force a man needs to exert (using a relieving tackle!) when steering with such a balanced rudder in a fresh wind, when it is at its best, as compared with a wide rudder hinged at its leading edge. Elsewhere he makes clear that it was impossible to prevent *Viking* turning up into the wind and coming aback, which the rudder was powerless to prevent. Our experience confirms both these observations. By the end of the trials it was possible, under the right conditions, with a minimum speed of four knots, to tack by helm alone without touching sail or oars, which I do not think has previously been successfully done by a viking ship replica. It is often not accomplished by the modern femboring with a stern rudder and higher aspect ratio rig. On the other hand on Tuesday the 8th we could easily have lost the ship had we been dependent on rudder alone in a fresh quartering wind.

Having got the rudder as effective as we could at this stage, we continued fitting out. The two anchors, one a plough for sandy bottom, the other a folding fisherman of the old Norwegian Patent type were stowed forward with their chain and nylon warp. During the trials we moved them aft alongside the engine, which not only enabled the rather low freeboard aft of the prow to lift more buoyantly, but also seemed to improve windward performance, perhaps by marginally increasing the rake of the keel's leading edge.

When the yard had finished caulking, and the seacocks for such underwater devices as log and echosounder were fitted, the *Raven* was ready to return to the water again. We launched at 1145 on a grey day with no crowd and no band, and a very fresh SW breeze funnelling up the fjord, so that we had to drop astern for half a mile before it to get room to turn. Then, going full speed with an after oar held firmly in the water at 45° to help the rudder, Eddie just managed to get her round to starboard in the width of the fjord, without having to go astern to complete a three point turn as we had had to do before. This may not seem large progress, but both rudder and propeller were on the inside of the turn and we expected a better performance with both in clearer water on the outside. Without the certainty that she could be turned under power it would scarcely have been justifiable to make our first sailing trial on such a day, and we were now impatient to start.

The presence of the instruments for the first time also cheered us by showing that the performance in this weather was in fact better than we had estimated. Inside the fjord we were doing 6 knots into a 20 knot wind with only half revolutions, say ten horse power or little more than we could deliver from the oars for an hour. As we emerged between the islands into the open fjord to the full fetch of the swell we found that we could still do 4.5 knots into a force 5 with two-metre-high steep waves, because the steering was now good enough to take them slightly on the bow instead of head on.

At 14 15 Eddie issued, for the first of many times, his usual cordial invitation, 'Right, get it up', and we began for the first time to take the weight of sail and yard, still stopped up, on the halyard, to begin the tricky task of easing it forward between mast and shrouds, to lie across the foredeck clear for hoisting. The ship was plunging and rolling as Eddie headed upwind to get a good offing and there were many trapped hands, breathless oaths and sprained wrists on the way. Eventually our considerate subtlety gave way to bad temper and brute force and we simply got hold of the nearest bit of sail, or arm holding onto the sail, and pulled as hard as we could. It was then necessary to take a rather cooler look at things as we tied down two reefs to ensure that bowline, sheets, tacks and braces were all clear and not included in the reef, and ran outside shrouds and halyard. Anyone who has handled a recalcitrant spinnaker for the first time can readily imagine what a foredeck is like with fifty square metres of heavy Terylene and a seven-metre solid pine spar scything around at shoulder height.

At 14 45 we hoisted sail in *Odin's Raven* for the first time and it went, as things usually did on the project, better than we'd hoped, billowing majestically out without breaking anything and accelerating the ship so rapidly that we had to lean forward or catch hold of a shroud to balance ourselves against the smoothly and silently increasing speed. We sailed around on various headings for two hours, soon discovering that the various tensioning devices of priare and duva had to be used to set the sail well for windward work, that tacking as yet needed two hefty men pulling their hardest on the two forward oars on the lee side, but with them was reliable enough, and that although the freeboard when heeled looked dangerously low, and water did indeed come in through the as yet uncovered oarports; she stayed fairly dry. This was partly because the hollow bow turned the water away to leeward so that she seemed capable, like a coble, of sailing with the rail level with the water as long as she was going fast enough, but mainly because the centre of effort of the double-reefed sail was so low that with sheets eased it lifted the light hull over the waves. We were reasonably contented this time when we returned to Rød jetty under power at 1705, though tired and sore handed, with a list of extra jobs like more rivets in the frames to which shrouds were secured, and, perennial problem, the rudder, which had not improved as much as we had expected.

That night we cleaned up and went for a celebratory dinner to the city hotel in Fredrikstad. Usually at Lilleby's we catered for ourselves. We took it in turns to make breakfast and dinner, with a certain competitiveness. Breakfast was a blend of Norwegian and English, including cereals, pickled herring and boiled eggs. A rough rule was that if an Englishman was cooking, the Norwegians would drink tea instead of coffee, and if a Norwegian was cooking the Englishmen would drink coffee instead of tea, but some were good at both. When we had relieved the watchmen at the ship to go into town for their breakfast I usually went with them to buy materials for a cold lunch and the evening meal. Of these the most interesting was Rolf Hansen's north Norwegian fish stew, requiring half a stone of cod and what seemed an almost equal amount of leeks, peppers and potatoes – for six of us! For the benefit of anyone who would like to try it, I insert the quantities scribbled on the back of a message-pad, the original shopping-list. Three kilos of potatoes, two kilos of cod (deep frozen or fresh), 2 lemons, 2 green peppers, 1 large leek, 4 onions, 4 tomatoes and half a pound of butter. The method is simplicity itself, as cooking usually coincided with the cocktail hour on return from a hard day's work and the cook was usually the centre of a genial group always ready with constructive suggestions about the broth as they queued for washplace and shower. Rolf fries all but the first two in the last, then adds the first two and enough water to cover, and cooks until the conviction of the majority that it *must* be done by now proves irresistible any longer. Even if you don't like cod, you may well like this, and even if you don't the absence of both dill and dried reindeer make it refreshing as a novelty in Norse cuisine. Once the whole crew was assembled it was no longer really practical to live in this way, and restaurant meals were more usual, if we did not eat our main meal on board as we often did. Odd Børstad, our cook, as well as acquiring a magnificent set of pans had bought himself, in a little black case, the most lethal array of cook's knives I have ever seen, so that with any motion on the ship his regular cry of 'Alan! Plaster' sounded like a leadsman chanting soundings. Eventually either his tough hide turned even these expensive edges or he got used to their sharpness, so that the tin of dressings in my oilskin pocket lasted the crossing, which at first had seemed unlikely.

On Saturday the 5th we left Rød at 13 30 and had the red spar buoy at the entrance abeam at 14 10. It was a much better day, as the wind though still fresher than I like for trials, had backed to the southward so that we could hoist sail at 14 20 more or less in the entrance. We paid for this brashness by getting it in a terrible mess with the yard foul of the forestay and a brace round it, which you would think was not possible without casting it off, deliberately passing it round, and then making fast again. We had to lower again and take the braces right aft to hold the yard clear whilst hoisting, and I seriously considered hoisting it in stops and breaking out when it was aloft, as we set the topsails in the STA schooners. It was probably the strain imposed by this frap which caused the fixed side of the rakke to come loose from the yard at 15 40, so that it blew away from the mast and had to be lowered once more. We soon had it up again, this time with the rope's end seized firmly to the standing part. The rakke is the wooden traveller which holds the yard to the mast. None was found at Gokstad and I am now doubtful whether the curved, almost horseshoe-shaped piece of wood from Oseberg, often called a rakke, can really be one. Magnar felt the curves to be so sharp that it would be likely to break across the grain and therefore laminated one, with a steel insert to this pattern, but we found it unusable as it seized on the mast in a very dangerous way, making it impossible to lower the yard quickly in a squall. The femborings have this trouble even though they use a more modern double traveller of wooden parrel beads with flat slats in between. They cope with it by having a downhaul block on the traveller so that two men can apply the force of four to heave it down. This still seems to me fairly dangerous in an unballasted ship like the *Raven*, and I therefore preferred the older Faeroese and Icelandic fashion, where one end of the rakke is fixed to the yard, but the other to a rope which leads over the yard and then down between it and the sail, behind the latter, to the foot of the mast. When this is slackened it allows the rakke to open away from the mast and the sail comes down without difficulty. Because this system was unfamiliar to the Norwegians we also had the femboring block on the rakke.

If we did not want to secure the tack to the samson post right forward, but have it further aft for a freer wind, we led it through the forward oarhole. This was where we shipped most water and it also meant that we could not use it for an oar with which to cast the head round. It was therefore decided to use the traditional north Norwegian seglstikke, and Rolf Hansen made a beautiful one. It is a steel rod about a foot long provided with a thick wooden handle about the same length. It is stuck out through a small hole in the upper plank and the tack is then hitched round its projecting outboard part, to be immediately released if you pull out the seglstikke. The small holes provide a range of adjustments for tack position without admitting water and without blocking oarholes. Erik Rudström suggested to me that the small holes in the bow of Skuldelev 3 could well be for a seglstikke of this kind and I think their position, agreeing very well with Andersen's results in Hals og Skaut, suggests that he is right. It is another instance, like the way the priare seems to be represented on the Gotland stones, of the way north Norwegian workingboat tradition has preserved features from the viking age. The ease with which the tack could be secured and cast off, and the short boards we were making in the fjord led us to neglect the duva as we called the three part tackle (*ref.* Q p. 97) which held the lower part of the luff vertical and to windward. The straightness from this to the bowline is well seen in (*ref.* P p. 97).

On a long open sea passage this comes into its own, but it is undeniably more troublesome than it is worth on short tacks, revealing the real disadvantage of the square sail, which whilst it can be trimmed to pull to windward, and gives more power than a fore-and-aft sail of reasonable height, unfortunately requires a lot of time-consuming and skilful trimming devices to do so.

On Sunday there were many visitors to the yard, including two from the Birka vikings of Sweden who hoped eventually to build a replica of one of the eastward viking ships which carried Swedes through Russia. Even in prosperous Sweden they had not yet found anyone to put up the funds, and in spite of our reservations about some aspects of Norwegian bureaucracy, notably the State Wine monopoly and the Customs, we felt that our reconstructed voyage was easier than one up the Neva and down the Dnieper. We were able to give them a thrilling sail before a rising force 6, with breakers running forward along the ship's side and then being left behind, as balanced on their face we accelerated away from them under reefed mainsail. It was on this occasion that I first noticed something for which I later discovered, discussing it in Shetland with Thomas Muncrieff, that the traditional Shetland term is 'water-loose'. At certain speeds the bottom planking throbs beneath your feet, and as the following wave runs forward (for the wind has to be free to attain these speeds) a sort of pattering can be heard running forward with it, as the lashings of bottom planking to frame snap tight in turn. If one is half-asleep on the deck at night it sounds like mice scampering back and forth beneath the planking, as if running from the luminous breaking wavecrest alongside. The stern of course lifts to the overtaking wave, and the bow dips. As the wave runs forward the bow begins to climb, but as the wave passes the mast the bow stops its climb, and even dips, before, with an accompanying change of sound in the bow wave, beginning to climb once more with an increasing speed. I wish I had some good theoretical explanation for this: it presumably has something to do with interference between the ship's wave-making pattern and the natural wave train which suddenly increases and then reduces the ship's resistance so that she accelerates even up the back of a wave. What makes the impression more vivid is that sometimes the dragon head at this point nods slightly, presumably because of the differential deflection of the weather and lee bows by the higher bow wave to leeward. The quivering of the whole body and the tossing head make one feel an immediacy and appropriateness in the legion of kennings for viking ships which make them sea horses, which had for me previously been merely conventional, but can now make me think of the *Raven* gathering herself for the jump when I see a horse going for a fence. 'Water-loose' is a good example of the power of many old expressions which are technical and poetical at the same time. Why should we regard the terms as opposed?

On this Sunday afternoon sail we decided we really must get a different recording head for the log, as for ten minutes at a time the needle was stuck against the pin at eight knots, the maximum recorded, and it was infuriating not to know how much more we were actually doing. The next model up ran to twenty knots, but my original estimate that I would be pleasantly surprised if we ever averaged seven knots over an hour had begun to seem very craven, and no one felt twenty knots was too much for a log for the *Raven*.

That night I returned to Oslo with Odd Børstad and the Swedes on a twilight journey that seemed sometimes a continuation of the afternoon's Flying Dutchman ride. I could only hope that the invulnerability of which Odd was obviously completely convinced extended to his passengers. There were various things to get on Monday that were not obtainable in Fredrikstad, whose great days as a port are past, or were more conveniently collected in Oslo. We needed a new main halyard as the original had been calculated to land the yard on the yard supports, but we had found that sail work at this height above the hull, as well as doing nothing for stability was not really justifiable in the weather we were experiencing. Sooner or later the odds were that someone would experience worse than a trapped hand: in fact I think we are prouder of our completely accident-free record than we are of other more romantic aspects, and it was achieved by remedying weaknesses immediately they were detected. We moved the lower block further aft to increase the distance from it to the mast head so that we could accommodate a longer tye which allowed us to lower the yard to the deck.

After only a week of the bunkhouse, as we called Lilleby's, it was odd to be once again in a civilised and ideal home sort of house. It had actually been an exhibition house before Odd bought it, and had more than once proved itself by accommodating a dozen of the project to dinner with less congestion than some of the old-style restaurants we favoured. In the morning we swept like a devouring flame through the Oslo ironmongers and shipchandlers, ticking off one item after another in the toolkit, deck and engine room stores, not forgetting nine fifty-gallon neoprene waterbags for fresh water which we acquired on a detour to a sort of maritime supermarket in an improbably picturesque village on the way back to the yard. As by some strange system everyone has been to school with everyone else in Norway, or at least with their sister (which when you think about it explains a good deal about Norwegian society) it was no surprise that Odd was on first-name terms with everyone in the place. We arrived at Rød in the sunny evening and plunged again into the mist of Trekkfast, having mercifully been absent for what had obviously been a Trekkfaster's field-day. It struck with increased effect after twenty-four hours breathing real air.

On Tuesday the 8th determination was in the air. An end to fooling about on our own doorstep. We were bound across the Oslofjord to have a look at Vestfold where the original Gokstad came from, and the coast we were to harry later on behalf of Den norske Creditbank. We left at 12 30, with the log reading 40, and ran north between the fortified island of Ravo and the mainland until at 14 05 we had the lighthouse on its northern tip abeam, and could head out across the Oslofjord. We were now setting out on our first real passage, hard on the wind, apparent wind on the meter 18 knots, 5 points (58°) on the port bow. The ship's head was west and we were not going to windward as well as it may seem, for we were making the ten degrees of leeway we regarded as desirable.

It may seem strange that we did so, and as this is one of the most important results of our trials, the reasons, though complicated and to some extent controversial, should be explained. If the ship is moving sideways through the water and not simply in the direction in which it is pointing, it is the lift to windward generated by this which resists the sideways pressure of the wind in the sails. As the angle of leeway increases so does this lift, but at the expense of greatly increased drag. At one particular angle the ratio between sideforce and drag is at its most advantageous, and both Paul Graville's theoretical tank testing and Erik Rudström's practical experience suggested that for our hull this was about ten degrees. If the leeway was much more or less than this, although the pointing to windward might *seem* better, the actual progress to windward would be less. Some of Graville's assumptions seemed to us optimistic, both about the power exerted by rowers and about sail area. He seemed to regard 120 sq m for a full size Gokstad as moderate, whilst we knew from experience that it was far larger than is either plausible or necessary. But his work spoke directly to our condition as they say, and his thesis can have had few more attentive and devoted readers. His demonstration that the difference in speed between a Gokstad sail area of 90 sq m and 130 sq m is only half a knot, whether to windward or downwind, depends of course on his assumption of a steady wind of fifteen knots in which we knew we would do much better speeds than his tank model had done, but it served to show that sheer sail area on a Gokstad hull is not as decisive as you might think at first. Even more striking are his figures for its ratio of side force to drag compared to modern yachts. In a six-metre racer the ratio might be 4.5, in an ordinary fin keel 3 and in a twin bilge-keel cruiser 2.5, compared with 6 for Gokstad. The obvious moral is that, whatever the manufacturer says, if you want to get ahead get a Gokstad, preferably a scaled-down one. The catch is of course that these ratios reflect the very low drag (at low speeds) of the Gokstad hull and its striking lightness, partly of construction (fibreglass is heavy) and partly of absent ballast (as I believe, though not all would agree). They also depend on assumptions which we were never quite able to match in practice, and whilst we will all readily agree that there are probably more skilled viking ship sailors in Europe, we would like them to publish their results in our painstaking detail. We could never get anywhere near three points off the wind, let alone do 6 knots on that heading from a 20 knot apparent wind, and rather doubt whether a full-size Gokstad, even over-rigged, could do, either. *If* you could lie that heading you perhaps could make the speed, but it would surely need an impractically flat-cut sail, if not a rigid aerofoil, and we cannot really imagine viking ships with the sail wardrobe of a Cowes week racer. The really interesting point of Graville's results is the very peaky shape of his graph of sideforce to resistance which looks more likely to be sought for than accidental. His suggestion that the comparatively small projection of the Gokstad keel from the hull works by generating a vortex so that the ship in effect sails on a keel of water is very attractive, and explains why it combines good windward performance with easy beaching, always a prime requirement.

In the clear waters of the Oslofjord we could see this vortex with its trapped air-bubbles emerging from the *Raven*'s keel under our quarter, and measure the angle between it and the keel. In spite of all this it seems unlikely, as this day was to show, that anyone ever left harbour in one of these ships deliberately to beat to windward. They either waited for the wind to change or, for a short distance, lowered the sail and rowed.

At 14 30 either the wind freed slightly or our sail trimming had improved, for we were able to alter course without loss of speed from W to W×S and an hour later had crossed the fjord and tacked just off the two factory chimneys which had previously been only two points on our western horizon. On the tack back to the eastern shore of the Oslofjord we had to clear the south point of Ravo from whose northern point we had set out. The distance made good in two tacks across the Oslofjord would then be the length of Ravo island, perhaps three miles, in three hours, as we took an hour and a half to cross the fjord and returned at the same speed. At 16 35 the south point of Ravo bore 120°M. At 16 45 the bearing was still 120°M. and it had not changed at all at 17 00. We were quite clearly not going to weather the south point of Ravo, towards which we had been sliding sideways for the last half-hour, and were now a little close to it to tack, which might involve a sternboard. Wearing involved turning towards it not away, but there was surf breaking on the rocks which looked increasingly unattractive, and there was no time to be lost, so we eased the sheet, swung the yard with the braces and put the helm hard up to wear ship with the speed about six knots. Absolutely nothing whatsoever happened to the ship's head, and *Odin's Raven* continued towards the south point of Ravo as if on tramlines. At 17 05 our guardian angel, the little Bukh diesel, was going full astern, prompted by Eddie's quick command and Dave Eames's equally brisk execution, and we were lowering sail, to hoist again at 17 30 with a safe offing past the south point of Ravo. At the spar buoy at the entrance (17 45) we began a post-mortem which lasted through tying up at Röd at 18 20, the usually silent drive into Fredrikstad, dinner at the Chinese restaurant on the dockside, and was only cut short by lights out at Lilleby's at eleven. Opinions varied as to whether what was needed was two rudders, more oars out, or a human sacrifice and if so who, but the last comment appeared to come from wartime comedian Jerry Colonna in his rueful catchphrase 'We learn sum'p'n noo *every day!*'

Wednesday the 9th was devoted, for psychological as well as practical reasons probably, to trying various of our post-mortem (nearly) ideas for getting the ship round. We wanted no more surprises of this kind and were after all having to do our learning in wind and sea conditions quite unusual for May, which did not permit of second thoughts. A check of positions entered yesterday on the chart by Brian Cousins (well done, B.C.!) showed that we had, even on the way out, only been making up to windward about 10° (i.e., 80° off the wind) no matter how close we had seemed to point. Some of this was probably the effect of waves knocking the head off, some the effect of surface drift after strong southwesterlies for almost a week, in a region of little tide. But we were after all sailing in the classic area for viking ships and this was a salutary demonstration of the difference between tank tests and the real world. Of course we all think now, that we would do much better if we went back now (and wish that we could!) but we could not do as well as the tank test suggests, or at least not more than once a century.

We left at 11 20, log 68, and hoisted sail at 12 15. By the time we were back alongside at 17 00 we had satisfied ourselves that with a couple of oars over the lee side, our inevitable resource, she could always be turned off the wind, most effectively if they were stern oars, which helped the stern to hang up whilst the bow blew off. The sudden acceleration which this could produce as the yard swung was reminiscent of the first day and could be quite alarming. The reason for the early finish was twofold. The rest of the crew was arriving from the Isle of Man with the last consignment of gear, and we wanted to be back at the bunkhouse to greet them and help them unload, and the following day, thus reinforced we were to go up the fjord to Horten to attack one of the Denmark–Oslo ferries and 'kidnap' some friends, including its captain. We had, as usual, stayed out too long, and it took some determined, though happily brief, driving on the left by Nigel to overtake the two crew-buses with the new arrivals. Their arrival at Lilleby's had the advantage over ours of daylight and sobriety, even if they found the warmest places already pre-empted. We were in any event to sleep away the following night, and leave for good two nights later.

Next day the extra bodies and full drinking water tanks, though not yet full stores or kit, put the freeboard down to 75 cm when we left at noon under oars, and I began to wonder whether we had not cut things rather fine for the crossing and ought not to lighten ship. We emerged, completely in piratical character, through the inconspicuous northern entrance, where we ran the engine for fifteen minutes and made sail at 13 25. We had to call in Engelsvik with its small fish quay to rendezvous with the TV team and therefore lowered sail at 13 50 and rowed in upwind. After lunching, and losing a fender, our first evidently deliberate sacrifice to Ran, Old Norse god of the sea, we left the quay under sail at three, the natural reward for having rowed in. Half an hour later we were reaching up the Oslofjord at a very satisfactory 8 knots in a light force 3. We found that bringing the wind on the quarter to run across to Horten, we could increase speed by slacking the forestay to increase the rake aft of the mast, and also shifting the tack aft, a good instance of the flexibility of the rig. We ran swiftly on until 18 50 when, the wind dropping, we lowered sail and ran the engine for half an hour round the south end of Basto island to pass between it and the western shore, rowing quietly into Horten at 19 50.

This was the first night the entire ship's company was aboard, and though later, in the North Sea, people collapsed on top of one another (warmer and softer than the deck planks!) here many of us chose to sleep on the jetty alongside, after the spare sail had been rigged as tent, and the hammocks in which Robin and Eddie manifested an uneasy eminence had been slung. On one or two occasions we really feared for their safety as they appeared to roll outside the rail, and accelerations in a viking ship at sea are so large that I think it must be doubtful whether the 'hudfat' of the sagas can really have been a hammock. It was a clear, cold night and I was glad to be wearing a wet suit inside my sleeping-bag.

At 04 15 on Friday May 11th we had coffee, and the Ravens changed into their viking gear for the forthcoming exploit, whilst I went on board Magnar Hansen's launch for a second breakfast and some grandstand photographs of the raid. The old maxim about shoemakers' children being ill-shod was patently untrue of all the staff of Rød boatyard, whose own craft all had the gleaming perfection in England seen only in the hands of millionaires or varnish advertisements. At 06 20 the boarding, painstakingly recorded by Norwegian TV, succeeded, across a pilot boat which had not been warned to expect anything out of the ordinary and offered a spirited resistance. There were the usual staged photographs unhappily inseparable from modern public relations, a ransom of beer and akvavit was handed over, mostly consumed by the chilly 'victims', and we returned to Horten. On the way in, a well-meant bit of tidying up resulted in the spear with the raven banner going over the side, but it was recovered within six minutes (good man-overboard drill) and at 07 15 the third sitting for breakfast began alongside in Horten.

We left at 08 20 to run some of our visitors across the fjord to Moss on the Eastern shore, leaving there at ten to sail back in a dying wind towards the burial mounds at Borre, where the TV crew wanted to film the mounds with a viking ship passing in the background, and shrewdly surmised that the chances of any other one coming along were slim. At 11 40 we toiled past Borre under oars, going aground briefly about 100 metres north of the harbour entrance. We cleared Borre at 13 10 and at 13 30 set course back home to Rød. It was a very hot day, the only one of the trials, and most of the crew were asleep when at 15 08 we had Vesle Kalv lighthouse abeam to starboard, having done ten miles in just over an hour and a half. At 17 00 we were in the north entrance and at 18 30 after a sudden shower, made a sensational arrival at the yard under sail, after ghosting down the fjord with oars as bearing-out spars to extend the foot of the sail. The wind freshening at last, we stormed between the yard's jetty and a fishing boat lying off it, with about a foot to spare on each side.

The following day, Saturday the 12th, we took Magnus Magnusson and a TV crew on board for filming as we sailed up Oslofjord to Engelsvik again. Conditions were ideal, with a freshening force 5 southerly off the land, which had not yet had time to raise much sea, and with this on our quarter we rapidly outran the escorting *Sunshine IV* which was at her maximum of 10.5 knots. As in one hour we ran two miles ahead, we must have averaged 12.5 knots for this hour, or almost twice the square root of our waterline, a speed which certainly requires such confirmation to be believed. Normally in that wind we would have reefed, and in any other conditions we would have had to. It made a fine farewell, part of the time with Ray Sutcliffe at the helm: Magnus and I were to fly back from Oslo that evening. It was also farewell to Lilleby's, for on the Monday, Tuesday and Wednesday, the *Raven* cruised to Sandefjord, Tonsberg and Horten again, on the way to Oslo in what was socially the most sparkling week of the voyage. Den norsk Creditbank entertained its friends and the *Raven*'s crew royally in all these places and the friends soon became close friends of the *Raven* as well. When I rejoined in Trondheim many crew members were still receiving letters and visits from friends made in these ports. At Horten the ship was entertained by the Norwegian Naval College, and many souvenirs, official and unofficial, were still in evidence. Only the rest which unaccustomed days in harbour from 10 30 to 17 00 afforded made possible the selfless and enthusiastic pursuit of social duty in the evenings. By Thursday, May 17th, the National Day, the *Raven* was in Oslo not far from the berth at which she was to be lifted onto the coaster *Slettner* for the trip up to Trondheim. A large and enthusiastic crowd swarmed around the ship to purchase posters and the products of a pop group calling themselves the Vikings.

The following day the crew, in costume, were presented to his Majesty King Olav, who was, as might be expected of a sailor of his eminence, interested particularly in how well the *Raven* sailed. As this seemed to all a very sensible thing to be interested in, the audience went with a swing and a good deal of laughter, and was a good deal more genuinely enjoyable than such honours often are. After leaving the palace some paid their respects to the original Gokstad out at Bygdoy, whilst others expressed the practice of the viking age by relieving the natives of various trophies which it is unlikely can ever be exhibited on board again. Then they set off to make their way to Trondheim by various interesting routes, for only Eddie was to travel on the coaster to keep a master's eye upon the ship, so well that after the stresses of loading and unloading, there was only a tiny crack near one oarport when she was once again in her natural element in Trondheim.

Here the final provisioning for the voyage was carried out, and the final checks from the somewhat over-protective Norwegian shipping inspection were successfully endured. These have had decisive consequences for some previous ventures, denied permission to sail because they lacked the requisite radio, life-rafts and pumps, and qualified personnel, or in other ways failed to satisfy the inspectorate which is so proud of the nation's maritime culture. We knew that we had the most seriously prepared and seaworthy viking ship this century has seen, and were pleased that the inspectorate saw it this way too.

5
The Crossing

The dawn of May 27th, sailing day, was certainly not smiling. A
heavy grey cloud over Trondheim checked any tendency to pale
brightness with its intermittent drizzle, and the same was true of
some valued members of the crew. Their celebrations of our crossing appeared to have been not only premature but injudicious, but
in the best Manx fashion they revealed it only by sighing, as they
carried a heavy load on board, 'I don't know what they put in the
beer here, it doesn't taste that strong, in fact I don't think it is'; to
receive from a comrade the undeniable but sympathetic reply, 'It's
just that there's so much of it'. All no doubt very viking age.

Breakfasts on the project had always been very expansive meals,
starting with two or three talking serious shop in subdued English
breakfast-room voices suggestive of bereavement, developing
through discussion of the relative merits of tea and coffee in England and Norway respectively (*very* respectively) and inevitably
ending up with a large circle of people, who reduced other paying
guests of the hotel to a minority whilst discussing the virtues of
smoked reindeer-meat for breakfast, in voices designed to carry
across an arctic fjord, only occasionally coughing on their cigar
smoke as they were struck by a joke, or the most recent arrival's
hearty accolade between the shoulder-blades.

Sailing day at the Prinsen in Trondheim was the last such breakfast in Norway, itself enough without the weather to damp the

spirits of Englishmen returning to *Guardian* and *Telegraph* instead of implausible but entertaining reminiscences of Spitzbergen. The talk was all of the chances of getting a tank lorry to top up the diesel tank, which no one took very seriously, and of synchronising the Norwegian radio coverage of our departure with the live Manx radio programme going out at lunch time in the island. In the event both proved easier than might have been expected, but were poor stuff compared to earlier epic breakfast conversations. A visit to the airport-like control tower from which the sole duty officer of the harbour board took a godlike view of the entrance produced the right telephone number for fuel, and when we rang it the voice at the other end observed that it was after all early Sunday morning, and wet with it, in a tone detached enough to imply neither criticism nor apology. It might take some time to get hold of the driver, but we could certainly have as much diesel as we could take at the floating pier before we were due to leave. This omniscience about where we were and when we were going to sail by now seemed to us natural: 'It's for the Manx Viking ship' enabled one to count on co-operation quite beyond the commercially expected and I only hope we did not abuse it.

The driver, like most people doing anything for the ship, brought his son along for the ride. The ten-year-old insisted on personally putting the nozzle into the tank, evidently because he felt he wouldn't otherwise have been allowed on board. We forbore to enlighten him on the ease of taking over such jobs on a Sunday morning from a hung-over crew, but it was charming to see how convinced he was that that he had out-manoeuvred the simple foreigners. His father winked, and impressed us more by unrolling quite unexpected lengths of delivery hose from what appeared an ordinary road tanker. There are many antique jetties in Norway which no prudent driver would venture a heavy vehicle upon, and he would certainly have capsized the floating pier had he driven on it.

In spite of the rain and the night before, by ten o' clock cheerfulness was beginning to break through among the Manx lads as it always did, and eventually their infectious example prevailed upon the weather, so that by the time the television crews had finished jockeying for position the rain had stopped. Among the gathering crowd were faces we had last seen weeks ago in the south, and scarcely expected to see again. Some of them, like our Swedish friends from the Birka vikings, were to be in the Isle of Man to greet the *Raven* on-her arrival there, some emphasised the completely casual nature of their presence on a wet Sunday morning by elaborately producing a long-standing obligation (at their wife's insistence of course, though her face scarcely confirmed this) to visit a wife's aunt in Trondheim as their reason for a thousand mile drive in a weekend. Their presence meant a lot to us: we had early learnt to recognise that to have a heart captured by the project, but to be reluctant to admit (or recognise?) the fact was as common outside the crew as within it. The ship could never have held all those who wished to sail or were qualified by their enthusiasm to do so, but contact with them always served to remind those who did of what a privilege they had, even on a wet Sunday morning in Trondheim. The floating pier there was a sort of classic collection of all our friends, still amiably but firmly regretting the shape of our oars, our rig, our engine, and still ready to drive a thousand miles to emphasise their point even though they knew by then that we were very unlikely to make any last-minute change.

There obviously weren't any survivors of previous voyages of this kind to Man and the Isles, but there was something as close to it as our century can produce. Remote, amused, a little eccentric and very proud of his coarse English, stood a pensioner with beard and broad-brimmed hat who had been a seaman on the Shetland bus and later gunner on the fast motorboats of the Royal Norwegian Navy which had run between Shetland and the Norwegian coast during the last war. His conversation was cordial and well-informed but humbling; 'I only wish more people would do it, before we forget how natural it is, always was: you have the right time of year exactly, though it is still cold, and a beautiful ship, though she is a bit crowded, but from Maaloy I suppose you won't want to sleep: we never used to in the boats.' Useless to remind such a veteran that the North Sea was now peaceful, and its only flames came from oil-rigs which made admirable half-way houses to Shetland: interesting that for him our attempt to evoke in a small wooden ship the voyages of a thousand years ago inevitably recalled the much more dangerous voyages in not very different ships forty years ago. Interesting also, even a little irritating, that he took it so much for granted that there was one way to Britain, down the leads to Maaloy, as ships had gone, without charts often enough, for at least a thousand years and perhaps for two. He embodied a good deal of history, and we were all sorry he wasn't sailing with us, for our sake as well as his own, as he spoke so knowledgeably of Baltasound and Lerwick, managing to make them sound like an American's version of Paris, but a good deal more sensibly. His last words to me, which next day seemed excessively pessimistic and the day after wildly optimistic, proved true in the end: 'Next Sunday you can go to church in Lerwick at the Norwegian church there, and with a bit of luck you can have a good drink in Lerwick on the Saturday night at the barbers', this last was a bit of living North Sea folklore (at first I took it for a riddling and traditionally obscure joke) which only explained itself after our arrival in Lerwick.

It was an abrupt change to leave him for the apparatus of a twentieth-century public event, which his departures had never been. The arrival of the band was followed by that of the bishop whose predecessors had consecrated Bishops of Man and the Southern Isles until the fourteenth century. Like most Scandinavian churchmen of our day he spoke English almost as well as his native tongue, and regarded the Church of England with the same serious respect that some of its Anglo-Catholic members give to Rome. Add to this the extent to which all churches in coastal Norway and Sweden are inevitably seamen's churches, and it was clear that his presence on board a Manx vessel sailing from Trondheim to Man was for him and his congregation no antiquarian formality. Not simply that he was repeating a visit his predecessor might have made six hundred years ago (he was too responsibly contemporary for that) but that any evocation of contact between Christians, in Norway, Man, India or Africa had a claim on the Bishop of Trond-heim, and one from Man most of all.

He was followed by the harbourmaster, all smiles and bearing a Trondheim coat of arms, and then the Norwegian ship inspector-ate, professionally unsmiling like their brethren the world over, but about to allow an authentic viking ship to sail from Norway, against their rather unfortunate precedents and perhaps the greatest testimonial to our various skills any of us will ever have. Next came the Lady Mayoress, like her sisterhood the world over and very unlike the shipping inspectorate, wearing a jolly and very feminine smile and a pair of most unsuitably high-heeled shoes for her municipal floating pier. A gallant rush to assist her on board was won (long merchant service experience) by our captain Eddie, and she was borne aboard in triumph and dry-shod.

The floating pier was by this time so crowded that some know-alls among the spectators were obviously re-considering their own safety relative to that of the crew of the *Raven*. The crew not only had a stable and buoyant hull beneath their feet (and the municipal floating pier seemed neither) but also had the for them unusual experience of looking at people with even less room to move about than they had. Even the freeboard of the hull seemed to be increasing as the pier, under the weight of the increasing crowd, sank lower.

The Bishop had brought us a stone from the original work in Trondheim cathedral, whose decoration and workmanship showed it to be carved by those workmen from Britain who built it, and thus a most appropriate gift to the old cathedral in Peel where we were bound. These masons had presumably arrived in Norway in ships very like that in which we were now to take back part of their work. How long had their voyage taken? Was it for them too a once-in-a-lifetime experience, or something they did each summer? It is the frequency of such voyages in the life of the individual or family that establishes that community across the sea which one feels today throughout the Old Norse world.

Everyone was by now eager to be away, and Robin Bigland's reply to Bishop and Mayor was even for him brief and restricted to essentials.

The band swung smoothly into 'God save the Queen' followed by the Norwegian national anthem during which a Norwegian flag amost half the size of the mainsail was unfurled by the Norwegian crew members. The rest of the *Raven*'s crew replied with the Manx national hymn, 'Eilen Vannin' (the Manx ensign was already floating at the stern ensign staff), and the gap between us and the quay widened rapidly as the four after oarsmen showed how rapidly with their winter's training behind them they could speed up a twelve-ton hull. At 12 55 the affecting exchange of farewells across the widening gap was interrupted, as so often in marine history, by a rasping request to get the mainsail up and sheeted home on the port tack. As it had been all ready for hoisting for the last quarter-hour, thanks to some unobtrusively irreverent activity during the parting ceremony, Capt. Eddie was able to give a convincing performance of not being staggered by the expedition and efficiency with which the job was done, over the toiling oarsmen's heads and between the swinging looms of their oars. Not for the first time it was clear that without the vertical yokes whose awkward presence at other times we cursed, smooth transition from oar to sail or vice versa would have been difficult, and tangles between sailing gear and the moving oars likely and dangerous. It obviously also helped to avoid this that the hull was so easily propelled that only the after oarsmen, least in the way, were rowing. More wind would have been desirable, but by the time she passed the end of the floating pier and turned toward the harbour entrance, the *Raven* was gathering speed under her swelling sail, and swept past the jetty end five minutes before the programmed time.

Though the ship had been ready to sail an hour earlier it had been necessary to wait, to keep faith with the public and the appointed time for various radio hook-ups. It also unfortunately meant that we could not miss a less happy appointment (supposed to surprise us) which some of us, conscious of how easily relationships can be curdled, would have preferred to avoid by sailing early. We had discovered that morning that a surprise ambush, boarding and reduction by a fleet of femborings was planned, and that *Odin's Raven* was to be attacked on leaving harbour. Some of the attackers we later found were carrying implements capable of causing pain and were prepared to use them – the borderline between vigorous horseplay and the violent expression of feelings their possessor may not even be conscious of harbouring is often a vague one. In the event things turned out rather well for us, and it might have been a pity to miss the taste of antique tactics involved, but it was fortunate that the *Raven* came through unscathed and did not have to embark on the open sea crossing with the damage to hull and rig sustained by the two femborings which made close contact.

Trondheim's fjord, and particularly the folk high school at Rissa, is the centre of the revivalist sport of sailing replicas, some built within the last few years, of the late-nineteenth-century femboring. They are open double-ended pulling boats with high stem and stern posts setting a high-aspect squaresail and topsail, and are for working craft extraordinarily beautiful and exciting boats, capable in skilled hands of sensational performance under sail, so light that

they can combine a good ballast-ratio, of more than half the displacement in recent examples, with a very rapid and sensitive
response to trim and helm. The visual impression of one hurtling
down the fjord hurling spray from the lee bow I suppose corresponds to an important image in the imagination of most Norwegians and anyone interested in antique craft. Our rig in *Odin's
Raven* followed femboring practice in many respects, not all inevitably advantageous, but we were all conscious of having much to
learn from the experience of these devoted sailors of a single
squaresail, which is soon to be made available in English. When we
were fitting out the *Raven* their pamphlet was only printed in an
almost impenetrable northern version of Ny Norsk, the most
aggressively individual version of Norwegian, not easily understood either by other Scandinavians or even Norwegians from Oslo.
We all felt, on the other hand, that by dint of hard work and practice
we had learnt quite a lot in a month about the handling of the rig by
the time we sailed from Trondheim.

It isn't surprising that some proud purists who couldn't really
believe that any Norwegian south of Trondheim could handle a
squaresail were slightly nettled at the easy assumption of a mainly
Manx crew that it was not only possible but pleasurable to acquire
the knack in a month. Genuinely regional culture in Britain has had
such a limited field since the Industrial Revolution that it is difficult
for us to understand the fierce Norse pride in even the drawbacks of
something felt to be truly a central part of the culture of a region.
For us the Scotsman who knew that no other land could compare
with Scotland in fruit-growing (he preferred gooseberries and he
preferred them sour) is a figure in a joke, and a conventional one at
that. In many parts of Scandinavia his attitude would I think be
found unreasonable (mainly because it was about fruit) but not
necessarily ludicrous or unadmirable. The students of the high
school had determined to attack the *Raven* as she left.

Another strand of feeling may well have involved aesthetic considerations, given as so often an inaccurate historical top-dressing.
The shields bearing the contemporary devices of those who had
made the ship possible, by no means all of them commercial companies' emblems, undoubtedly jarred upon some. It is ironical that
it is because the devices were contemporary and comprehensible
that they were objected to. Had they been those more garish

recorded from the eleventh century and presumably as readily identifiable then, there would probably have been less objection though the strictly visual effect would have been the same. This seems to affect the view of every aspect of the Middle Ages in our day. We often forget as we view a medieval abbey of subtly weathered stonework set in smooth Ministry of Works lawns and peopled by antiquarians in quiet heather-mixture tweeds, that in its prime the stonework was garishly striped with the brightest colours available, and carpeted with rushes only partly hiding rejected fragments of meat whose spices had not concealed its highness. All this did not matter so much then, for our forefathers, as far as we can see, lacked our discreet good taste. Some of the unimportant features of the *Raven* were in important respects more genuine than the purists' preferred alternatives.

It may be that the high-school students concentrated on shields and figurehead because they are features important to the image of a viking ship which do not occur in the modern femborings. The figurehead was not intended as a replica of one the Gokstad ship might have carried, but as a genuine twentieth-century piece of art, a re-creative exercise within the old tradition, not a plaster cast. It was unashamedly the twentieth-century dragon head of a twentieth-century ship, just as the stern ornament was firmly based upon the only surviving authentic example from the Ile de Groix burnt ship-burial, but redistributed the three circles inside the toothed outside one to recall the Manx Millennium emblem.

The claim that a ship with shields and figureheads constituted a challenge and an insult to the locals under Old Norse law which was the ostensible reason for the attack was probably, insofar as it was seriously held at all, based on a misunderstanding. It might have been an inaccurate memory of a hazy reference to Ulfljots Law. This is an early and not very reliable antiquarian text which we find in various fictional contexts in the sagas, which has some interesting details about various aspects of viking life, for instance the sacred gold arm ring of the leader, which are supported by casual sidelights in more serious sources in Old English and Latin. From it we also learn that ships with gaping dragon figureheads (which *Odin's Raven* certainly had) were to remove them when approaching Iceland (*not* 'when leaving Trondheim') in case they frightened away the guardian spirits of the land. Quite apart from the reflection that one might be better rid of such poor-spirited guardians, the form taken by these spirits, of lion, bull, eagle and man's head is so clearly that of the traditional four Evangelist symbols that it is impossible to believe that they are of any very high antiquity in Old Norse paganism. The figureheads were no doubt removable, it would be in any case impossible as well as pointless to make them in one piece with the stem, and may well in their role as standard have embodied the assertion of their owner's power, with some magical overtones as seems to have been the case with the high-seat pillars and in particular the nails ('God nails' or 'mighty nails') decoratively hammered in.

To carry the shields displayed along the rail at sea *was* sometimes regarded as a sign of uppishness, so that one Bjorn acquired the ironically derisive nickname 'Shield-Bjorn' because he did so, but the pictorial and documentary evidence is overwhelming that chieftains' ships did have shields rigged like that in harbour and fjord.

Thus the historical element, which unfortunately some of the attackers seemed to take quite seriously, was barely adequate even for a student rag. Such episodes have to be judged to some extent as a 'happening' or a sort of living art, just like the voyage itself, and from this point of view the fleet of dark square sails approaching us from the north shore of the fjord certainly added drama to our departure from Trondheim.

The attack had probably been intended to board us fairly close to the harbour, where the coast road westward out towards Agdenes climbs the headland outside Trondheim. It would have provided an admirable grandstand and was jammed with spectators' cars when we sailed past. In the event the femborings had overestimated their speed and underestimated ours, though a large and persistent television camera cruiser certainly did his best to redress the balance by repeatedly closing us to windward and blanketing our sail. I don't know how long he succeeded in persuading himself that our gestures were friendly, but when they eventually became such as to make his film unusable for family viewing he at last sheered off, smiling to the last.

To start with the wind was light and fluky, and the femborings further out in the fjord were holding a better wind whilst we were still in the shadow of the land. It was infuriating to see their mainsails swelling firmly when one's ears were assailed by the occasional sulky thud of ours falling against the mast as we rolled, before it filled again. But eventually the *Raven*'s larger area of well-cut and well-set sailcloth of the most modern type (for our main concern was the successful recreation of a voyage, not just a ship) began to tell. It also had the advantage of being set as a single sail with an unbroken windward edge, whereas the femborings carried baggy sails of antique cut, and topsails which were there to make possible the rapid reduction of the sail area, really too much for the hull, but were not the best way of setting that total area on the wind. As we got further out into the fjord the wind scarcely freshened but became at any rate steadier in strength and direction, important for our heavier gear and fuller hull. For the approaching femborings to have any hope of intercepting us required a substantial alteration of their course, and even after this we had been under way for an hour before the leading femboring, having outdistanced the others, came up with us.

By this time we were reaching down the fjord at a steady six knots, speed increasing as the force three southerly wind sped the small white cumulus clouds across a cold pale blue sky the colour of the fjord water which still in places reflected the white patches of snow lying low on the surrounding slopes. To fight even a phony running battle in viking ships at this sort of speed is a risky business, and not really like Bermudan-rigged dinghies jockeying round a buoy. If one side persistently over-estimates its own performance and underestimates the other's, there is a real danger of serious damage.

Our two adversaries were *Munin* and *Siste Viking*, both of them redoubtable little ships with voyages to Iceland to their credit. *Munin* was one of Odin's Ravens, and therefore alleged that the name had been stolen. *Siste Viking* (The last Viking) was named after Bojer's famous novel of a Trondelag fishing family, but was fairly obviously feeling that after the last viking one shouldn't have any more. When it appeared that boarding was impossible, and that the femborings, in spite of finer lines and better ballast ratio, had their work cut out to keep up with the *Raven*, *Munin* managed to draw slowly down our windward port side landing one or two birch blows on our people in the stern. The breeze freshened slightly and *Munin*, struggling hard to get ahead, was led into the fatal temptation to bear away from the wind slightly to increase speed. Her

captain may have hoped to accelerate rapidly enough relative to
the *Raven* to draw clear ahead of us, but his optimism proved
unfounded. Those of us in the bow had the happily unusual experience, for which nothing in Tall Ships races really prepares you, of
seeing, with incredulity soon giving way to real concern for the
other's welfare, a ship attempting to overtake along our port side
and turn sharp to starboard across our bow! Once committed to
this desperate manoeuvre their only hope of keeping damage down
was to keep their speed up, if necessary by turning even more
sharply. We risked going aback (though not frankly inclined to risk
too much to save others from their actions) by luffing, but the
freshening wind working upon the *Raven*'s better sail accelerated
her at least as rapidly as the femboring. It all happened a good deal
more quickly than it takes to describe: I recall looking down from
our curving prow onto *Munin*'s stern as our bow wave suddenly
steepened, funnelled between the two hulls, just before we touched.
All in all they were very lucky to get away with a cracked rudder-
head. The femboring rudder like that of all post-medieval ships is
hung centrally on a sternpost, and one of the Ravens unsympathetically observed that if femborings had not gone in for such
new-fangled innovations, but stuck to a viking side-rudder like our
own, they would not have damaged it.

Whilst *Munin* was stopped to leeward examining the damaged
rudder and effecting temporary repairs, *Siste Viking* came ranging
up on our quarter to windward from the same angle as *Munin* had
done. This is after all the only way for an attacker of approximately
equal speed to have any hope of laying alongside an enemy. She
looked most impressive as she heeled towards us in the now appreciably stronger wind, her mainsail bellying out and overshadowing
those crew in the *Raven*'s stern. As she moved forward it began to
blanket our mainsail and her relative motion increased as we
slowed down. From our place in the bow we could see beneath our
mainsail her high prow moving down our port side with increasing
speed until, level with our mast, it seemed to come to a surprisingly
sudden stop, though we felt no collision. Then it dropped rapidly
back until we eventually sailed out clear ahead and our mainsail
filled again. Looking beneath it we could see a great vertical gash in
Siste Viking's mainsail rapidly spreading up and down until it ran
from headrope to footrope. As her swelling sail had pressed over

our stern it had caught up either on the triangular points of the dragon-tail stern ornament or one of the spears stowed there, and the small tear produced had rapidly spread in a sail full of wind.

I don't think it would be from one episode of this kind historically justifiable to conclude either that stern ornaments were as a general rule made of this form with defensive purposes in mind, or that the bundle of spears carried in this position in more than one picture of a viking ship on Gotland stones was there for the same purpose, but it is an interesting consequence and one worth reporting. Any viking ship approaching along the windward side heels towards its opponent exposing the whole interior of the hull in a way that makes it very desirable to have shields handy along the rail. A stern ornament of Ile de Groix type, or a bundle of spears stowed in the same place, makes it very difficult for the hostile ship to approach close on the weather quarter without losing the mainsail: in both cases the crucial role of the three or four men at each end of the ship, the *stafnbuar* of the sagas, is clear. The ornament or spears are not of course in the way if both ships round up to windward and slacken speed slightly, as we later proved. After a declaration from Robin Bigland hostilities terminated and we took Jon Godal, who has written much about femborings, off his craft for lunch on board *Raven* with us.

We were all the time flying down the fjord with a freshening wind, and at 15 30 *Siste Viking* was far astern as she turned into Statbygd on the NE shore to land her vociferous students. *Munin* accompanied us until 16 00 when she too went into her home port of Rissa, and we said farewell to Trondheim fjord when we rounded Agdenes lighthouse at 17 20. We received a complicated salute on its vast foghorn to which even Knut Skogøy's considerable powers of obbligato on our cowshorn seemed almost inadequate in reply: usually he could put to shame the most expensive gas operated chromium-plated hooters. We were considerably relieved to find that once outside the fjord we could just about lay the course down the lead without speed dropping off, though if the wind did draw ahead more southerly as was forecast it would be a different story. We had been doing a steady eight knots for the last two hours, but if we had to tack down the lead the *Raven* was not precisely at her best, particularly as we did not know how far we could steal out of the channel before going about, and the system of marking in the

The end of the jousting under oars against *Goosander*

Approaching H.M.S. *Odin*

Robin Bigland in a helmet from the film *The Viking*, 1957 (courtesy of Kirk Douglas and Thurstan Binns)

Facing North Sea dawn

First class sleepers

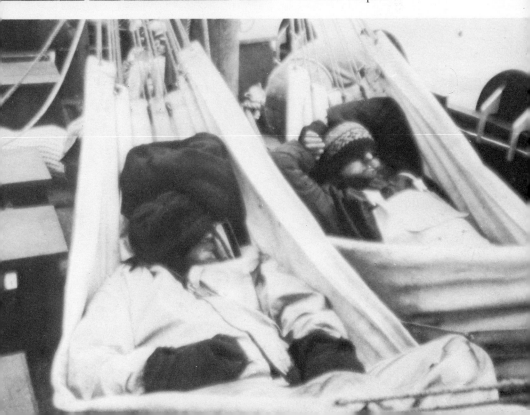

Welcome home!

leads (the passages inside the islands) is mainly designed to keep you on the recommended track. The sunshine and jolly little white clouds which had given such an exhilarating run down the fjord were now replaced by a return to the calm grey depression weather of the morning, and for the next two hours we had to be content with five knots. It was all in the right direction, with no tacking needed, so that by 19 30 we had Kongsvold lighthouse abeam to port, and the log reading 30. That meant that since leaving Trondheim at 12 55 we had averaged 5 knots, the traditional speed of the *doegr sigling* of the sagas. Again it would be absurd to attach too much importance to one single instance, but it is striking that even if we had not had help from log or lighthouses the traditional estimate of our distance made good, and therefore position, would have been accurate.

Like many of the lighthouses in the leads, Kongsvold light is to English eyes very low down. On such a deeply intersected coast there is little point in trying to ensure that the light can be seen from a great distance, and lights high up are not only less certain points to head for, but more likely to be obscured by the frequent low cloud. What is important is that one always has, on rounding a corner in the twisting channel, a mark ahead to steer for to take one clear of the many rocks at or just beneath the surface, with which even the main lead is in some places liberally scattered. This is achieved by various coloured sectors in the light, often much more complicated than anything you will meet with on the British coast. Agdenes light, for instance, when seen from the west shows red, then white, red, white, red, white, green, white, and shows as red again when you see it from the southward. When it is bearing south from you the question of which precise white or red sector you are in is very important. Kongsvold light only shows through 180° of which 90° show white, but the other 90° red, white, green, white, red. In summer in these latitudes the Norwegians economically do not exhibit the light anyway, so you are spared the elaboration of the sectors and navigate perforce by lining up headlands and prominent peaks in the old-fashioned way.

The lines given by such alignments are called in Norwegian 'med': the corresponding word in English is 'meet' but this sense is now obsolete, though it is probably punned on when Hamlet says: 'When in one line two craft directly meet.' The lines have their own names, some very primitive in form, and likely to be at least from the viking age, and are printed on the older Norwegian charts, though not on the Admiralty ones, of the Norwegian coast. The fascinating thing about them is that some of them relate features of the submarine contours two hundred fathoms beneath the surface to the peak of a mountain fifty miles away seen above the north end of an island twenty miles away. This sort of navigation is both made possible and, at the same time, necessitated by the steep-to nature of the Norwegian coast, a beautiful example of how early seafarers seem to have lived and worked in a way as rigorously determined by the natural environment, and as beautifully adapted to it, as any animal. The Old English navigator seems to have used soundings more and anchored more than his viking opposite number, both a good deal easier and more useful in our shallow sandy seas. A Norwegian fisherman, before the advent of the echo-sounder, could scarcely expect to find his way to his fishing-ground by soundings: to get reliable soundings in two hundred fathoms with a hand lead would involve stopping the vessel for perhaps half an hour each time. Hence his preference for the 'meet' system and its lively survival in Norway, Iceland and Faeroe, partly a matter of culture and history, part determined by the unchanging natural environment. It is used by British inshore fishermen as well, and some of the most vividly pictorial 'meet' names in Iceland and Faeroe such as 'the attic window' or 'the old armchair' seem to be the creation of British fishermen in the late nineteenth century. They could not rely implicitly on their compasses (there are many more magnetic anomalies in high latitudes off the coast of Iceland or Norway) and one great advantage of the meet system is that as well as giving you a position it gives you the course to steer, and track to be maintained, to get there. This is obviously an important matter if you have no compass to steer by, and the last, the ability to check the track actually made good, is crucial for low-powered vessels perpetually being set sideways by wind and current, and only rarely travelling exactly the way they seem to be pointing. As we were soon to find out.

The wind was freshening as the sun began to sink towards the northern horizon, and we fetched from Kongsvold light to the cable markers at the south end of Leksen island in fifteen minutes, a speed of eight knots over the two miles of ground. This was satisfactory in many ways. The sail was now set up as close-hauled as we had ever found it profitable to carry it on the trials, and eight knots for a fifty-foot overall sailing vessel under these circumstances is a very respectable speed not always surpassed by our crack sail training schooners. Also, it showed that our log was reading correctly, and that we had not, as yet, any of the unpleasant and almost unpredict-able adverse currents which once established can continue even during periods of theoretically favourable tidal stream. The satis-faction was short-lived, for the wind died away as rapidly as it had arisen: the weather seemed fairly unstable, even for a region where it changes more rapidly than in Britain, and the next six miles down the lead took us two hours to Skogøy lighthouse which we reached at 21 50. Knut Skogøy inevitably greeted it as an ancestral home, though, no doubt, of the Mediterranean branch of his family, for he, like all the Norwegian members of the crew, was from the far north of Norway, and this Skogøy was closer to England than to his birthplace. Norway is in fact well-endowed with places called 'skogoy'. This is not surprising, as it means 'wooded island': a title which could be denied to few Norwegian islands apart from the outermost, bare, wave-swept skerries.

From Skogøy light there followed a very frustrating hour's sail, for which I suppose I may be partly to blame, as a more intelligent interest in place-names might have suggested a more successful course. My excuse must be that the Admiralty chart form of Nor-wegian placenames is usually the nineteenth-century literary form, which in Norway is several spelling reforms ago, and bears remark-ably little relation to pronunciation on this part of the coast any-way. In consequence I had read off the Admiralty chart from which we navigated only the names of the major islands and lights down the leads, and established with our Norse colleagues an acceptable compromise pronunciation so that they and we knew what we and they meant by our not always identical versions of the Norwegian names. I hadn't bothered to go through every name on either side of what is a pretty long sample of Admiralty Norwegian, and therefore had no idea of the name of the headland at which the giant hand reached out and grabbed us.

I mean this in the Michael Green sense, not the Excalibur one. Most amateur sailors feel indebted to him for his invention of this use of the phrase, and explanation of its general usefulness, in his

Coarse Cruising. It can turn the explanation of an error into a challenging grasping of the nettle, because it challenges your of course ostensibly sympathetic listener to dare to disagree or disbelieve. Green says he first used the phrase 'it was as if the ship had been seized by a giant hand' to explain going aground in an eddy on the Norfolk Broads, but it is truly, as he claims, the great general-purpose description for the many surprising things that can happen to small sailing ships, and I hope he will not resent our use of it to account for instance for our discovery at journey's end of whole paddy-fields of rice in the bilge.

What happened was that an hour after passing Skogøy light we were approaching the entrance to Hevnefjord about half past ten, to cross it and continue southwards. We were discussing whether there was likely to be an indraught, in which case we should stand well off the point, or whether the wind, funnelling down the fjord, might be expected to freshen to a good breeze, which we sorely needed for the next, rather tricky, stretch. In that case it would be best to stay close to the south side of the lead, close in to the point and upwind of the island of Terningen. The name means 'dice' and hints at a gamble: we did not wish to be pushed to the northward so that we had to take the rocky passage between it and the island of Hitteren which had been to starboard all the way down the lead so far. It was quite evident from the difference in the water surface ahead, off the point, where dark concave wavelets contrasted with the shining silver of the fjord, that there must be *some* change of wind or current. At 22 40 the matter was taken briskly out of our hands, and we were turning to our first real work since leaving Trondheim at one.

The wind headed us as it came curving round the point, and at the same time the *Raven*, with sail flat aback, turned further into it, curving to port, towards the rocks, even against full starboard rudder. At low speeds the rudder was never very effective, and with the sail aback steerage way was rapidly diminishing, so Eddie wasted no time in giving the order to tack. Pleased to have something to do, chilled hands (for there was still snow lying at sea level) cast off the port tack, passed forward the starboard clew to set up as the new tack, swung the main yard with the braces and waited breathlessly for the sail to fill again. It did so quickly, almost suspiciously quickly, and the *Raven*, by now clearly in the grip of that old giant hand, continued to turn with immense dignity but right against the helm, until the stern came through the wind and she was pointing back to Trondheim. We swung the yard once again and this time got the oars ready as well, remembering from the episode during the trials that the rudder alone would not force her to pay away before the rocky corner. The familiar and hallowed order 'Give way together' echoed crisply across the water, followed by the regular and oddly musical dip of blade in water and creak of pine in oarport, and the *Raven* headed back for the middle of the lead and safe room to manoeuvre, away from what I too late discovered, when I later consulted a Norwegian chart, was the headland of Stromness, or 'Current point'. Once clear, with sail drawing again, the oars came in and we stood towards the north side of the lead, the inside shore of the island of Hitteren. We tacked back only a quarter of an hour after being seized in the eddy, and at 22 55 were back on our course southward down the lead towards Stromness, but losing ground now all the time against an increasing stream. At 23 15 we were back once again where we had been at 22 00 and still going backwards over the ground. This is not a particularly unusual experience for a small sailing ship, but it is one the wise mariner does not prolong unless he has to. Unfortunately this section of the lead is not a particularly healthy one either to anchor or attempt to beach, and it seemed a pity to drift safely back to Kongsvold, so just before midnight we started the engine and with its aid were able to get round the eddy, now much stronger, on its northern edge, in half an hour under power.

Once past it the way was clear, but the wind was dying and visibility deteriorating, not so much from failing light but increasing haze, so at two in the morning of Monday, May 28th, we decided that we would choose the next suitable cove we came to and could enter, to lie up for four hours' sleep. This proved to be Kjorsvik (63° 25' N, 8° 44' E) which is in no sense a harbour, we did not even see the common village quay; but it does have one of the lead light-houses at its entrance so that you know which of the many apparently identical inlets you are in, and it has an anchorage in three fathoms with a small beach at its head, sheltered from all quarters. It has obviously been a way station for ships like the *Raven* for thousands of years, though only for those as fast as her (and with engine help past the eddy) is it within twelve hours of Trondheim.

When at six that morning we woke to the sun already high burning off the night mist it would not have been surprising to see one of Flecker's Old Ships revealed drawn up on the beach. We however had to be in Shetland by the end of the week, and so we left Kjorsvik at 06 30, just able to make three knots along Skibnesstranden, being abeam of the radio mast on Mellandsfjell at 08 20. At 09 00 we were passed by a Norwegian coaster who gave us his latest weather report for the area between us and Stadland. It was ideal for the crossing to Shetland. Visibility was moderate to good, and the southwesterly winds which had plagued us for a month seemed to be breaking up at last. The forecast was for the longed-for north-easter, 1 to 2 m per second (Beaufort Force 2). This well-meant friendly help with a forecast true for his area of interest, but fundamentally misleading, might easily have proved fatal, had we not that evening received important additions (and a welcome gift of fresh fish) from the trawler we met as we set off for Shetland.

The morning however was calm and fine, so it was decided to change our original intention of continuing down the lead, break-fasting as we went, to Kristiansund N. Instead we were to take what seemed a good chance to make the open-sea crossing to Shetland. I see from my notepad that in Kristiansund we were to get a transistor radio and batteries to pick up the weather forecasts, as the *Raven*'s radio, protected only by loose deck-boards, was already giving trouble. At 09 35 we had Tyrhaug light abeam to starboard and at 11 30 Skjerving light abeam to port, an average of five knots, including a hole in the wind where we rowed for fifteen minutes, encouraged by the hooter of a north-bound passenger ship we met.

We now headed out towards a slim pillar on the western horizon, the solitary lighthouse of Grip, a tower 150 ft high perched on a small and rocky island group. The sharply pointed gable ends of old wooden houses made the low rocky skyline seem even more jagged. There had once been a sizeable fishing village, but the islands were now completely deserted, even the lighthouse fully automated. Through binoculars we scanned a Marie Celeste island of still neat and weatherproof houses no longer attractive to fishermen who can push out from the mainland in two hours with powerful diesels. Before they had such engines they could sometimes save a whole day by living on Grip, or make the difference between getting five days work in the week and only one, among the rapidly succeeding depressions which curve across this part of the coast. The traditional jumping-off place for crossing to the Shetlands was further south, where the distance was less and where the depressions were more likely to pass to the northward. It has been argued that these storm paths lay further north anyway in the viking age, but it is impossible to be certain on the tenuous evidence available. No doubt the weather was better in Northern Europe round about the end of the first millennium in AD 1000, perhaps as much as 4 degrees centigrade (9°F), so that corn ripened in Iceland and grapes in York. But the satisfactory evidence for these milder conditions on shore, and clearer sunnier skies, does not necessarily imply, as some have urged, the settled sea and favouring northeasterly winds we associate with such spells of sunny weather in our modern summers.

The sea round Grip is encumbered by many skerries and shoals, the path through which is critical if one cannot stay firmly in the main fairway as we could not, so it seemed best to run the engine again, very uncomfortably, into a long high swell which sent the spray flying over both ship and islands, and suggested that unpleasant weather to the SW was still building the seas produced by the strong winds from that quarter over the past month. Odd Børstad accomplished wonders from his tiny galley in the circumstances. It was as well that he had chosen cooking pots so extraordinarily broad that they could not shift in the alloy chest containing the burners, and so high that soup for the whole crew could tilt fourteen degrees without approaching the rim. It was his proud boast that the ship would take water over the side before anything spilt in his galley: perhaps fortunately, no one was attempting to cook in the squall off Skye which did heel her so far. Snorri Sturlason in the Prose Edda uses the term 'just a good rim left for carrying a drinking horn' to describe the disappointing effect on a mead-horn of what Thor had intended to be a great gulp draining it off in one mighty draught. Odd's cooking pots presented a similarly magical challenge. A stew of saga-like size, carved from a whole side of reindeer, would cower in the bottom of a vast gas-holder-like cauldron surely bigger than that of the original full-size Gokstad, which they must have used only ashore, for any fire large enough to warm it would have been dangerous to the ship. Even seventeen second helpings for hungry oarsmen sometimes seemed to lower it suspiciously little, so vast was the area of the base, and one looked to see whether Odd, like Utgardar-Loki, had managed to get the sea itself to fill up the receptacle as we drank. As we had been under way since 6 00 a.m. without a meal, it would have taken more than the prevailing seas to take the edge off our appetites, though not since the early days of the trials had we experienced the *Raven*'s rocking-horse motion as she powered into a head sea. But even when sail was hoisted again on clearing Grip at 13 30 the corkscrew pitching roll tended to throw the wind out of the sail, and it was very slowly that Grip disappeared astern. Had we been sailing against a viking-age knarr with her slower more ponderous motion she might well have had the sort of advantage over us that we had enjoyed over the femborings the day before. In this respect the knarr's weight, which made it too heavy to be propelled by oars, at any rate had some compensations in light wind and confused sea.

It was noticeable that once we had cleared the skerries and fairly emerged from the inner lead out to the usual north-south offshore route, the very marked tree-line on the high bare coast was just above the horizon. This gives a fairly accurate measure of the distance off the coast at which vessels are not only clear of offlying obstructions but also in the best belt of usable winds, outside the wind-shadow of the high coast in offshore winds, and the area in which the wind is tending to rise off the surface of the sea in onshore ones. It was fascinating to speculate whether this critical distance may, on coasting voyages, have been what was meant by such traditional Old Norse phrases as 'to put the land in the water' or 'to let the sheet run along the land'. It seems natural to suppose that the first means to make the land sink beneath the horizon, but however much our imagination is seized by the bold sea crossings we should remember that the majority of instances, which is what determines speech usage, were of coastal voyages. When Old Norse sailing directions speak of having the sea 'half-way up the mountains' it is quite clear that the course is parallel to them. It is obviously easier to observe, as we were doing, the coincidence of horizon and tree-line than to estimate half-way up a mountain of unknown height with its base below the horizon. In this part of the Norwegian coast, from which so many voyages to Iceland and Faeroe set out, the tree-line seen from seaward is in fact about half-way between sea level and the summits. A vessel running down the coast and not as we were directly away from it would, as it rolled, bring the lower corner of its sail down across the land on the horizon. Closer in, the lower corner is always against a background of cliff, further out it will only rarely seem to touch the land in occasional heavy rolling. To evaluate phrases like this it is indispensable to put oneself into the context of the situation in which they were developed, as I have found with the somewhat similar terms used by modern fishermen. These two Old Norse phrases are unlikely to have been any vaguer than the present-day ones, which seem imprecise to outsiders because they do not understand that a very precise shade of meaning is in them attached, by traditional usage, to words often elsewhere used vaguely. 'About a boat's length' (how long was a boat? What sort of boat? When?) is a good instance of an apparently hopeless description of the distance an islet ten miles off should project beyond a cape nine miles off! Yet to those brought up with the usage from childhood it enables them to locate their ship upon exactly the right spot on a tiny fishing bank without the help of compass or sounding. The pity is that we cannot recover the precise significance of 'letting the sheet run along the land', but only speculate about it when we recognise the same circumstances.

By early evening we were about half-way out to Storeggen, the Big Edge, the edge of the Continental Shelf where the bottom drops from 80 fathoms to 450 fathoms within five miles and the upwelling waters produce a rich fish pasture. After the long westerlies the fish were evidently well inside the edge, for we could see two or three Norwegian trawlers slowly towing their gear to the southward. The sun was shining pleasantly, but from a hard blue sky and on an unpleasantly steep sea when we closed one of them to get the weather forecast we had been going to pick up had we gone to Kristiansund. It was as well we did so, for her skipper's views were clear and firm. Because of the last two forecasts he was going into port and so were his friends in the other ships. With characteristic Norwegian instinctive respect for the independence of others he simply observed in no patronising manner that though we obviously had a splendid vessel, in our place he would do the same. Southwest gales were forecast for the area between us and Shetland, and had been since morning.

The general trend of the Norwegian coast from Grip down to Maaloy whence we originally intended to turn off to Shetland is itself SW. We could thus continue for another couple of days to close the distance to Shetland by continuing down the sheltered lead we had hopefully left that morning, and there really was no question that this was the most sensible thing to do. The best entrance back into it was about twenty miles south of us, and once in we could continue on the lookout for opportunities to break out to Shetland with the first favourable slant of wind, as our predecessors had presumably done. It is a much better feeling to be reeling off the miles on roughly the right course in comfort than to be hove-to in a gale blowing rapidly back to your starting point, or sitting in harbour waiting for the wind to change. And so, whilst we did not turn south with alacrity, it was not with resignation either. Our idea was now to make Aalesund and there get some sleep and the radio that we certainly needed for weather forecasts. At 19 20 with the log reading 126.2 we turned on to a course of south by east, and at 19 40 the sail was already filling to a familiar and increasing southwester. The shades of the northeaster we had been promised that morning disappeared with their north-bound prophet along the stretch of coastal water to Trondheim for which they may have been true enough. We now settled down to an interesting but scarcely favourite evening's occupation, running in across a rising wind towards a rocky coast to hit off a narrow and unfamiliar entrance, by no means a main one, to the sheltered lead behind the skerries and islands on which we could see occasional breakers. By 21 00 we were close enough to land to see an unwelcome church: unwelcome because, though the captain was tolerably sure of his reckoning, and there was a church at Bud, on the north side of the entrance we were making for, it should have been still concealed behind the projecting shoulder of the great mountain to the north of it. It is the last infirmity of a navigator to suppose that any explanation of such a discrepancy is more likely than the obvious one that the ship is not where he thinks it is. If that *was* Bud church where were we? Luckily it was *not* Bud church, but the one at Fagervik, much less prominent on the Admiralty chart and three miles north of the gap we were seeking. With the freshening wind now well abaft the beam we were sailing on in fine style, but were naturally anxious about approaching the coast too soon, downwind of the entrance. The last half-hour of the approach, even with a diesel motor to fall back on and save the ship if need be, was a rare excitement. It is known I think outside small sailing ships only to glider and light aircraft pilots. This is not at all a silly attempt to devalue the rapid reactions of the professional seafarer or pilot of our century, with thousands of horse power (and pounds, dollars, lives) in his charge. But the satisfaction of playing off crosswind against current to come into the gap that you have chosen belongs to those without so much power at their disposal, a triumph of adaptation to the environment not domination of it.

The relaxation of the tension is perhaps the best thing about it. At 21 35 the crucial whistle buoy was at last firmly identified fine on the port bow, and we could see a large lighthouse beyond it. That was not yet certainly nameable, but the buoy to port meant that we were successfully round a chain of skerries it would have been risky to blunder across, and we knew we had a safe line in towards the light. An added blessing was a southbound coaster coming down on us from the northward. We were not too proud to reflect that followed for so long as we could hold her in sight, she should certainly get us through the initial complexities of the turn into the main lead, before she disappeared ahead, and so it proved.

After this eventful day the second night out from Trondheim began idyllically. At 22 45 Bjornsund light was abeam to port, with the log on 148.5 still showing good agreement with the saga's traditional *doegr sigling*, for the time under way from Trondheim was thirty hours, when the four hours at anchor in Kjorsvik is deducted. Once past Bjornsund light the coaster increased speed and rapidly outdistanced us, but we could see her sternlight leaving the islands of Lyngvaer to port and Orten to starboard and therefore did the same. The navigational hazards were now past and most of the crew, with only four hours' sleep and two meals in the last thirty-six hours, experimented to find the most comfortable, or least uncomfortable, disposition of twelve off-watch bodies. The Harofjord is wide, free of obstructions and well sheltered from the rapidly rising SW wind by a continuous chain of islands of which Haro is the largest though Sando the northernmost. The course was south by west until we came to Bjorno light (Bear Island, but not the one best known in Hull) at 03 50. The name reminded those about to go off watch of the Bjornsund light we had passed on entering five hours earlier, and suggests that the whole passage was for our predecessors 'The way to Bear Island' where you alter course to slightly east of south, diverging from Bredsund (The Broad sound) and the direct route down the coast.

We arrived in Aalesund at 05 00, waved enthusiastically onward to the very centre of town by the only living soul on the pierhead, to tie up in the narrow channel which cuts through from north to south and bisects the town and the long island on which it is built. As the ship's requirements could not be obtained before the shops opened at 9.00 a.m. the immediate priority was to establish which dockside café opened first. It proved to be an impressively glossy first-floor room at the end of the fish pier overlooking the harbour. Robin Bigland invited the crew to breakfast there, with traditional magnificence: that saddest of viking-age chieftain's nicknames, 'the mild but meat-stingy', could never have been applied to him. The crew needed no second bidding, though many second helpings, so that it sometimes seemed that our leading oarsmen were treading a sort of Faeroese ring dance from serving counter to table and back again. The rising wind blew sharp bursts of rain against the windows steamed up with the mixture of coffee and the omnipresent old-style shag tobacco smoked in pipe or cigarette, which replaces fish in the atmosphere when you get inside a Norwegian harbour café.

With a good breakfast under our belts we turned to our various jobs. Lying alongside in the centre of town we needed the spare sail rigged as an awning the length of the ship: there was no privacy on board amongst ourselves, but felt we had better not start by taking a whole town into the family circle. Captain Eddie was waylaid for an interview by the local paper, *Sunnmorsposten*, which he dealt with like a Yorkshire batsman facing some would-be subtle bowling. He explained simply that whilst it might well be necessary to ride out a gale in the open sea, nobody in their senses does so off a rocky lee shore with good shelter twenty miles away. Furthermore Aalesund had nothing to fear, as any rape and pillage would be carried out as peacefully as possible and one of our main targets was baths, as we did not want people to smell us before they could see us. At the time Eddie was saying this he did not know of the loss of two large yachts with only three survivors in what would have been our position had we continued southwestwards after our meeting with the fishing boat twelve hours before. It was characteristic of local journalism as we found it everywhere in Norway that before we left, early next morning, every crew member was given a copy for himself of the front page. It was well illustrated with photos of the *Raven*, and of Odd Børstad and Arne Wisth (as Odd's assistant cook, a well-known news photographer) consecrating as an honorary viking the leader of a visiting circus. Arnaldo paid his footing with invitations to that night's performance, and it was clear from the way the weather was developing and reports of ships in trouble were coming in, that we would still be in Aalesund that night.

There was a local exhibition on, as well, so all the hotels were fully booked, but we managed to negotiate the use of showers in both of them, and the Salvation Army very generously allowed those who wished to, to stretch out their bedrolls in the meeting-room and catch up on their sleep. Life beneath the traditionally striped boat tent was even by our standards cramped, and the spare mainyard which took up a good deal of deck space was advanta-geously disposed of to a contractor and turned into consumable stores, which were then consumed. It is a well authenticated way of passing time for sailing ships windbound in harbour. During the afternoon the original Colin Archer sailing lifeboat, now a yacht, came in and tied up astern of us. As she was the progenitor of such a noble brood which is to be found all over the world she was naturally of great interest to any sailing enthusiast, and the fact that under her old-fashioned but tremendously strong rig she had just arrived from the south lead where we were bound made her doubly interesting to us. The Norwegian Lifeboat Institution grant her, exceptionally, as the first of their line, the right to fly the lifeboat flag, and we were therefore in some confusion when she entered with the local lifeboat. They had had a hair-raising arrival ten hours after us and therefore through heavier seas.

The start of the circus was delayed that night, as we all stood in the crowd, swapping our various experiences during the day and looking at the clouds racing across the sky. The local fire-brigade were expensively hosing down the big top to shrink its flapping canvas, not nearly as well cut as our spare sail. It seemed ironical that the same wind which had made it possible for us to accept the tickets was about to prevent the performance to which they would admit us, but eventually the authorities were satisfied that the tent was safe, and the performance could begin. Small towns in Scan-dinavia must surely be the ideal field for circus in our century, and we vastly enjoyed the skill and humour which it is the essence of circus to convey across language barriers by not depending on language. The same methods proved efficacious for our younger Manxmen, and as some of us settled down on board that night to doze we could hear with sleepy amusement the return of other crew with new-found friends tempted by the prospect of viewing a viking ship by night. Some of the crew made out surprisingly well with the little Norwegian they had picked up, and probably did not sleep at all.

It seemed in some ways a pity that my more extensive knowledge of the language had to be devoted to a long conversation with the Bergen forecast office about their ideas on the weather for the next few days. Their head forecaster took a great interest in our voyage and went to considerable trouble to give us one of the best weather briefings I have ever had in the technical sense, though it was not a very promising one. The depression of 994 millibars just E of Shetland which was giving our present southwesterlies was only part of a larger depression stretching from Scotland to Norway and Iceland, with SW winds of 20 metres per second (or gale force 8 in English). The situation was fluid, but there was no question of departure before Wednesday morning at the soonest.

South of Aalesund you have to leave the shelter of the lead whether you will or not, for here the notorious cape of Stadland juts out through the coastal belt, making its exposed forked tip a sharp dividing line between the northern and the southern leads. This fifteen mile projection seaward has often played a decisive role in Norwegian history when some leader, stuck on the wrong side of Stad by contrary winds, has had to wait helplessly for his fate to be decided or the wind to change. The song of eleventh-century vikings in England, the *Lithsmannaflokkr*, shows that Stad was the recognised divide.

We left Aalesund for this, our next hurdle, at 06 00 on May 30th, log 185, with the forecast promising winds down to force 5. Our way out was simply to continue down the narrow channel through town in which we were tied up emerge on the south side of the island into Aspevagen. We turned to starboard round its western headland, Slinningsodden and headed down Heissafjord to yet another Broad sound, though this time spelt Breisund. Once round the point the course was dead to windward for the first fifteen miles to the bridge between Rimoy and Bolandet under which we passed at

10 00 into the Voldsundet. At the small port of Fosnavag, with the log reading 205.7, we paused for breakfast and a phone call to the Isle of Man to give our position and bring the office up to date on our present plans. We left at 11 35 under the southern bridge between Bergsoy and Nerlandsoy out into Heroyfjord. From here our course was southward down the fjord until at 13 30 we turned SW across the entrance to Rovdefjord and into Haugsfjord, skirting as closely as we dare round the little island group which gives the fjord its name. It was a bright and exhilarating day, and in these fjords the fresh wind raised only amiable little wavelets until we emerged into the two-mile-wide Vanylvgapet, south of the island of Kvamsoy, where the cloud coming up from the south was boiling down over the 1200-feet high mountains on that side, and a longer higher swell was curving round the Kvitnes or White Head towards which we were heading. Perhaps named from the white spray thrown up from the rocks at Kvitnesflu.

In the next hour the sea increased considerably as we came out of the lee of Stadland, which sheltered us at the same time as it obstructed our way south. Once clear of Kvitnes we could alter slightly back to the west again, to round Staalrev, the Steel Reef, which forms the northwest corner of Stadland itself, and we had this abeam to port at 16 00 on Wednesday May 30th. The *Raven* in the confused sea off the point was rising and falling, sometimes dropping into the same hole, sometimes shipping water over the rail between the first of the shields on the starboard side and the steeply rising prow. It was a disadvantage of being a two-thirds Gokstad that she had as it were a big ship's bow on a small hull; the more evenly rising sheer which a viking ship of fifty feet would probably have had would have kept her dry even in these conditions. But though not pleasant, and very very cold, the water shipped was not particularly alarming, and judicious use of our anachronistic but sensible lifeboat pump every half-hour kept the bilges dry. What was depressing was that it was quite clear that in these conditions we could make no way to the southward, and therefore could not possibly round Stad. It was small consolation that the two powered vessels we saw were making much worse weather of it than we were, throwing clouds of spray over their wheelhouses when they came over to have a look at us, and give us encouraging siren blasts. They were able to push straight into the seas, whereas we could barely hold our own, and even if with moderating seas we could get down to the south corner, we could certainly not weather the exposed thirteen-mile lee shore on the south side before reaching the lee of Vaagsoy, which at our present rate of progress was going to take more than twelve hours!

At the very tip of Stadland, between its two claws, is a small bay, Stadvaag, with an anchorage in the indentation on its western side, the traditional refuge for vessels in our position to avoid losing all they have won by running back into the Haug islands. The Norwegian chart of Stad (but not unfortunately the Admiralty one we had on board) gives a splendid 1:25,000 insert of this anchorage and the various skerries and submerged rocks at its mouth. We were clearly getting nowhere where we were, so at 16 10 put the helm up and went storming down the unpromising and wind-funnelling gap towards Stadvaag. As the soundings decreased from a hundred fathoms to twenty the seas naturally got steeper. We were now running before them, sometimes almost surfing, and Eddie, unrelieved at the helm, had beads of sweat on his forehead from the physical effort of holding her dead steady towards the spar buoy we were to round. Once inside the bay the seas diminished, and we began to look for the beach at its head on which, if the anchor would not hold her, we could run the *Raven*. Disappointment: no beach, but a wall of stone against which the waves from time to time foamed white, but never in one place there in the middle. Up on the hillside behind that place two large white triangles: seen through binoculars they are pyramidal beacons. They are the leading marks to the place where the waves never break. Rapture! The little side cove has been vastly improved by the addition of two solid breakwaters, overlapping one another from opposite thousand-foot high sides down which the low grey cloud spills onto the darker grey sea. The *Raven* slid through the gap and just carried her way to tie up alongside a local fishing boat somewhat anxious for his newly applied paint at the little jetty with its general store.

At 17 40 when we made fast (Log 231.5) there was not a soul in sight, but as usual in these apparently depopulated solitudes, by six o'clock every schoolchild in the country had brought his friends to sit on the fishing-boat rail and pass well-informed comment, some positive, some not, but all fortunately incomprehensible. Ten minutes later they were joined by those of their parents whose dignity had not permitted them to run or cycle, and more welcome to us, the shopkeeper, to re-open his shop in case we felt like a run ashore. We did, and Statvaag (or Honningsvaag as Eddie, with some support from locals, persisted in calling it) settled down to preparing to fit an extra day in between Wednesday and Thursday. By seven the arrangements for a beach barbecue of either half a sheep or twenty chickens were well under way, postcards were being bought and despatched, and *Odin's Raven* had almost disappeared beneath a cloud of drying clothing and sleeping-bags. Those of the crew interested in the World Cup were able to get invitations to watch it on the vast colour television sets which to a romantic taste might have seemed incongruous in this fastness. The night was obviously going to be a very cold one, but the vacant bunks in two fishing boats were available, so that only four slept on the *Raven*'s cluttered decks for the coldest night of the trip.

The festivities that night were not completely unclouded. The 18 00 BBC forecast, picked up without difficulty on the new transistor set we had bought in Aalesund had given SW force 5 to 6 for the Viking and Forties areas. The pressure round Britain was high enough, but between us and Shetland still lay an active trough. There was frost on our sleeping-bags next morning at six, and the flesh being weak we missed the Norwegian forecast from sheer inability to force already freezing hands out of the relative warmth of the sleeping-bag. Luckily by seven o' clock not only had conscience triumphed but the sun was higher and the air warmer. The forecast was well worth taking. We had become somewhat sceptical about them in this area of rapidly changing weather, but never of course doubted their descriptions of present weather, which was given as flat calm in both Trondheim to our north and Bergen to the south. Our experience the day before had convinced us that this was the weather we preferred for Stad, where there is always some wind, and the forecast had only moderate winds, all with some East in them. It looked like the sort of break in the weather we were looking out for, and we decided to start the crossing.

At 09 25 on Thursday May 31st we cleared from Stadvaag (Honningsvaag) with the log reading 231.5, and passed close to the south cliff, at the entrance from which the schoolchildren, given the day off to see us leave, waved enthusiastically. With a smiling sky and light south-easterly breeze it was difficult to recognise the Wagnerian landscape of yesterday. We had been told that the two new breakwaters through which we passed had cost two million kroner last year, and were all convinced supporters of what, as far as we were concerned, was the best investment the Norwegian government could have made. By 11 30 we were round Stadland, in 62° 09′ N, 5′ E and called up the Norwegian coastguard to tell them we were heading out for Shetland, or rather first the oilrigs, where we had an appointment to keep.

This time the weather forecast was as good as its word, apart from the so-called showers which as we neared the trough turned to a continuous drizzle, strangely more penetrating than sea spray, as the wind veered first southerly and then, to no one's particular surprise, to the west of south again. This was not however enough to bother us on our heading of West by South (Mag). We had rigged the spare mainsail as a bow dodger over a line running from forward yoke to bow, and though nothing like Magnus Andersen's water-tight cambered deck on *Viking*, it did provide a sheltered forecastle which had only one unforeseen disadvantage: it was so much the warmest and most attractive spot in the ship that an impromptu census at 04 00 on Friday June 1st showed that of the seventeen on board, twelve were sleeping, three deep in places, in the forward third of the ship, with effects on trim, rudder immersion, steering and general handling which may be imagined. Our total displacement at this time was probably a little under twelve tons, and the most tactful friend of our crew could scarcely reckon twelve of them at less than a ton. So it was necessary for the watch to spend an invigorating hour shifting all the sea chests as far aft as possible to balance this, improving the trim, but not doing much for the compass, where the helmsman craned over sea chests stacked on deck in two tiers. We must have looked like the first viking container ship on the North Sea route, and rolled steadily onwards at our by-now-taken-for-granted five knots, until the grey wet dawn of Friday found us faced with another humiliating navigational conundrum. I think it was Sir Alker Tripp who observed that the only thing calculated to make running aground more embarrassing is uncertainty about which continent is involved. Our triumphant joy at sighting the first oil rig at 08 15 on June 1st was slightly modified by complete uncertainty about whether it was the right one, or indeed which field it was in. More orange flames appeared through the grey drizzle ahead, a twentieth-century throwback to the beacon fires of old, and cynics asked how the vikings managed to find the way without these invaluable aids. By holding the reserve VHF carefully shrouded in plastic dustbin liners on one's knees it was possible to communicate with the rig radio operators but not to reach many firm conclusions about our position or which way to go.

No doubt future generations, if the rigs last so long, will develop a terminology, known to all, which can distinguish them, words like cutter, ketch and sloop, but at present, certainly to the Ravens, an oil rig is an oil rig is an oil rig, particularly glimpsed from sea level through drizzling mist. Their operators' classification of them by structure and burn-off boom meant little to us at first, but as Trekkfast observed, 'it's surprising how quickly you learn in this ship'. Our position signal, relayed to Kathy Lewis in the Isle of Man office at 09 00, gave it as simply 'in the Brent oilfield' (just about true, probably, by then) but we learnt quickly that Friday morning, picking our way through the artificial volcanic archipelago towards Ninian. It did help position-finding that the rigs have their name and number painted in large letters on the side. We were often inspected by the large crew-change helicopters on their continuous back and forth service but made our rendezvous with 'our' helicopter just after three in the afternoon.

There followed some very interesting manoeuvring which all previous viking ship seamen have been spared, for which viking ships do not seem well suited. What comes down must go sideways, the down-draught of the helicopter at the sea surface spreads rapidly outwards in all directions so that every helicopter carries its own little portable squall beneath it. As it banks away the air draught swings towards the ship, and you see the dark ruffled patch of water scurrying towards you. In the *Raven* we were pleased they were determined to take pictures that did us justice, but wished they would use a longer tele-lens, as the chopper was sometimes so close that not only did its draught disturb the set of the sail, but one had very little time to do much before hit by its departing airthrust as it banked away. The contrast between old and new in the North Sea was to be emphasised by a picture of our viking ship sailing beneath the burn-off flame of an oilrig, not an easy shot for the helicopter to take or for that matter for us to make possible. The rig's commander was naturally anxious about allowing a dangerous and unhandy anachronism anywhere near his rig's sensitive and expensive apparatus, and with his overheads per minute could scarcely welcome any interruption of work. He particularly did not want us anywhere near the flame, which is cooled by an injection of water which falls out from its underside as boiling droplets, so that the *Raven*'s passage beneath it, even for an oilskin-clad crew by now as inured to public relations men as to the hardships of the deep, was a real baptism of fire. This tense Wagnerian hour of very skilled shiphandling was forgiven by the rig, which hospitably enquired about the state of our supplies. As the rig was dry they could not supply the beer which we felt ready for, but their inflatable speedboat came bouncing after us with chilled soft drinks and warm sandwiches of superb steak in fresh bread. It was pleasant to see in close-up the rigs we had only previously known from above the clouds, and a better and more welcoming halfway house one could not wish to have. It meant that we viewed the crossing as made up of two separate steps, and we were high-spirited, refreshed and cheerful as, one more appointment ticked off, we set off from Ninian to Shetland at 16 15, log reading 402.

This complacency was momentarily upset an hour and a half later, when the helmsman, Richard, found the tiller waving wildly in his hands. The leather strop round the upper part of the rudder, in spite of all its careful anointing with preparations claiming to surpass the most expensive skin lotions, had broken where it was secured to the hull. It was fortunately not the main pivot, which had given so much trouble during the trials, but once got right had functioned perfectly ever since. At 17 45 we were lying stopped for repairs with 409 on the log, but with enough strong arms to hold the rudder in place it was not difficult to release the broken strap, pull more of it through the slot in the rail, and bore fresh holes for the securing bolts. It had been deliberately made long enough in the first place to allow this to be done, in case of need, and we re-assembled it without the metal plate beneath the bolt heads which, intended to spread the load on the strap, had actually done more harm than good by its unrounded edge. In little over a month the leather had cut itself through at this point, where rudder and leather flexed. We should of course have been inspecting it regularly for wear, but the problems with the main pivot had forced themselves on our attention by the deterioration in steering power, and I suppose we had begun to assume that what did not give trouble must be allright. At 18 10 we were under way again, pleased with the rapidity of the repair (which still showed no sign of wear on arrival at Peel) as we switchbacked slowly over a long swell. The wind was freshening from just west of south, and the rig had advised us that it might continue to do so, but as we were by this time only sixty miles from Shetland we had good hopes of being at least well in under the lee before the wind could become either strong enough or west enough to bother us. In the event it did neither, and the last night of the crossing was ideal.

The sunrise was beautiful, and over a perfectly clear horizon, enabling us to observe a good amplitude at 04 00 with the sun bearing 51°. Our course of Southwest by west magnetic on the steering compass was evidently equivalent to 250° True, and on this heading it had a deviation approaching 8° W, not surprising considering the many changes in stowage, and responsible for some of our difficulties the previous morning. We had shifted the heavy spare anchor and one of the liferafts (with its gas cylinder) right aft to just beneath the steering position. This was obviously not the ideal place, but room was so tight, and stability so important, that it had to be accepted.

Radio bearings with the Heron DF at 04 46 (Muckle Flugga 335M Bressay 250M) put us, optimistically it turned out, only 22 miles east of the nearest point in Shetland. At 05 00 the log reading 467 credited us with 65 miles through the water in the last thirteen hours, demonstrating once again that though it is very pleasant to have such aids as compass, radio DF and electronic log, there would have been scarcely any practical difference on such a voyage if one had worked off the traditional sun azimuth and the average five knot speed of the *doegr sigling*. And both these, unlike some more fanciful devices, *were* certainly known to viking navigators.

Just before six in the morning we could see, fine on the starboard bow, the white tower of the Out Skerries lighthouse brilliantly reflecting the rays of the sun shining down on it through the haze which to our incredulous delight gave promise of one of those ideally hot summer days that come so seldom to the northern isles but are so perfect when they do. By the time we could make out Whalsay and the high Kames on the Mainland beyond, at 8.0 a.m., there was no doubt about it. Our chilled and stiff limbs were thawing out rapidly and some cavillers were observing that it was going to be a very long and hot row in.

They were right. As it seemed most appropriate we were to enter Lerwick from the North, round the north end of Bressay and into Bressay sound between it and Easter Rova head on the Mainland. This meant heading into the northgoing stream and overcoming it. Out in the open sea it was not strong enough to require the unbroken efforts of sixteen men at the oars. We were thus able to enjoy the generous gift of the Scottish reporter who returned to Lerwick with enviable dash in his speedboat, and brought out to us some very welcome beer. From time to time Eddie could order those of us rowing forward of the mast to take in our oars, laying them across the ship, and relax for five minutes and as much beer as we felt was judicious in the forenoon beneath a blazing sun with many miles still to row. After half an hour it would be the turn of those abaft the mast to have their rest. The energy demanded of each oarsman when the sea is smooth and all hands are at the oars is not, over the four hours the approach to Lerwick took, exhausting, and the wit and beer flowed freely enough to underline that unique feature of Norse oared warships, that the rowers were, as far as we know, free men and not galley-slaves. Only in the last half-hour where the narrowing sound concentrated the adverse current did we fall silent and tug with a certain desperation at the oars.

At nine we were nowhere near the Sound, and the sun beamed on sky and sea of a fierce unbroken blue, both equally smooth and unbroken, except for the widening circles behind a playful porpoise to our left. The rings coalesced into a serpent pattern: the ship was covered with mildewed leathers and shapeless nameless sprawls of shaggy sheepskin which constituted shore-going viking costume, exhumed from beneath the deck-boards, and evidently denied the healthy light of day for far too long. The *Raven* at sea was never much of a treat for sensitive nostrils, and wherever viking ships carried their dried raw fish, it should now I think be regarded as settled that it was not hanging in the shrouds, where in drizzle it is apt to soften, stink, and drop gently on the deck or any sleepers below. But that Saturday morning was something special, and we had general sympathy, though some ribald disagreement, for the sensitive viking who declared roundly as he viewed his costume with horror 'This lot should have been up here, and me down there, – I don't need airing!'.

As we rounded the north tip of Bressay, the Lerwick pilot cutter leading us in with great skill and understanding motioned to us to move out on his quarter into some slacker water, a seamanlike welcome for which we were duly grateful, as we toiled away along the inner shore of Bressay to get enough upstream of Lerwick to display the sail as we stood across, to fulfil people's expectations of a viking ship. There was barely enough wind to fill the sail and even the graceful Shetland racing skiffs with their huge high-peaked sails over traditional double-ended clinker hulls could not make up against wind and that tide together. It was an interesting demonstration of the importance of oar and sail together to a viking ship, but we were all thankful when we could bring the oars in and hoist the sail.

The rather forbidding grey waterfront of Lerwick was concealed at ground level by an unbroken crowd the whole length of the extensive quays, and above them by brightly coloured bunting. As in Trondheim there was a band, and representatives of the Harbour Trust, but what caught the eye was the Up Helly Aa vikings, a good deal more resplendent and less mildewed than the Ravens. They were literally dazzling as they reflected the brilliant sunshine. After the briefest of welcomes we were led through the crowd to cars waiting to take us to the Galley Shed, where the Up Helly Aa galley is kept, for our first taste of Shetland hospitality. It proved almost overpowering, even for a crew in good physical fitness parched by a week's salt air and trained on Norwegian akvavit. Each crew man had been allocated to a Shetland host, and we went from the Galley Shed to our respective houses to bath and 'snatch ten minutes every ten', as our ship's jargon had it. (Robin had incautiously, in a radio conversation about how we slept, talked of 'snatching ten minutes from time to time'. The phrase was joyfully seized on and applied to those who would sleep for twelve hours on going to sea to repair the ravages of shore exertions. They simply snatched ten minutes every ten.)

In the evening we reassembled for a reception: refreshed by sleep we were soon to be even more refreshed by the magnificent cold table provided in the new Evening centre. After a week of conversing only with our fellows we all enjoyed meeting our hosts' friends on other tables and joining in different conversations. It often struck me in the course of the voyage that the organisation of social life in small harbours actually provides a much more relaxing sequel for a ship's company than the anonymous commercial provisions of a large port, such as, to take an example quite at random, the Hawk Club in Fredrikstad. Walking back along the quays at midnight and looking at the black bulk of Bressay on the other side of the sound, with the Up Helly Aa songs still in our ears (we had demanded them again and again from our hosts) we could reflect that we had reached the crossroads of the Scandinavian North Sea. If you set dividers at 200 miles with the centre on Bressay Sound, the circle you describe, two days and the intervening brief night of summer *doegr sigling*, will touch the Faeroes and Aberdeen as well as Bergen. It is this geographical position as well as the historical inheritance of the Norse Earls which explains the very special relation to Norway which one feels everywhere in Shetland. We went contented to sleep: in the words of *Beowulf* 'Tha waes sund liden, eoletes aet ende': the sea was crossed, water-travel over.

6

Lerwick to Skye

The stay in Shetland will never be forgotten by any of the crew, at least not the parts of it they remember. Our hosts took us around the islands on Sunday, and in the evening we all gathered again in the Galley Shed, the most appropriate setting imaginable, and swopped experiences and stories. By now we were all enthusiasts, almost addicts, for the Up Helly Aa songs and must have caused some pain to our generous hosts by our repeated insistence that they sing them again, when we invariably joined in ourselves and destroyed their own really professional polish. One musical Raven observed that they didn't just look like Wagner, they sounded like Wagner and he at any rate meant it as a sincere compliment. On this Sunday evening it was interesting to observe that the older and more experienced seafarers had attempted to turn out as smartly as possible in the circumstances, the younger and more informally minded in ordinary shipboard rig minus oilskins, wearing what had become almost *Odin's Raven* uniform, denims and a Helly-Hansen polar jacket. As 'uniform' was in the majority, those rash enough to turn out in suits paid the penalty at a late stage of the evening, or morning.

The morning, June 4th, was sailing day, though this time only for the hundred miles to Kirkwall in Orkney. As the arrival there was to be after midday, and the wind was at last easterly and moderate, an evening departure seemed best, taking the open sea during the night. The quay was as crowded as it had been for the arrival, and everyone who had a boat, which in Lerwick is almost everyone, was ready to escort the *Raven* on her departure, even on a cool grey evening with the halcyon weather of the last two days now over. Some were no doubt surprised to find they had difficulty in keeping up, as she stood across Bressay Sound under tightly braced sail just after 1900. Two faultless tacks without any assistance from the oars showed the onlookers, and the three Up Helly Aa vikings taking passage on board to Orkney, where two of them had never been before, how handy a vessel like the *Raven* can be, in spite of (or because of?) her antique rig. I was sorry to be seeing her from outside for the first time, from one of the escorting craft, as I had to leave to return to Hull University, which had allowed me almost a month's leave from a busy term to help with the first stages of the trials and voyage. But it was very good to see how closely she pointed and how certainly she stayed. As she cleared the south end of Bressay and emerged into the swell beyond, we were almost the last of the escort to leave her: that honour belonged to a small inflatable speedboat which bounced from wave-top to wave-top carrying the indefatigable accordionist jarl up the Up Helly Aa to give the *Raven* the most appropriate send-off imaginable, another generous dram and the strains of the well-loved songs once more. It took more than low grey clouds and occasional rain-flurries to damp the spirit engendered in that brief stay, particularly when the rain was carried on a good usable wind giving a six-knot speed as far as Fair Isle, abeam at 0100 Tuesday, June 5th. This good run was achieved in spite of the usual problem of the steady drift forward of a significant part of the weight, all seeking the best sleeping positions in the bow, with consequent effects on the trim which we had experienced on the crossing from Norway. Towards morning the wind dropped and so did the cloud, some of it to sea-level, giving patches of clinging damp mist which struck home after the glorious weather of the last two days which had already erased memories of the cloud and drizzle which had been unbroken before them.

As you travel southward in these latitudes at this time of year, particularly in a completely open vessel with no deck lighting, dawn comes to have more meaning, and soon after dawn North Ronaldshay could be seen through the mist and cloud with a sudden

definition that showed how far south we had come from Trondheim. The estimated time of arrival could now be passed to Kirkwall Harbour master, and was faithfully relayed by local radio
throughout the Northern Isles, but to keep it required use of the
engine again as the wind died completely, and the optimistic forecast could not be kept to under oars alone. The drizzle had now set
in with that gentle persistence which is so characteristic of the
Northern Isles, and perhaps of their inhabitants as well, so that
those who had acquired new jerseys in Shetland (and where better?)
had reason to be glad of them. In an open boat rain is less menacing
than wind, but not less chilling and uncomfortable, for it reaches
you even under the weather gunwale where wind and spray cannot,
and you must have something which retains its insulating properties
even when soaked, which many modern materials do not. It was a
welcome lift to the spirits of all on board to see how many people
who did not need to endure it had turned out in that weather to
welcome the ship in. You can argue that they are used to it, as foxes
are to being hunted (though I doubt that either can really claim to
enjoy it) but it is still a sort of courtesy peculiar to places where the
ship is the irreplaceable communication between scattered communities. Every harbour is scanned eagerly by people approaching
it from sea, never more so than when one fears to see a rival's
topmasts smugly projecting above the sheds. But as the *Raven* had
no rivals it was a detached curiosity which led to the lively discussion on board about the gaff-rigged red sails in Kirkwall. There
were enough connoisseurs of that rig aboard to recognise the
genuine signs of a vanished craft not yet ancient enough for anyone
to replicate as we had done with the *Raven*. It could only be a
Grimsby fishing-smack of the late nineteenth century, a sort of craft
which with crew scarcely less piratical than vikings, had also sailed
to Norway, often surreptitiously importing pianos! And then, with
the money, they bought lobsters to take home alive. In her way she
represented a culture which touched that of *Odin's Raven* and was
almost as remote from the present day North Sea. She was, of
course, Faeroese. Many of these old smacks, outdated by steam
when they were still in their prime, were sold to Faeroe, cheap, and
found there owners whose respect for them was such that some are
still afloat in Faeroe though none in England. They all have engines
now, much needed in the strong tides and sudden windshifts of their

new home, and would scarcely have survived without them. Local respect for the tradition embodied in the smacks sometimes took strange forms. A Faeroese friend (I cannot remember whether it was Sverre Dahl or Bjarni Niclasen, but name both to the saga to show my bona-fides) once told me that as teapots were found on the vessels when they were taken over in Grimsby – and who can imagine a British trawler without a teapot? – the new crews, although they drank their favourite strong coffee when fishing in their own fashion with longlines, would always brew up tea in the teapot when they were trawling, a good example of the continuous creation of fishermen's superstitions about how to ensure good luck at the fishery, though indignantly denied by all involved!

In relatively sparsely settled countries the accommodation of visiting voyagers has always presented problems. We can see from sagas and some provisions in early Norse shipping laws that it was usual for the crew to be widely distributed among hosts whose homes were often far from the ship, and so it was in Orkney. This dispersal, followed by concentration, is something that recurred in our voyage as well. One of the effects of living close together and completely mutually dependent during the voyage is that the greatest delight of arrival on shore is to split up and talk to strangers: for one evening, after which one misses the company of people who know the ship's reality, the in-jokes, who don't need to be any more considered than oneself in deciding whether to say or do anything. It was always glorious to arrive, change, bath and we were very lucky everywhere to find hosts, or, as we got south, hotels, to fall in with our needs. But everyone also welcomed the re-assemblies such as that at the Orkney civic reception on June 6th. The fish lunch was superb, even to people accustomed to Norwegian fish cookery and patriotically ready to defend its unapproachable superiority. But it was oddly moving to visit Maeshowe before it. The Runic graffiti there were left by Norsemen who had voyaged a good deal further than the Ravens, on this trip at least, for they had been to the Holy Land and back. A strange feature is the information that one of the inscriptions was cut with the axe that Gaut Trandilsson, a famous figure of the sagas, had owned before his violent death. Was it inherited or plundered? It must in any case have been more than a century old when it was used to scratch these graffiti on the stone walls of this dark burial chamber. That evening the crew of the

Faeroes 'slup', who were not fishing, but voyaging to the other North Sea islands in much the same spirit as the *Raven*, entertained us on board to some of those Faeroese delicacies which are, to the inexperienced English palate, worthy competitors of their Norwegian rivals. Perhaps the one least likely to appear as a dehydrated convenience food for the hasty gourmet is spik, the blubber of the grind whale, which has been compared, not invariably to its advantage, to fat Yorkshire farmhouse bacon in the days before Danish competition had compelled its improvement. The grind are caught by being shepherded ashore (by deadly shepherds) at the head of a fjord: a crowd of small boats, easily overturnable, blocks the exit to the open sea and beats the water with oars to frighten the grind ashore. Then the crews jump into the waist-deep water to kill the thick-packed whales. I've never taken part in one of these hunts though I have arrived the day after (a Sunday as it happened) on a beach whose sand was turned to mud by the blood of hundreds of grind. Even now, the grind is an important food resource, taken in a way that has not changed in a thousand years – no explosives, no electrics – and I find it odd that many good people who get their food in tins or health-food shops, want to intervene in this indisputably nauseating but, unhappily for this culture, essential scene. The past is much less offensive in museums, but it may be most important to notice that it is not yet dead outside them. Probably more of the everyday culture of the viking age is preserved in Faeroe, for good or ill (in fact, for both) than anywhere else outside museums. It was this sort of complex historical hangover (in every sense) which led to the running battle on the *Raven* at four next morning.

Six hours later, on Thursday, June 7th, the *Raven* sailed for the small island of Rousay, in acceptance of the kind invitation delivered by Major Ritchie, and arrived at 1330 minus two crewmen who had to follow by launch. The island has 200 inhabitants and one pub, and after a sensibly brief welcome the whole crew and the majority of the population adjourned there as a welcome refuge from the chilling mist. The attraction these islands had for migrants in the viking age is evidently not yet exhausted: many of the crofters on Rousay are emigrants, I had almost written refugees, from the great cities of the south. As the ship was not to leave Orkney until Saturday, some of the crew returned to the relative fleshpots of Kirkwall next day, whilst others dived after scallops which made a memorable meal cooked that evening in the pub. As so often on the voyage those who dived certainly got no wetter than those who remained above water, and the *ceilidh* which closed the day went on until long after midnight.

On Saturday, July 9th, the crew was complete again, and the course once more westward, at first with a fresh breeze on the quarter which later drew more and more ahead. The local crab-canning factory presented the ship with a large bag of crab-meat, but calculating eyes concentrated on the Fortnum and Mason hamper Robin had received, no doubt intended to console him for weeks of dried reindeer. He generously shared it, and one crew-member waxes lyrical about pâté de foie gras spread on oatcakes with a rusty sheath-knife and washed down with champagne and malt whisky whilst seated on the pitching gunwale of a viking ship. It is such an obvious entry for a 'memorable meal' contest that only the chilling recognition of what it would cost prevents me from trying to go one better. It is certain that no previous viking ship crew had such a meal, but surely equally certain that if they had had the chance they would have jumped at it?

The Pentland Firth can under the right (or wrong?) circumstances be as unpleasant as anywhere in the North Sea or Atlantic whose tides rush back and forth through it, so it was fortunate that Saturday was a better day than any since the previous Saturday when the *Raven* arrived in Lerwick. The sunset was almost too like a painting to be believable, and at midnight the dramatic silhouette of Sule Skerry with its isolated lighthouse was still clear against the afterglow in the west-north-west. We called it up on the VHF only to receive a reply from Oban coastguard, monitoring the calling channel, that the lighthouse, like that at Grip where we had first left Norway, is no longer manned. The steep cliffs, fitfully illuminated by flashes from the light, and the curious seals unpredictably pop-ping up to inspect the strange ship, formed a dramatic setting and it was hard to resist the temptation to go ashore. But there is no safe anchorage and with considerable regret, for thanks to the good weather there was plenty of time in hand, course was set for the Isle of Lewis once again.

The morning of Sunday, June 10, dawned fine, calm and clear, with the mirror surface disturbed only by a school of dolphins. Encouraged by the friendly silence with which *Odin's Raven*

advanced they came much closer than to a large power vessel, and
gave a display of various tricks which they seemed to enjoy as much
as the crew. In spite of learned comment that the attempted tail-
stands and clownish backward loops were done for various scientific reasons it seemed clear that the display was primarily what in a
human would have to be called sport. The continuous clicking of
cameras for almost an hour seemed only to urge them on to further
efforts. Can it be that these intelligent creatures are already cor-
rupted by human vanity? The point of view from which you see
things is often decisive, and only when you are so close to the sea
that you are standing on a deck actually at water-level, as was the
case in the *Raven*, do you really get the feeling of being at home, one
of the inhabitants, and not an outside intruder. The dolphins alas
were too wary to follow the *Raven* too close to land, and by
mid-morning dropped astern.

At midday a most attractive anchorage appeared, in the small bay
of Shefhader. As always, the arrival of a strange ship soon collected
a growing group on the headland, and the inflatable workboat was
excavated from the tight-packed stowage beneath the deck-
planking for a run ashore to the little jetty, so reminiscent of
Norway. The careful English of the older speakers was also oddly
reminiscent of Norway, but this time for a different reason. Gaelic is
still the first language for many in Lewis, and another fresher
memory of the western half of the Old Norse world was the technique of cutting peat in the moor above the anchorage, which we
had last seen outside Lerwick. The carefully kept island Sabbath
was distinguished by a welcome and thoroughly scriptural miracle
when crewmen who had thirstily accepted with gratitude an invitation to a glass of water found to their delight that between the tap
and their lips it had turned to a delicious lager beer.

It was a calm warm evening and the tent rigged from the striped
storm sail was perfectly reflected in the water seen from the dinghy
which was rowed away with plankton net in tow for a bit of marine
biology encouraged by invitations to bring us back a dolphin. These
idyllic interludes with the ship alone in a peaceful cove were always
welcome for the chance to sort out and repair gear and generally
clean up, which never seemed possible in the bustle in harbour,
and with sixteen men in such small space was only possible under
ideal conditions at sea. It was one of the times when the sense of

sharing the experience of previous voyagers was at its strongest.

Monday, June 11th, was fine and sunny to begin with, and the *Raven* was not due in Stornoway until 10 30. Mike and Colin put on their diving gear to inspect the 'straw-keel' added in Trondheim which gave an extra 6 in draught amidships. It was still firmly held by the metal brackets and screws into the side of the main keel. There was no wind, so the entry into Stornoway had to be made under oars and it was not even possible, as in Lerwick, to hoist the sail at the last minute, for it would only have flapped idly, and one may surmise that this too was common on earlier voyages. Only under ideal wind conditions can these ships have followed under sail the narrow path that leads into many northern harbours.

The Corporation of Stornoway entertained the ship's company to the traditional dram of welcome in the harbour master's office. It certainly did no harm at all to have a harbour master as captain, though loose talk of a harbour masters' mafia is much exaggerated. The crew, with careful tact, were distributed between three billets, one a castle. They were an old people's home, a school hostel, and a home for battered wives! The allocation must have caused some careful thought. The usual rhythm was repeated, of relieved dispersal soon followed by joyous reunion at the hotel where the reception was complete with piper and interchange of song and stories. It was after only the shortest of sleeps that the crew got up into viking gear for a raid on the local primary school which seemed more enjoyed by the sparkling-eyed 'victims' than the rather duller-eyed raiders. The aggressively cheerful victims were then carried off to sea in the *Raven* and demanded huge ransoms in the shape of autographs from their captors before they would consent reluctantly to go ashore again. That night, to give a change to the doughty cook and his assistant, dinner was in the hotel before sailing for Skye at 22 00 with a BBC 1 sound crew on board. The obvious dangers of this timing were not avoided, but are a part of such voyages. However unlucky it may be to sail on a Friday, anyone who has sailed at all knows that it is much unluckier to sail at closing time and so it proved. One of the very rare disciplinary interventions on the voyage was required, and like most thunderstorms it cleared the air. Cleared it indeed to such an extent that the rest of that night is one of the happiest memories of the voyage for many, with the *Raven* slipping along at three knots with six oars manned, bottles passing down the row of swinging oars at moderate pace, and those not rowing joining in the conversation from their sleeping place before rising to take a friend's place for an hour or so.

By dawn Skye was well abeam, and though it was the thirteenth it was Wednesday, Odin's own. To celebrate, and recuperate, the *Raven* anchored in a small cove beneath steep grass slopes and the crew went ashore to stretch their legs, some to fish, some to light a fire on the beach, and some to talk to the people who inevitably turned up from previously deserted landscapes whenever the ship halted. Seen from the summit of the precipitous pastures daringly grazed by a few agile sheep, the *Raven* with a fire burning beside her on the beach looked, as indeed she was, an emblem of the viking age. She attracted the eye of the master of the local school, as well as the BBC TV camera, and soon smoked mutton and dried reindeer-meat were being cautiously sampled by his more daring pupils in the cause of history or geography or curiosity. One unforeseen spin-off of the voyage was the presentation of a clear and material picture of their own past and the former importance of their own bay to the children of flourishing but secluded schools for whom the television world is, though familiar, far away. This too was one of the links between one side of the North Sea and the other.

It was extremely unfortunate that the arrival in Portree was not to be until after 18 00 as the weather got steadily worse all day, and the steep hills above the bay, earlier so green and beautiful, were by sailing time beginning to lose their clear outlines beneath cloaks of grey cloud, and looked depressingly reminiscent of the cliffs on the north side of Stad when there was a gale on the south side. The *Raven* arrived at Portree at 19 00 in pouring rain and a distinctly choppy sea, but the number of people who had turned out to welcome her had its usual reviving effect upon the crew. As the rain increased in virulence the crew left the quay at a brisk and purposeful trot, more shelter-seeking than storming: as most were already soaked they managed to get to the hotel without getting any wetter, and gave a foretaste of the spirited performance put up at the dance that night, when cold cramped limbs rapidly loosened in some unusually lively reels.

Next morning, Thursday, June 14, the rain was still falling on the ship and the duty watch, but it did not discourage the crowds of child visitors, who took some shifting at midday when the job began of making ready for what was obviously going to be a tricky afternoon's filming for BBC TV. The assessment was such that even adult visitors were told that they could not be taken. Only six of the crew were going and the decks were cleared for action by landing some kists as the sea chests were often called. It was thus with braced nerves that they took *Odin's Raven* out to see what could be done in wind and sea as bad as anything yet, and as they were to discover, more treacherous. One almost has to draw on the terms of Old English poetry, always good at combining exultation in the beauty of a ship with a sense of foreboding, to describe the *Raven* as she shot southward, slicing through the waves as she was still sheltered by the hills. But these hills make their own whirlpools in the air, and one of these 'scarcely charted currents of air' swept round the ship as she tacked, changing its direction and backing so suddenly that the ship went right round through more than 180 degrees with the sail still full and drawing on the same tack before at last the mainsail reluctantly filled on the new tack. The BBC were delighted with the dramatic quality of the footage, and the *Raven* had barely recovered from this tack, when the wind suddenly veered, flying back to its earlier direction and shooting up to near gale force. The tack was right forward and the sheet hard in to fill the sail as close to the wind as possible, when the wind freed. The endless sheet running from one clew to the other is a feature of the femboring rig which saves some time in rapid short tacking with a small crew but has drawbacks in such a crisis. Even when the sheet was fully out the priare still held three-quarters of the sail full of wind, and as the hull had little way through the water there was inertia to overcome before she could start moving and absorb the increased energy by acceleration as she usually did when she was flying along in winds of this strength. It is an inescapable limitation of light craft without ballast keels that they can exploit successfully incredible strengths of wind providing they are not dead abeam, as every sailing dinghy sailor knows or soon discovers. All hc has to use instead of such a ballast keel with its leverage is his own weight. A viking ship caught like this is like a vast racing dinghy knocked down, and that she is also her crew's home is their misfortune not the wind's. Robin recalls the first little white flecks of water spurting through the oarports, and of recognising the reflection in other faces of his own incredulity, before the darker green water curled in over the rail and down through the loose deck-planks like a wave about to break. To ensure that no one was carried down with the ship if it went, all went into the water over the lee rail as it went under and got clear, to avoid being tangled in the rigging. The only casualty to suffer that fate was Robin's woolly hat, an ancient friend and comforter which got caught up on one of the shroud blocks as he was returning to the surface. In less than a minute everyone was back on board, though this time outside the hull, perched on its upturned starboard side, reflecting philosophically that they were really not that much wetter than usual, and the water was nowhere near as cold as they had feared. But everything that would float was washing away as the *Raven* lay on her side with the mast lying on the surface of the water.

The cameramen, in the best traditions of cameramen the world over, took no notice and went on filming, occasionally no doubt complaining about the quality of the light or the angle of the hull. A camera viewfinder isolates you from the rest of humanity almost as much as a gunsight: I once saw a grandfather filming his beloved grandson riding his new tricycle round a garden swimming-pool and eventually into the deep end, and I could still hear the camera running as I reached across to lift the lad out. Once the footage is secured there is nothing actually in their contract which specifically forbids saving life at sea, so the BBC ship approached the by now somewhat impatient *Raven*'s crewmen, whose first expectation was that they were probably going to be asked to do it again so the cameramen could get one or two reverse shots. This was unfair as the eternal quest for perfection took second place to realisation that to do that would involve righting the *Raven* first: it was also a pity as the Ravens had devoted some time to polishing the finer points of possible replies as they strove to keep as much as possible reasonably close to the ship.

Two attempts to right the *Raven* were made with a rope over the hull but both failed and it was evident that with the means disposed of there was little hope of success in the seas which the freshening wind had raised. Though no one would undertake such an experiment deliberately it was good to know that a viking ship of this type in full cruising trim with drinking water etc will float even when flooded with enough of the hull above water for the crew to perch on. This would scarcely much prolong their expectation of life in mid-Atlantic, but it must be remembered that the majority of viking voyages were coasting ones and almost always in company with other ships, so that the difference between a collected crew well out of the water and scattered individuals swimming around with only their heads visible is a very important one. It also has obvious implications for the question of ballast and probably some bearing on the loose deckplanks. Modern femborings and cobles carry their ballast in the form of large stones off the beach so that if they do go over the ballast may spill out and the ship still float. It is tempting to speculate (but not at all tempting to try) that a full crew of oarsmen, trained to the job, *might* be able to right the hull with the mast down. The important feature is that the *Raven* floats with mast level so that in a long drift she would be likely to take the shore with her keel against it. There are many stories in sagas and later accounts of crews being rescued from such hulls, and whilst they are obviously not lifeboats their ultimate safety in suitable waters is probably higher than later successors.

The only thing to be done was to tow the *Raven* back to Portree, a difficult job in which more damage might easily have been done: but she was always lucky in the skippers who towed her, and the skipper of the *Ferrara* was no exception. One of the liferafts of the *Raven* was inflated to provide a floating stowage for the various items spreading from her hull like a surrealist oil-slick of *objets trouvés*. The only oil on board was a souvenir bottle of North Sea oil given us by the oil rig. Robin had actually been able to get his hand to it as he surfaced but was unable to climb back on to the hull with it, but very many things that might have gone were saved, including, surprisingly, both stones from Trondheim cathedral and, eventually, the tree as well. The *Ferrara*'s inflatable workboat was launched in a sort of mad whale-hunt after wallowing sea chests and half-empty plastic water-tanks.

It proved impossible to raise Portree harbour on the VHF, but a friendly and helpful fishing vessel replied instead and did yeoman work collecting more of the floating gear. By evening the *Raven* was back alongside in Portree, upright once more but on the bottom with only mast and stems above the water to show her position. The rest of the crew sadly looked down at their submerged home, like men visiting a sick relative in hospital, before going in no very festive mood to the dance at which they had to choose a 'Viking Princess'. They did much more than look, but set to work themselves to effect the cure. There was much to be done before low water at 4.00 am, and Robin had some tricky phone calls to make almost before he had dried out. The Fire Brigade agreed to attend at low water as the speediest way to get the hull pumped out, and Macrae's garage, recommended as the best people for the job, lived up to their reputation by agreeing to start stripping out the diesel as it emerged above water. Robin rang his wife to ensure that crew families in the Isle of Man knew exactly what had happened and were not shocked by the inevitably dramatised accounts in the press.

What had happened was dramatic enough in all conscience and had done considerable damage to the modern features of the ship, and to some works of art like the weathervane, lost in the capsize, as was the spare sail which doubled as boat-tent. But the ship herself and her basic propulsion of sail and oar were undamaged and a viking ship of this type in the tenth century might well have been able to continue her voyage next day. By five in the morning the *Raven*, after a night's work by the whole crew and many friends, was beginning to lift to the incoming tide, and as one of her crew brightly observed was in no worse shape than some scruffy viking ships had been at their best, though now without engine, radio and electronics.

Friday, June 15th was the sort of day that many previous viking voyages must have experienced. Every skill to be found among the very variously capable crew was exercised to the full, and many had to develop skills they didn't know they had. First the *Raven* had to be thoroughly cleaned out, for even the clear deep Atlantic water of the west has a surprising amount of material in suspension, and the water of Portree harbour is even richer in nutrients. Some wit observed that Mike's plankton net should have reaped its richest harvest of the trip. Those with any claim to manual dexterity set to work to repair the chests that had come apart after their battering, others sawed deck planks to replace those that had floated away. Two returned in triumph in a dinghy with two local lads, having retrieved an oar that would have taken hours to fashion afresh. Next day was Saturday but work continued unabated: instead of salt crystals in the hair it was now sawdust, but the resistance to the

passage of a comb was the same. Robin had an infinity of arrangements to make, which all fortunately functioned properly, so it was
as well that he was eventually able to unwind at an overnight *ceilidh*
which finished at eight in the morning as a celebration of the success
of the magisterial improvisation of the day, or dawn before.

One reason why almost all who sailed in the *Raven* are a trifle
impatient with people who say, as many still do, 'You really
shouldn't have had an engine', is that quite apart from the factors
discussed earlier we all regard the engineers at Bukh as some of the
most reliable friends we have. A telex which arrived with them at an
ungodly hour elicited the rapid response that there was a newly-sold
engine of our model in Glasgow, but that they were getting in touch
with its new owner to assure him of airmail replacement of any part
he would allow the service people to cannibalise off his engine on to
ours. Fortunately he generously fell in with the proposal, and
Macraes' sent a car to Fort William to meet him, so that by 11.00
am the old love-hat relationship was in full swing again, as after
twelve hours' total immersion the sound our purist vikings loathed
and our old hands were glad to fall back on was reflected off the
quay wall. It couldn't prevent a capsize of course, and represented a
substantial part of the work necessitated after one, but it was still
the knowledge that it was there that made the voyage defensible.

In deference to local sentiment, and also exhaustion of the flesh,
Sunday was at least half a day of rest, though on their various
excursions people kept their eyes open around the beaches for items
of the ship's gear and had some successes. Odd and Shane arrived
back with a sleeping-bag and an oar looking rather like the traditional disgruntled seaman off on his way inland determined not to
stop until someone asked him what that thing was for.

Monday, June 18th, was celebrated with a jousting match under
oars against the crew of *Goosander*, and the finishing touches in
securing new gear in place of that lost, so that on Tuesday the
nineteenth *Odin's Raven* was ready to sail again after four days of
unremitting work by all concerned and many generous friends who
put themselves to much trouble to share that concern. In the early
morning the last replacement joinery was collected from the work-
shop and bags of shingle ballast loaded to lock the stable door. It
was 14 00 when a large, sympathetic and cheerful crowd watched
the *Raven*'s indomitable crew row her out of Portree. Soon after

that another important item of her complement was restored by the passing ferry which had picked it up after the capsize, and the small Norwegian tree which had been doing a little independent voyaging of its own (a very Norwegian thing to do) completed the tally of the gifts being brought from Trondheim. A fitful wind was only occasionally usable to help the *Raven* on her way south to Tobermory, but she was under way again.

7

Mull to Man

The Isle of Mull came into sight as darkness came, but the *Raven* was not due in Tobermory until 10 30 the following morning. It was soon too dark to find the way safely into any creek that would give a sheltered anchorage, and the gathering clouds which had speeded the onset of darkness shed a persistent West Highland drizzle on the *Raven* and her crew as they stood on and off between the headlands on opposite sides of the sound, and waited for the dawn. The position was five miles north of Tobermory, and the course straight over someone's unbuoyed crab-pots, picking up a piece of buoyant rope and bending the propeller shaft in the process. Next time the engine was tried, on leaving Tobermory, it had to be run at no more than half revolutions, and remained like that until the end of the voyage. The ship was put alongside a small jetty for breakfast, and the frying-pan went over the side. In spite of determined efforts it proved impossible to recover it from the icy water which seemed at least as cold as in Trondheim. Not much of a night was the general opinion. The arrival in Tobermory was somewhat dampened too: partly by the weather, partly by the uncomfortable and sleepless night and partly no doubt by the reaction after the efforts in remedying the capsize. The BBC Scotland TV unit, perhaps feeling that they had some leeway to make up, were assiduous in filming, and interviewed those crew members who wanted to talk to them. Another unit, from the programme 'Look North', had been lucky in getting extremely beautiful shots of the dramatic coast of Skye, and came to Tobermory to round off their film as well.

Thursday June 21st began with the invariable chore of pumping out the overnight rainwater from the ship, but as the rain continued the crew returned to the Western Isles Hotel, where a notable champagne banquet did wonders for their morale that evening. It will be interesting to see whether the TV footage of Odd dancing stripped to the waist and accompanied by Arne on a xylophone of vodka and orange glasses can ever be released for family viewing.

On Friday a large crowd gathered on the quayside in spite of the adverse weather, to watch the *Raven* depart into a freshening 4–5. The evident expectations of the more sensation-seeking were disappointed; 'there were no wrecks and no one got drownded, in fact nothing to laugh at at all'. A gale was forecast, but everyone was keen to get on to Oban. The Highland Tourist Board's twin-hulled thirty-knot *Highland Speedbird*, out ahead, reported that the wind was in fact moderating, and down to Force 2, so the Ravens pressed on through the rain to arrive wet and bedraggled in Oban only eight hours after leaving Tobermory.

After the plush environment of the previous nights the hard floor of the youth club basement was a shock to the system as well as the hipbone, though no harder than the *Raven*'s deck, and the older members of the crew eagerly accepted invitations from rapidly cultivated acquaintances to sleep elsewhere. The next day, June 23rd, was a Saturday and as Oban was full of tourists, many of them American, the ship being tied up alongside the quay had a continuous stream of visitors whose zest for questions about the voyage was never-tiring. The same could not be said of most of the crew, who had been answering such questions for a month already, but some good-heartedly donned their viking gear, to the warmly expressed appreciation of the visitors. The most widespread cliché in the eighteenth-century picture of the viking was that he looked forward to drinking from the skull of his enemy in Valhalla. It was a misunderstanding of a complicated Old Norse poetic kenning or metaphor which called a drinking horn 'the ornament of the skull'. It threw an odd light on that old confusion to see Americans eagerly photographing one shameless crewman whose helmet had been filled with beer in a local bar, so that he could drink from it. It is to be hoped the pictures do not figure in the controversy about whether vikings had horned helmets and if so whether they drank out of them (the answer is no).

On Sunday, June 24th the crew dispersed to follow their own inclinations which took Shane and Knut to Fingal's Cave and others to less augustly romantic destinations, but as usual all gathered in the evening at a reception. At the same time those on watch on board were able to arrange, with the enthusiastic co-operation of the local police, a less formal reception on board. Partly because of this, and partly to avoid arriving too early in Port Ellen, the ship did not leave Oban until 3.0 pm on June 25th. The weather was as usual blustery, with gusting squalls of rain, and the spectators could certainly not accuse the Ravens of being only fair weather yachtsmen. The way to Islay took the ship past the Small Isles, and the teacher there had asked her to sail close inshore so that his school too could get a good view of something that formed part of their history. The children, waving energetically from the jetty, seemed no more than matchstick figures that had escaped from the towering mills of a Lowry painting to a freer world where the masses and chimneys were islands and rocks.

Between the north tip of Jura and the steep-sided island of Scarba is the infamous whirlpool of Corrievrechan. The experience of sailing by it in an open and flexible hull is unforgettable. It is easy to get used to the rhythmic noises as the ship lifts to the swell in the open sea, but here the water from time to time goes glassy smooth, until a new crest seems to unfurl from somewhere deep below the seething surface, bending the ship and next minute rising into a five- or six-foot breaking wave. The waves seem stationary, and it is only when you lift your fascinated eyes from the continually changing surface that you see how the rocks close to shore are racing by, and realise from the foam creaming up the distant cliffs how large the sea outside the hurrying stream is, and how rapid is the ship's onward rush. The 'giant hand' is less of a joke in Corrievrechan, when you can feel it plucking at the bottom of the rudder, tugging at its fastenings, and vibrating the tiller in the steersman's hand. How, we wondered, did the killer whale passing us feel when he dived into such turbulence? Was it at all like the unexpected ups and downs of an aircraft flying through a front?

Safely past the whirlpool it was time to anchor at midnight when in these southern latitudes one can no longer safely manoeuvre near

to rocky coasts. That night the temperature fell below freezing
again for the first time since we left Stad, and it was a stiffly
reluctant crew, still bent into the crouches in which they had spent
the night, that crawled about the ship at 10.00 am on the morning
of the 26th to weigh anchor and move on to Port Ellen. Between
Jura and Islay there were five Campbeltown fishing vessels happily
engaged in cutting their own throats by illegal scallop-fishing in
broad daylight. This illegal over-fishing is something that short-
sighted fishermen have always done, unless prevented by their own,
or someone else's patrol boats. They had many sackfuls piled up on
deck and would probably argue that as the overfishing was going to
happen anyway they had to get them whilst they could. The same
men would of course have been playing the martyred saint to their
MP had a single foreign skipper been found doing the same, but if
fishermen were not blind to long-term returns they probably
wouldn't be fishermen. With the VHF on the fishing boat channel it
was possible to savour the intership discussion about the *Raven* and
the probable sanity of her crew. Lord knows what they must have
made of the next passers-by, a small fleet of kayaks which caught up
with us soon afterwards, reminding more than one of the very
similar scene in the Vinland sagas. These hardy souls, unlike the
Skraelings in every way but one, were not interested in strips of red
cloth, but did, like them, accept food and drink. They got very wet,
as in that lop the *Raven* was knocking up a very confused wash
along her lee side and it was an unusual and warming experience for
her crew to see people colder, wetter and even closer to the water
than they were; everyone was sorry to part from them in sight of
Port Ellen.

The crowd waiting on the jetty there made a striking splash of
colour, standing out against the no-nonsense background of the
town. The welcome had the extra warmth associated with an island
one, for the attitude of island communities to voyaging in a traditional ship is inevitably different from that of mainland towns
whose inhabitants have no need to voyage if they don't want to.
There was a piper, and though the lilting voices of the school choir
could not of course begin to compare with the stentorian Up Helly
Aa vikings of Lerwick, the song the children sang had more to do
with the old Kingdom of Man and the Isles, than Wagner and
Sullivan. It was the song of Gorry Crovan, the perfect choice,

reflecting the serious and intelligent interest in their past which keeps the past alive, in an un-museum-like way, in all the Northern Isles. Gorry Crovan is the Gaelic Hebridean form of the great King Orry of Manx tradition, who died in Islay after ruling sixteen years. The crew visited his grave later, and though he would probably have preferred something stronger than a bunch of flowers, it is likely that he welcomed a token from a ship that had sailed from Trondheim and was bound to Man.

Robin Bigland's meeting with an old friend, Rod Walker, was an echo of a more recent and very different world. They had last met in Piccadilly, where Rod was deputy general manager of the Athenaeum Hotel, and both were wearing city suits. Now he ran the Machrie Hotel, in Islay, and the crew, falling on their feet as usual, moved joyfully in to the comfortable small cottages attached to it, to savour once again the luxury and good food so much more enjoyed after a day or two in the ship. The golfers on board went for a round or two on the famous Machrie links (not, mercifully, in their viking gear: an instinctive reverence told them that some things are too serious for joking) and returned for a *ceilidh* on the evening of the 27th which marked the first meeting with the crew of HMS *Odin*, and showed the wisdom of accommodating melodious mariners away from the main building of the hotel.

Next morning no one, including the hotel staff, was very interested in early rising, but two resourceful and relatively clear-headed Ravens, Robin Bigland and Shane Lucas, got the preparation of breakfast under way in the hotel kitchen to be joined in turn by various members of the staff who were not, as they might have been, put out at finding their kitchen taken over. After breakfast *Odin's Raven* sailed in search of *Odin*. The fog was thick enough in places to make it seem that the raven might have to fly back the way it had come as Floki's did, but eventually this quest, a strange one for a viking ship (like looking for a submarine in an archipelago, someone complained) was successful, and she came up with *Odin* some two miles offshore. Even more eventually the BBC helicopter, rather a failure in the submarine-spotter role, was talked to the spot by its two victims on their VHFs, and filming in every direction began. Crews were exchanged: *Odin* only had one crewmen dressed as a viking. Thanks to the prompt generosity of the Up Helly Aa vikings the damage of the capsize to the appearance of the

Ravens had been remedied by the loan of some of their gear from Shetland. Both crews once on board the other ship marvelled how its crew could stand it, and once back on board their own expatiated on the decadent luxury they had found on the other. *Odin* dived and surfaced, and the Ravens in her were amazed to find people with even less spare room than they had, though, as one wistfully observed, a lot less fresh air as well. *Odin*'s crew, on the look-out for signs of the usual claustrophobia in the crew of *Odin's Raven*, concluded that providing the air was warm and not doing twenty knots round his bearskin the average viking didn't bother greatly about its pressure or fume content, after a month's North Sea air in embarrassing quantities. Whilst dived, the Ravens had the anachronistic pleasure of viewing a viking ship through an attack periscope – a war film yet to be made, but a sure-fire combination of cinematic clichés.

On return to terra firma there was an inspired visit to an hospitable distillery, the one institution to which you could take the crew of *Odin's Raven* in the hope that they would show as much enthusiasm and discrimination as in a maritime museum. In both they spoke with the authority befitting an end consumer talking to suppliers, and a consumer of wide experience at that. There are still museum directors with viking ship models in their collections who remember the day they explained an interesting feature of its rig to a Manx viking, and almost the only topic on which the crew had more opinionated prejudices than the rigging of viking ships was malt whisky. The Norwegians had largely been protected by the fiscal policy of a kindly government which made it almost impossible for them to get any experience of it, even at fifteen pounds a bottle, but it is always possible for a Norwegian to argue from principle if experiment is lacking, and the visit of *Odin's Raven* to Bowmore distillery had a predestined appropriateness about it. The distilleries in Islay are justly famous and their products are exported all over the world, difficult as this is to credit when you see how much is consumed locally. It should not be assumed that the consumption in celebrating the arrival of a shipload of guests is a measure of the normal: for it could not be and still leave a surplus for export. The crew of *Odin's Raven* were capable of holding their own in most companies, and it was rarely that the ship left an island without some rueful local champion, arm round one's shoulder for support as much as friendship, confiding that the ship's visit had been the session of his life. Even old men were heard to compare events with the best years of the herring fishery, and in the Northern Isles that, if not necessarily praise exactly, at any rate means that something out of the ordinary has happened.

It was with considerable regret that the *Raven* left Port Ellen at 3.0 pm on June 30th before a freshening northerly wind for a splendid sail past the now regrettably well-known Mull of Kintyre. An unidentifiable submarine, not our friendly *Odin*, surfaced and her crew waved silently, only four cables off our port side. By nightfall the wind had backed to NW and raised a steep following sea. To keep the ship dead before it required constant attention to trim as well as rudder, and on one occasion sleeping crew men were rudely awakened by a wave which broke all along the starboard side and sent a fair amount of water over them, requiring the exercise afforded by pumping to warm them up again. It was probably a cross-sea reflected off a face some distance away, but indicated another reason why, on an intersected coast like this or the Norwegian, it was not regarded as a good idea to sail at night when the run of the sea, particularly astern, cannot be seen as clearly as these hulls require to meet it properly.

The seventy miles to Port Patrick took just over twelve hours (a good *doegr sigling*), so it was just after three in the morning when some nightowls of the little port reassured one another that that was indeed a viking ship nosing between the piers. They found this an excuse to prolong a party and insisted on a representative delegation from the ship accompanying them. After twelve hours before a cold north wind the prospect of warmth was quite inviting, so Colin, David and Robin agreed to accompany them whilst others settled down to sleep and others prepared a raid on one of the Manx yachts which had come up to meet the *Raven*. Their excuse, delivered with anticipatory glee, was that the victims were friends of theirs. How, I wonder, would they treat an enemy? After sampling the hospitality of Port Patrick, the delegation made the best breakfast it could in the Port Patrick Hotel under the attentions of a waiter who seemed to be an ex-TV chatshow compere who had been fired for garrulousness and lack of subtlety. But that may be just their impression: it takes a light hand to carry off jokes about ascribed sexual prowess at breakfast-time, particularly to total strangers who have been up all night.

After breakfast the local torture chamber was put at the delegation's disposal: a small bedroom cunningly situated at the foot of
the main staircase which was in constant use by children intent on
seeing whether they could manage the last four stairs in one jump,
and quick to denounce any cheat who only jumped three. After a
stormy night even this failed to prevent sleep for long, but it was
agony whilst it lasted. When sleep did come it was interrupted at the
request of one of the local council who was disturbed to see that a
vessel for which a civic reception at three pm had been carefully
prepared (including, guess what, TELEVISION!) was already tied
up in the inner harbour, with its crew sleeping off their various
exertions in full view of everybody, thus compromising that sus-
pense so vital to a good public event. The idea that in a strong
northwester in the night, with nowhere else to go, one might as it
were enter Port Patrick *faute de mieux*, was to him novel, but he was
touched by an account of hardships undergone that had even Trekkfast reaching for his handkerchief, and even more touched by the
offer to go away and come in again at the right time.

So out to sea again went the *Raven*, to be escorted in by the
lifeboat, an escort unnecessary for the *Raven* but no doubt welcomed by the Manx pleasure boat whose passengers crowding to
the side with a good view of the *Raven* gave it an alarming list. On
this occasion there was a pipe band and a rather more formal
reception than that twelve hours earlier. Eddie brought the *Raven* in
under sail not only through the narrow outer entrance but right up
to the inner harbour, a good demonstration of what can be done by
these hulls with a suitably handy rig and an experienced crew,
which shows that it was well worth rigging them like this and that
some were probably so rigged.

On Monday a rehearsal was held for the arrival at Peel. The
harbour was now full of Manx yachts which had come to meet the
Raven, and to enable all the crew to play their parts, friends from
the Isle of Man, John Martin, Stuart Callister and Jan Maughan
played the parts of the Bishop, the Governor and Lady Paul. The
Raven was beached with two crewmen wading ashore with springs
to hold her steady, the crew formed a half-circle and the chief
rehearsed his speech and the presentation. It was to be a sort of
ironic revenge for those few occasions on which the *Raven* had not

precisely fitted in with the careful ceremonial plans of others that
her arrival at Peel was to produce such genuine mass enthusiasm
that this carefully rehearsed ceremony almost became a beach battle
such as the Old English Chronicle describes, and the chief had to
make his presentation whilst fending off a small boy who was
attempting to relieve him of his sword.

That night, for the last time on the voyage, Robin Bigland entertained the crew to dinner with his usual combination of generous
hospitality and good sense. The former, in the provision of one
bottle of chablis and one of claret 'at each rowlock' as the old
formula has it, and the pre-prandial champagne and canapés. The
latter, in his private intimation to the management that it might be
as well if the banquet were to be held somewhere off the beaten
track rather than in the main dining-room, where other guests
might not always understand. In this he did both the crew and the
other guests an injustice. As the evening wore on the whole hotel
was inevitably sucked into the vortex, and the guests were to be seen
watching with a horrified fascination every detail of the proceed-
ings around, on, and under, the surface of the hotel's swimming
pool. The prudence of those vikings who thought to remove any of
their clothing before entering the danger area was rendered nugat-
ory by diligent galley-boy/photo-journalist Arne Wisth, who moved
around the pool like a small troll from a Marx brothers' *Peer Gynt*,
carefully collecting the neat piles and consigning them too to the
deep. Even the hotel manager arrived in time to join in the fun,
though there can be no excuse for the loss of his jacket sleeves which
he very fortunately took in good part.

This was clearly a difficult party to follow, but when it dispersed
in various degrees of viking dress, denims and dampness, it was still
early enough for normal sane guests (as they would no doubt put it
themselves) to be still around in the corridors with smiles ranging
from the awed to the nervously ingratiating. Several Ravens felt that
these good kind people really wanted to join in and should not be
left as outsiders, but they were fortunately overpowered by vikings
with a surer social grasp, and the crew adjourned without further
incident to several very successful sequels on Manx yachts in the
harbour.

The long voyage of 1,800 miles in an open boat and the six weeks
of hard living and common effort required some lightning discharge

and could not have had a better one. Nor could it have been at a better-chosen time. The following day was free, to recuperate, except for a brief rehearsal, and on the evening of July 3rd dinner was a very sober affair. After the exultation, and the relief that nothing had gone irreparably wrong, and that the voyage in spite of foul weather had been successfully accomplished to schedule, came the sadness of recognition that it was over, and anxieties about the daily progress of the ship were overtaken by the concerns of life to which the crew were returning. How had things gone in their absence? Not only or primarily the things that can be discussed and accounted for, but personal attitudes and views. It must have been easier in the past for women to accept a man's absence on a voyage which was accepted as an economic necessity, than it is today, on one which was regarded by many as a costly eccentricity. It says much for the wives and girl-friends of our crew that they all good-humouredly absorbed the thousand niggling annoyances that the voyage caused them. Their experience of coping with house and children and parties, without the presence of a partner, was not the least genuine part of the voyage. It was unhappily typical of what happens to people whose consent is vital, but who are not of interest to the media, that they were not even allowed to enjoy the welcome home. The crowd of spectators was so large that it swamped the place on Peel sands reserved for them, a poor return for the part they had taken in making the voyage possible and enjoyable. No one would dare to treat a reporter or a cameraman like that.

It was three o'clock on a windless dawn when the last stage of the voyage began. Even at that hour a crowd of well-wishers was on hand to pelt the departing ship with rice – whose nuptial signifi-cance was not lost upon the crew – which soon joined the other flora and fauna of the bilges, by now an ecological study in them-selves. As the ship got closer to home, attention from the press in various boats, planes and helicopters increased and eventually became continuous, so that the crew found some embarrassment in relieving themselves over the side, as was customary and indeed the only way out, on *Odin's Raven*. One of nature's gentlemen was so reluctant to spoil a photograph that he attempted with back-breaking difficulty to use one of the oarports instead, feeling that this would be less conspicuous. In the event, the genuine interest in the practicability of this solution, evinced by everyone else on board, inevitably directs attention to him, as his bowed head towards which all faces are turned becomes the focal point of the photograph.

As some wind began to come as the sun rose higher, the weather was nearly ideal. Much more wind than welcome came on two or three occasions from a large Norwegian helicopter, which required a smart lowering of the mainsail several times. The *Raven* still arrived off Peel well before the scheduled time, and stood on and off the land in a light breeze just sufficient to show off the perfect set of her mainsail and the precision and certainty with which she tacked and wore. This gave great satisfaction to all concerned with it as we took turns putting 5p pieces into the large slot-machine binoculars on the promenade until we discovered they were inferior to our own. Kathy Lewis, who ran the Isle of Man end of things, was briefing pressmen from the small office at the end of the pier, and the Peel viking ships from the port's annual festival were being anchored off the entrance to provide a triumphal avenue up to the part of the beach where the *Raven* was to land. Large, imperturbable and somehow antique looking Manx policemen imperturbably ignored the fact that the roped-off enclosures on the beach were being completely disregarded by everyone but those locals who could do with a bit of rope. They were probably right to do so. The crowd was very good-humoured but it *was* very large, evidently much larger than the authorities had really expected. This was another indication that, though the voyage certainly had plenty of critics among the enlightened who rather pooh-poohed it, most people approved of it and understood it without footling reservations: the very different coverage in different newspapers points the same way.

By the time, dead on time, the *Raven*'s prow first touched the sand of her home port, those who had led the crowd's advance were in danger of being pushed into the water by the crowd behind them, and were cheering on the *Raven* with understandable enthusiasm. I could still just see the Bishop, the Governor and Lady Paul, but also observed the crew wives were very properly refusing to commit their children to the scrum of two thousand or so on the beach. Nor did they choose to fight for some place among the thousands more on the promenade. Being the nobly sensible and altogether admirable women they are, they retired philosophically, smouldering, to the bar in the viking longhouse where the arrival party was to be held.

The bowmen leapt and splashed ashore with the ropes that had been run out to so many different holding points in the past. The rest of the crew followed, and without using their weapons, or at any rate the sharper parts of them, managed to form what was, if not the prescribed half-circle, at any rate a sort of elliptical dotted line, and the chief presented the stones from Trondheim cathedral to the Bishop. They were to form part of St Germans, which is to be the new cathedral of Man: they had shared many cold and wet nights with the crew and had even (miraculously, as the Middle Ages would certainly have said) survived the capsize. Then the crew and ship were presented, after prayers, to the Governor and Lady Paul, their patron and godmother. As the pressure from the crowd was steadily increasing, and its motto seemed to be the Old English one of not allowing the vikings a single foot of land, the crew re-boarded to row into the harbour with alacrity. It is not easy to get back on board from waist deep water even over a freeboard as low as the *Raven*'s, and whilst illustrators always show viking ships beached at right angles it would probably be more sensible to do as most beach boats do at the present day, and allow the stern to swing so that the inshore side of the hull tilts down to bring the rail lower.

The more persistent small boys were still adhering to the *Raven* as she backed off the beach, and the crew swung to their oars to row round the pier and into the harbour, to the steps by the longhouse where they were to land through a crowd in which their wives, playing on what was now their home ground, had resolutely secured the best places.

Inside the longhouse the party was just like that at Fredrikstad, Hørten, Sandefjord, Tonsberg, Oslo, Trondheim, Lerwick, Kirkwall, Rousay, Stornoway, Portree, Tobermory, Oban, Port Ellen, Port Patrick: familiar faces, steadily more sunburnt, engaged in serious discussion or dead-pan anecdote, now slowly indoctrinating their partner into a new set of in-jokes. A large number of the couples were telling one another how well they looked, evidently each having expected to meet an emaciated wreck: a nice example of assurances of mutual dependence, that each expected absence to endanger health, but was pleasantly surprised to find it hadn't. It was a pleasure too for the English and Manx guests, so often out of their gastronomic depth in Norway, to see well-remembered Scandinavian faces frowning uncertainly over such exotic delicacies as bridge-rolls, or gamely throwing down a brown sherry as chaser to a pint of mild.

Everyone was glad to be back, and because they were, people for the first time on the voyage (and the last) started slipping away from the party. They were, after all, not going back to the ship. They were going home.

References

Chapter 1

P. G. FOOTE and D. M. WILSON, *The Viking Achievement*, 1970.

E. V. WRIGHT, *The North Ferriby Boats*, Maritime Monographs No. 23, 1976, National Maritime Museum.

K. ELDJARN, *Gengith a Reka*, 1948.

P. BANBURY, *Man and the Sea from the Ice Age to the Norman Conquest*, 1975.

D. A. WHITE, *Litus Saxonicum*, Wisconsin Univ. 1961.

J. A. GILES, *Six Old English Chronicles* (Ethelwerd, Asser, Gildas, Nennius) 1848.

A. GRIMBLE, *Migrations, Myth and Magic from the Gilbert Islands*, 1972.

G. N. GARMONSWAY, *The Anglo-Saxon Chronicle*, translated with an introduction, Everyman's Library, 1953.

P. J. C. BOELES, *Friesland tot de eelfde eeuw*, 1950.

J. J. KALMA, *Geschiedenis van Friesland*, 1968.

J. BØE, *Jernalderens Keramikk i Norge*, Bergens Museums Skrifter 14, 1931.

H. ÅKERLUND, *Nydamskeppen*, Sjöfarts Museum i Göteborg, 1963.

R. BRUCE-MITFORD, *The Sutton Hoo Ship-Burial, I*. B.M. Publications, 1975.

T. RAMSKOU, *Lindholm Høje*, 1960.

D. WHITELOCK, *The beginnings of English Society*, Pelican 1952.

C. GREEN, *Sutton Hoo, The Excavation of a Royal Ship-Burial*, 1968.

Chapter 2

R. HAMER, *Anglo-Saxon Verse*, 1970.

G. BONE, *Anglo-Saxon Poetry*, 1943.

C. L. WRENN, *Beowulf*, 1953.

BEDE, *Ecclesiastical History of the English People*, translated A. M. Sellar, 1907.

H. ARBMAN, *The Vikings* (ed. and transl. A. L. Binns), 1961.

C. SANDISON, *The Sixareen and her Racing Descendants*, Lerwick 1954.

D. WHITELOCK in *Studies in the Early Cultures of NW Europe presented to H. M. Chadwick* (ed. C. Fox), 1950.

D. LEWIS, *We, the Navigators*, Australian National Univ., 1973.

E. J. MARCH, *Inshore Craft of Britain in the Days of Sail and Oar*, 1970

E. HJÄRNE, 'Vederlag och sjöväsen', *Namn och Bygd*, 17.3, 1930.

M. OLSEN, 'Fra Norges kystled', *Namn och Bygd*, 4.1, 1916.

A. S. COOK, *The Possible Begetter of O. E. Beowulf*, Connecticut Academy, 25, 1922.

GOLDSMITH, 'The Seafarer and The Birds', *Review of English Studies 5*, 1954.

W. F. BOLTON, *Alcuin and Beowulf*, 1979.

Chapter 3

T. ANDERSON (ed), *The Vikings*, Symposium Uppsala, 1978.

P. H. SAWYER, *The Age of the Vikings*, 1962.

H. R. LOYN, 'The Vikings in Wales', Univ. Coll. London, Dorothea Coke lecture, 1976.

A. L. BINNS, 'The Navigation of Viking ships round the British Isles' in Fifth Viking Congress, Torshavn, 1968;

'The ships of the Vikings, were they "Viking Ships"?' Eighth Viking Congress Aarhus, 1980;

'Ohthere's Northern Voyage', English and Germanic Studies 7, 1961.

R. EKBLOM, 'Idris Map of Scandinavia', *Namn och Bygd*, 19.1, 1931.

Chapter 4

G. BERSU, D. WILSON, 'Three Viking Graves from the Isle of Man', Soc. for Med. Archaeology, Monograph 1, 1966.

R. H. M. DOLLEY, *The Hiberno-Norse coins in the British Museum*, 1966.

M. MAGNUSSON and H. PALSSON, *The Vinland Sagas*, Penguin Classics, 1965.

L. KRISTJANSSON, *Graenlenzki Landnemaflotinn in Arbok hins Islenzka Fornleifafelags*, 1964 (English summary pp. 64–8).

B. THORSTEINSSON, 'Observations on the Discoveries and Cultural history of the Norsemen', in *Saga-book* 16.2, Viking Society, 1964.

J. R. ENTERLINE, *Viking America*, 1972.

D. ELLMERS, *Fruhmittelälterliche Handelsschiffahrt*.

A. NAESS, *Hvor La Vinland?* 1954.

Chapter 5

H. R. LOYN, *The Vikings in Britain*, 1977.

I. MORRISON, *The North Sea Earls*, 1973.

G. BRODERICK, *Cronica Regum Mannie et Insularum* (ed. and transl.), Manx Museum and National Trust, 1979.

M. CHIBNALL, *Ordericus Vitalis* (ed. and transl.), 1969.

AELNOTH, 'Hist. Sct. Canuti Regis', in *Scriptores Rerum Danicarum Med. Aev.*, ed. Langebek.

C. af PETERSON, *Knytlinga saga*, SUGNL, 1919.

Chapter 6

U. SCHNALL, 'Navigation der Wikinger', *Schriften des Deutschen Schiffahrts Museums* 6, 1975.

G. J. MARCUS, *The Course for Greenland, Saga-Book 14*, Viking Society 1957;

'The Navigation of the Norsemen', *Mariner's Mirror* 39, 1953.

C. SØLVER, 'Vikingernes Kompas', *Naturens Verden* 26, 1942;

Vestervejen, 1954;

'Leitharsteinn, the compass of the Vikings', Viking Society *Old Lore* series 75, 1946.

C. SØLVER and G. J. MARCUS, 'Dead Reckoning', in *Mariner's Mirror* 44, 1958.

T. RAMSKOU, *Solstenen*, 1969.

H. WINTER, 'Die Nautik der Wikinger', *Hansische Geschichtesblätter* 62, 1937.

N. WINTHER, *Faerøernes Oldtid*, 1875.

P. G. FOOTE, 'Solarsteinn', in *Arv* 12, 1956.

A. L. BINNS, 'Sun Navigation in the Viking Age', *Acta Archaeologica* 42, 1971.

J. HORNELL, 'The Role of Birds in Early Navigation', *Antiquity* 20, 1946.

Chapter 7

M. ANDERSEN, *Vikingefaerden*, 1895.

A. W. BRØGGER and H. SHETELIG, *Vikingeskipene, deres forgjengere og etterfolgere*, 1950.

A. E. CHRISTENSEN, *Boats of the North*, 1968.

O. OLSEN and O. CRUMLIN-PEDERSEN, 'The Skuldelev Ships', *Acta Archaeologica* 38, 1967.

O. CRUMLIN-PEDERSEN, 'Das Haithabuschiff', *Haithabu Berichte* 3, 1969.

S. MCGRAIL, 'The Gokstad Faering', Part 1.

E. MCKEE, 'The Gokstad Faering', Part 2, *Maritime Monographs* 11, 1974, National Maritime Museum.

Chapter 8

B. GREENHILL (ed.), 'Aspects of the History of Wooden Shipbuilding', *Maritime Monographs* 1, 1970, National Maritime Museum.

E. MCKEE, 'Clenched Lap or Clinker', 1972, National Maritime Museum.

E. SUNDT, *Det Norske Arbejde, Nordlandsbaaden, Folkevennen*, 1865.

S. HAASUM, *Vikingatidens Segling och Navigation*, 1974.

H. ÅKERLUND, 'Ass och Beiti-ass', in *Unda Maris*, 1956; 'Vikingatidens Sjöväsen', in *Svenska Kryssarklybbens Arskrift*, 1959.

N. TUXEN, 'De Nordiske Langskib', in *Aarbog for Nordisk Oldkyndighed*, 1886.

ROYAL INSTITUTE OF NAVIGATION, 'The practicability of Commercial Sail', in *Journal of Navigation*, 30, 1977.

Chapter 9

S. NORDAL, *Islensk Menning*, 1942.

P. GRAVILLE, 'Performance Prediction for the Gokstad Ship', unpubl. thesis, Southampton University, 1976.

C. FELL, *Egils Saga* (transl.), Everyman's Library, 1976.

Chapter 10

A. CHRISTENSEN and I. MORRISON, *International Journal of Nautical Archaeology*, 5, 1976.

N. RASMUSSEN, *Vikingeskibehallen-en orientering*, Roskild, 1973.

H. FALK, 'Altnordisches Seewesen', *Wörter u Sachen* 4, 1912.

R. BRUCE, 'More about Sixerns', *Mariner's Mirror* 20, 1934.

Chapter 11

B. CADORET (ed.), 'La Tradition Nordique', in *Le Petit Perroquet*, 17, 1975.

J. GODAL, *Kort Instruksjon i Sigling med Afjordsfemboring*, Batlaget, 1976.

A. L. BINNS, 'Ulfljot's Law in The Story of Thorsteinn Uxafot', *Sagabook of Viking Society*, 14, 1955.

O. BRIEM, *Heithinn Sithur a Islandi*, 1945.

P. HOVDA, 'Norske Fiskemed', *Stadnamnarkiv* 2, 1961.

J. LEATHER, *Colin Archer and the Seaworthy double-ender*, 1979.

Acknowledgements

HIS EXCELLENCY THE LIEUTENANT GOVERNOR – *Patron* (Sir John Paul, GCMG., OBE., MC.)
LADY PAUL – *Godmother*
RT. REV. VERNON S. NICHOLLS – *Bishop of Sodor and Man*
SIR CHARLES KERRUISH – *Speaker, House of Keys*
ROY MacDONALD – *Chairman, Harbour Board*
G. BURDON – *Chairman of Peel Town Commissioners*
L. QUILLIAM – *Chairman of Peel Vikings*
I.O.M. POSTAL AUTHORITY
FRANK WEEDON – *Chief Constable*
ALAN DAVIS – *Education*

Millennium Committee
MRS BETTY HANSON – *Chairman*
MAJOR CRELLIN
CLIFFORD IRVING – *Chairman of Tourist Board*
R. E. KERRUISH
PETER KNEALE – *Manx Radio*
CELTIC VIKING ASSOCIATION
ARCHDEACON GLASS
I.O.M. HARBOURMASTERS
I.O.M. COASTGUARDS
J. F. KISSACK – *Government Property Trustees*
PAUL DWYER – *Business Expansion Ltd.*

Manx Millennium Viking Voyage Committee
R. N. S. BIGLAND – *Project Organiser*
I. W. B. K. BROWN
MRS K. L. LEWIS – *Project Administrator*
J. F. NELSON
R. QUAYLE – *Clerk of Tynwald*
T. SAYLE
MRS E. SALMOND
WILLIAMS & GLYN'S BANK (I.O.M.) LTD
DAVID SWINTON

Thanks for supplying illustrations are due to:

(photographs)

(drawings)

ARNE WISTH

ALAN BINNS AND D. A. WAITE

SHANE LUCAS

MICHAEL INGRAM

(maps)

COLIN BOWEN

MISS A. M. FERRAR — *Map Curator,*

BBC

Hull University

Special thanks are also due to:

MONA NAPES

ALAN BERG

SIMON GALLIVER — *Ashley Hill School, Onchan*

ALAN BINNS

H.M. FORCES

H.M. KING OLAF OF NORWAY

LADY MAYOR AND PEOPLE OF TRONDHEIM

SPEAKER OF NORWEGIAN STORTINGET

NORWEGIAN POSTAL AUTHORITY

RØD BATBYGGERI BOATYARD

HANKÖ YACHT CLUB

REV. GOUDAL — *Bishop of Mid Norway*

Shetland — Lerwick

DON LESLIE — *Up Helly Aa Committee*

JIM NICOLSON — *Guizer Jarl, Up Helly Aa Committee*

PETER MALCOLMSON — *Up Helly Aa*

H. GRAY — *Chairman, Harbour Board*

DAVID POLSON — *Harbour Master*

Orkney — Rousay, Kirkwall

MAJOR & MRS RIO RITCHIE — *Rousay*

BRIGADIER & MRS S. B. ROBERTSON — *Kirkwall*

ROWAN MCCALLUM — *Director, Orkney Islands Council, Kirkwall*

E. R. EUNSON — *Convenor, Orkney Island Council, Kirkwall*

COL & MRS R. A. S. MACRAE — *Orphir, Orkney*

HARBOUR MASTER — *Kirkwall*

Lewis — Stornoway

CAPTAIN ANGUS M. MACKENZIE — *Harbour Master, Stornoway*

REV. D. MACAULEY — *(Western Islands Council), Stornoway*

D. A. MACLEAN — *Western Isles Islands Council, Stornoway*

Skye — Portree

MESSRS E. & D. MACRAE — *West End Garage), Portree*

ARCHIE ANNAN – *Skye and Lochalsh District Council, Portree*
HARBOUR MASTER – *Portree*

Mull – Tobermory
MR MCKENZIE – *Caledonian Macbrayne Limited, Argyll*
MICHAEL GOSSIP – *Argyll & Bute District Council*
HARBOUR MASTER – *Tobermory*

Islay
ROD WALKER – *Manager, Machrie Hotel*
HARBOUR MASTER – *Islay*

Sponsors

Shields
BIGLAND	THERMO-SKYSHIPS
HOUSLEY HEATH & CO. LTD	GORE TEX
COSTAIN FAMILY	BRITISH MIDLAND AIRWAYS
ROYAL TRUST BANK	ISLAND EXPRESS
DEN NORSKE CREDIT BANK	MARKS AND SPENCERS LTD
BUKH	MR & MRS R. F. OXLEY
SPERRY UNIVAC	HAMBROS BANK
SHEILA MATHESON TRAVEL	MR & MRS ALAN FAIRLEY
OKELL & SON LTD	MR & MRS BERNARD SWAIN
POBJOY MINT	SIR DOUGLAS CLAGUE

Oars
MRS NIKIMAA	ALAN SUTTON
MR H. H. BIBBY	SAVINGS AND INVESTMENT BANK
CANON CUBBON	R. L. LAMMING
A. L. LONG	TREVOR BAINES
W. A. NICOL	I.O.M. POSTAL AUTHORITY
SCHOLL (U.K.) LTD	COSTAIN FAMILY
G. W. JOYNSON & CO. LTD	HOUSLEY HEATH & CO.
R. L. STOTT & CO.	

Main Sponsors
J. E. O. ARNOLD

Sundry anonymous donations

Index